Accompany John Rensenbrink on a 15-year sojourn through US Green history, from its joyful ingenuous beginnings in 1984, its near fatal rift in 1991, and its innovative Party-building break-through in 1996 — the Draft Nader for President campaign. Rensenbrink coaches us to see the US political anomaly through a prism of clear-headed logic.

Linda Martin, Past Co-Chair, Association of State Green Parties (USA), National Coordinator of the Draft Nader for President Campaign 1996, and Hawaii Green Party Candidate for US Senate 1992.

Who better to bring us up to date on the growing and important Green movement than U.S. Green Party co-founder, theoretician, and U.S. Senate candidate John Rensenbrink? Lively, informative, provocative, and inspiring, this book is a must-read for anyone interested in third parties, grass-roots democracy, ecology, social transformation, and the state of the world.

Michael S. Cummings, Professor and Chair, Political Science Department, University of Colorado at Denver

Anyone wanting to know how Green politics in the US has developed, hould read this interesting account from a person who "was there." Rensenbrink has been involved in promoting Green politics in America for many years and more recently a driving force in the forming and development of the Association of State Green Parties. ASGP has become the vehicle that can make the Greens a major political force for change. The Green struggle in America is much more difficult than in Europe where both proportional representation and government funding have helped Green Parties enter 17 Parliaments and 7 governments. However, the rise of a strong Green Party movement in the world's only superpower is viewed by the European Greens as crucial to the success of Green politics worldwide. In cooperation with the Green Parties in Europe, North and South America, Australia, Africa, and Asia, the ASGP can bring Green change globally.

Ralph Monoe, Secretary-General, Federation of European Green Parties

*This book is dedicated
to all men and women everywhere
who seek and fight for the life of
the free citizen.*

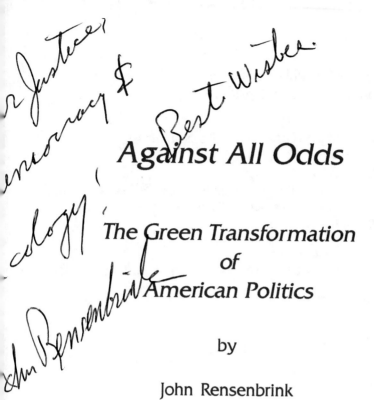

Against All Odds

The Green Transformation
of
American Politics

by

John Rensenbrink

Foreword by
Ralph Nader

Leopold Press, Inc.
Raymond, Maine 1999

Library of Congress Cataloging in Publication Data

Rensenbrink , John .
    Against all odds : the green transformation of American politics /
by John Rensenbrink : foreword by Ralph Nader
        p.   cm.
    Includes bibliographical references .
    ISBN 0-9660629-1-4 (alk . paper)
    1 . Green Movement . 2 . Green Movement--United States . I . Title .
JA75.8.R44 1999
363.7'0525'0973--dc21   99-19472

                    10   9   8   7   6   5   4   3   2   1

Printed in the United States by employee owned United Graphics,
Inc. 2916 Marshall Ave. P.O. Box 559, Mattoon, IL 61938

Cover design: Michael Yoder

                        Published in the U.S.A. by
                            Leopold Press, Inc
                              PO Box 1237
                        Raymond, Maine 04071-1237
                            (207) 655-4715
                            draper@ime.net

About the Author

John Rensenbrink, fifth of seven children born to Dutch immigrant parents, grew up on a dairy farm in Minnesota. For his high school education he completed a four-year correspondence course. He attended Calvin College in Grand Rapids, Michigan, majoring in History and Political Science, and served as Editor of the college newspaper during his last two years. He took degrees in Political Science from the University of Michigan (M.A.) and the University of Chicago (Ph.D), and spent a year in Amsterdam as a Fulbright scholar. He taught at Coe College and Williams College before going to Bowdoin College in 1961. At Bowdoin he taught political science in the Department of Government and interdisciplinary studies in the Environmental Studies Program until he retired in 1993. He spent three years in East Africa in the early Sixties working in the Ministries of Education in Kenya and Tanzania, and a half year doing research on social change in Poland in the early 1980's.

He and Carla Washburne of Williamstown, Massachusetts were married in 1959 and they have three daughters, Kathryn, Margaret, and Elizabeth.

In the late Sixties, John helped found the Bath-Brunswick regional anti-poverty program in Maine, was a leading force in the anti-Vietnam War campaign, and helped organize the Reform Democrats of Maine, a short-lived dissident group within the Maine Democratic Party. He continued his activism in the 1970s on economic and social issues in Maine, both within and without the Democratic Party, and helped lead the effort to shut down the Maine Yankee nuclear power plant in the early 1980s. In January, 1984 he co-founded the Maine Green Party/Movement and thereafter focussed most of his activist energies on building the Maine Green Party and, at the national level, building what is now the Association of State Green Parties (ASGP). He currently serves as one of Maine's two representatives to the latter's Coordinating Council, and is Co-Chair of its International Committee. He was the Maine Green Party's candidate for U.S. Senate in 1996 and served as Pat LaMarche's campaign manager in her bid for Governor in 1998, a campaign in which her 7% of the votes restored official ballot status to the Maine Green Party.

John is author of two books: *Poland Challenges a Divided World*, Louisiana State University Press, Baton Rouge:1988; and *The Greens and the Politics of Transformation*, R & E Miles, San Pedro, CA: 1992. He is the Editor of *Green Horizon*, a national quarterly journal of news and commentary. He has written and published many papers, mostly in connection with his membership in the International Society for Universalism and its journal *Dialogue and Universalism* (published in Warsaw); and in the American Political Science Association's Organized Section on Ecology and Transformational Politics. From the latter he received a Praxis Award in 1994 for his work in relating theory and practice, scholarly work and political engagement.

It must be considered that there is nothing more difficult to carry out, nor more doubtful of success, nor more dangerous to handle, than to initiate a new order of things. For the reformer has enemies in all those who profit by the old order, and only lukewarm defenders in all those who would profit by the new order, this lukewarmness arising partly from fear of their adversaries, who have the laws in the favor; and partly from the incredulity of mankind, who do not truly believe in anything new until they have had actual experience of it. Thus it arises that on every opportunity for attacking the reformer, his opponents do so with the zeal of partisans, the others only defend him halfheartedly, so that between them he runs great danger.

Niccolò Machiavelli
From *The Prince*, Chapter VI

Socrates: There are those who have tasted how sweet and blessed a possession philosophy is, and have also seen enough of the madness of the multitude; and they know that no politician is honest, nor is there any champion of justice at whose side they may fight and be saved. Such a one may be compared to a man who has fallen among wild beasts—he will not join in the wickedness of his fellows, but neither is he able singly to resist all their fierce natures, and therefore seeing that he would be of no use to the State [the polis], or to his friends... he holds his peace, and goes his own way. He is like one who, in the storm and dust and sleet which the driving wind hurries along, retires under the shelter of a wall; and seeing the rest of humankind full of wickedness, he is content, if only he can live his own life and be pure from evil or unrighteousness, and depart in peace and goodwill, with bright hopes.
Adeimantus: Yes, and he will have done a great work before he departs.
Socrates: A great work —yes; but not the greatest, unless he find a polis suitable to him; for in a polis which is suitable to him, he will have a larger growth and be the savior of his country, as well as of himself.

Plato From *The Republic*, Book VI

We whose names are underwritten...having undertaken...a voyage to plant the first colony in the northern parts of Virginia, do by these presents solemnly and mutually in the presence of God, and one of another, covenant and combine ourselves together into a civil body politic, for our better ordering and preservation and furtherance of the ends aforesaid; and by virtue hereof to enact, constitute and frame such just and equal laws, ordinances, acts, constitutions, and offices, from time to time, as shall be thought most meet and convenient for the general good....

Mayflower Compact
November 11, 1620

Contents

Acknowledgments

I write this in early January 1999. I look back over the 15 years since the Saturday in January 1984 in Augusta, Maine when, as we now surmise, the first organized meeting of Greens in the United States took place. I think of all the women and men with whom I have worked to build a Green movement and a Green Party from Maine to California, from Georgia to Hawai'i and Alaska; and I think of Greens in Europe, Latin America, Australia, New Zealand, Asia and Africa from whom I have found so much to admire and emulate. Some have died and bequeathed to us their indomitable spirit of dedication and laughter. Some have left to do other things. And most are still at work, in the trenches as we say, persevering and building, doing it without pay and often without any recognition from the society they are seeking to arouse to our common peril and our common opportunity for greatness.

We have argued, we have struggled, we have moved forward side by side. None of us has not been changed, and all of us have learned much about organizing, about the world, and about ourselves. And, whether in the future, we continue side by side, or we move on different pathways, we will not forget these fifteen years of love and anger, hope and despair, fear and courage. In some very profound ways, I have not been alone in writing this book; the book has been written by all of us.

I want particularly to thank my companions in the Green Politics Network, now re-named the Green Network. We worked together closely to help nurture into being the Association of State Green Parties. They gave me much support in the writing of this book, reading different portions of the manunscript and providing valuable information, corrections, and comment.

Of course, the approach I take to our common story and the manner of telling it is my responsibility. Others write from their recollection and understanding of our history and its meaning. Each is a contribution to the unfolding story of the Green Movment/Party in the United States.

Foreword

In making the case for Green politics and the Green Party in the United States, John Rensenbrink necessarily writes out of multiple contexts for a dramatic democracy of renewal and foresight.

Our country's politics are dismal. They are duopolistic and indentured to the concentration of power and the control of private and public wealth.

Greens appear to be acutely aware of the true yardsticks that speak to gross poverty, the injustices, and the exclusion of the majority of Americans from the GNP gains of the past quarter century. They score the damage to worker and consumer rights, the looting of the small taxpayers by politically influential corporate welfarists, the corporate control of what people own as a commonwealth, the nullification of voters by seamy money in elections, and the general dismantling of our democracy by multinational companies whose global maneuvers preclude allegiances to community and public voice.

Certainly, Greens are keenly troubled by pell mell rush into unsustainable technologies and ecological crises while appropriate technologies and sustainable economic practices are suppressed, shunted aside, or not allowed a level playing field.

Unfortunately, however, the simple preconditions by members of the Green Party that would expand the party quantitatively and qualitatively are not being met. Given the sense of urgency expressed by the Greens, it is inconceivable that assumptions about membership do not include minimum annual contributions of 100 volunteer hours and the raising of $100, with suitable exemptions from the latter in special circumstances. A party can have discipline without traditional hierarchies if there is an exemplary measure of self-discipline, if each Green Party member becomes an epicenter of activity among neighbors, friends, relatives and co-workers.

Self-discipline invites attention, recognition, and emulation. The ensuing ripples will grow into waves for change. In the midst of Green growing pains and internal controversies over organizational structure and procedures, priorities and strategies, the minimum commitments by members should remain constants.

Dedicated to the proposition that a major purpose of leaders is to produce more leaders, the Green Party could well adopt a salutation such as: "Hello, how's your epicenter doing?"

Greens seek to persuade others that following the "least of the worst" rationale for voting Democrat or Republican, while both become worse every four years, is a prescription for a sliding paralysis. But to make the persuasion successful, the Green Party must be different between elections and not just with its candidates and platform. Contrasts with the two major parties are easy to draw. Be being a party of civic advocacy and civic service, the Green Party can become the party of a resurgent civic culture far beyond the contemporary politics of frenzied television ads and sloganeering over differences that turn out to be without much difference— much like tweedle-dum and tweedle-dee.

The new Connecticut Green Party has chosen to focus on electricity deregulation which bails out imprudent utility investments (called stranded costs) such as nuclear power plants on the backs of the taxpayers and consumers. It is the Green Party, not the Connecticut Democrats or Connecticut Republicans, who are mobilizing opposition and informing the public about alternative, superior pro-consumer and environment policies.

Greens can think about many energetic ways for the party to be a civic movement, a consumer movement, a taxpayers' movement, a workers movement, an environmental movement. All these highlight everyday injustices and events that cry out for engagement, compassion, knowledge and determination. Just read the daily newspapers—with all their warts—and see how they reflect in their stories such a large unmet demand for justice.

Greenmobiles (with least polluting fuels) to elicit citizen input, Green storefronts, Green hotlines, Green Cable TV programs (public access), Green volunteers on local boards and commissions will add up to a massive contrast with the somnolent major parties who wake up before elections to shake the PAC trees for their cash register politics.

Having abandoned the neighborhoods for electronic TV combat, the two major parties have also abandoned the very notion of party competition in many electoral districts by ceding the dominant party's hegemony. So voters are left with no major party candidate on the ballot for the lesser party; or are left with a nominal challenger by a candidate who wants some visibility for his or her business or profession. Greens can only relish the massive vacuums out there in the country, the absence of competition for many dimensions of democratic politics.

But it is well to distinguish between concern, seriousness, and resolute commitments to work and action. They are by no means part of an inevitable sequential flow of behavior. The number of people who take concern up to a level of seriousness and then to a level of resolute commitments dwindles too much in any civic and or political initiative. Greens should be far more acutely aware of the need to overcome such attrition.

It helps to construct scenarios of the possible in the various futures that reflect the Green Party's political philosophy and platform. When people see what wonderful futures can be theirs and their children's in concrete imagery, in operating models and experience, the civic resignation that feeds apathy and makes oligarchy and plutocracy more dominant begins to wither away.

The discriminatory divisions that now separate people so uselessly and cruelly begin to recede as the "indiscriminate injustice" heaped on all of them by the major power brokers provides a unifying movement of people taking back their society, their government, their economy, and their environment. A way of life emerges that becomes a labor of love invigorating a productive civic culture which fulfills human possibilities of, by, and for the people.

Read slowly and carefully John Rensenbrink's observations, thoughts, and urgings until you reach the frontiers of your own imaginations and energies and head into them confidently toward what Abraham Lincoln called "a new birth of freedom" for a just and self-renewing society. And remember that the only place where democracy comes before work is in the dictionary!

Ralph Nader
December 1998

We live in times that exhilarate us and also make us shudder. It's as if the human family is on the verge of a magnificent breakthrough precisely at the moment when its very future is in doubt. No citizen of his or her nation, no person able to reflect on the state of our planet, can hide from themselves the awesome fact that we human beings have a stark choice to make. It is a choice for life or for death.

But whether the choice we make is for one or the other, the inescapable truth is that it is a choice that confronts us. Though we do not make our destiny, as if out of whole cloth, our destiny nevertheless is inextricably interwoven with the reality of choice. Organisms are not just predetermined entities whose trajectory is fully contracted for by inertial forces or inscrutable divinity. We are organisms and we make choices as we participate in our own development and evolution. We participate in our destiny. That destiny necessarily includes not just us humans but all life on this planet—and perhaps beings on planets we now as yet know nothing of.

There is a movement of people on the earth, in every part of the earth, who are waking up to the fact of our choice for life or death. They perceive now, very deeply, the need to participate effectively with their neighbors and their neighbors' neighbors, and with all plant and animal life on earth, in choosing for sustained and healthy living for all and not for death. That movement is the Green movement.

The Green movement has taken hold in every continent. Rooted in that movement, Green parties have formed in over 75 countries worldwide. This is not unremarkable, considering the fact that most of these parties have come into being only within the last two decades. The Values Party in New Zealand, organized in 1967 and now called the Green Party, was a harbinger of things to come. Another harbinger was the formation of an Ecology Party in the United Kingdom in 1972, they having now also adopted the Green Party name. Later in that decade, 1979, a Green group, Die Grünen, formed in what was then West Germany. They made their way into the German Parliament in a startling electoral success in the spring of 1983.

Green parties then began sprouting up in all parts of Europe, and also in Africa, Asia, and the Americas, North and South. There is now a Federation of European Green Parties, comprising Green parties in 28 European countries, and loose-knit federations are forming in Africa and in the Americas.

In the United States, Green organizations only made their appearance for the first time in 1984. Their evolution towards a fully formed nation-

1

wide Green Party, based on an association of state Green parties, and drawing its strength from a developing Green movement, is the major subject of this book.

In one sense, this worldwide development has happened spontaneously. There has not been a center from which all this activity was spurred and directed. In each country, indeed in each state of the Untied States as well, small groups formed and then organizational links among these groups. They got together to do something about the ecological crisis facing their communities, their regions, and the planet.

But, though spontaneous, this worldwide development has a common origin in a new state of awareness, an ecological consciousness. It is this that makes the Green phenomenon a new and creative force, both now and for the long term future.

Ecological consciousness is not the same as environmentalism. Environmentalism is what is thought and practiced by Republicans and Democrats, by many scholars and journalists, and by their analogues in other countries of the world. Often they categorize "the environment" as one interest among many other interests that politicians and academics must now give heed to. In so doing they fit environmental interests into established intellectual, moral, economic, and political assumptions and institutions.

Some, and this includes many environmental activists, do go further and show genuine concern about the pollution, mindless extraction, and waste of natural resources and many abhor the aesthetic effects of environmental degradation. But, for the most part, their struggle remains a matter of particular causes. There is little hint from them of thinking outside the box, of asking and trying to answer fundamental questions. Questions such as how we human beings are to live on this planet if we are to survive, much less prosper; and what is wrong with our institutions and power structures that have led to such unthinkable consequences as the possible destruction of our species and even of the planet itself. Such questions touch on everything and reach to all the complex scientific, economic, political, and spiritual issues that perennially confound our species' attempts at civilization.

An ecological consciousness is a holistic consciousness grounded in values and in an entirely new understanding of the human place within nature and of the relation of human to human. Ecology invites us, pushes us, into a new paradigm that in turn has implications for every field of human endeavor. Ecology points us in new directions in economics, ethics, religion, art, politics, in how we think about thinking (epistemology), and indeed in every science. It confronts us with the necessity to look again, and look deeply, at ourselves, why we are here, and what we are doing with our lives.

It is because of this that the Green phenomenon has come into the world; why it critiques the world fundamentally; and why it has the staying power to endure as a worldwide movement. It is because of this that Green Parties aim to be, and bid fair to become, parties of a different kind. They don't fit the conventional wisdom or conventional pattern of what a party is "supposed to be." Their goal is to transform the way politics is carried on and to transform the relation of people and their government. They have this goal because they are rooted in an ecological consciousness.

This book begins, therefore, in Part I with chapters on reclaiming politics. The first is a theoretical excursion. It examines how ecology enables us to think creatively and transformatively about the political realm. It describes how ecology provides us with the philosophic foundation to reclaim and deepen the tradition of the free citizen. The second, building on Ralph Nader's bid for the presidency in 1996 under the banner of the Green Party, describes an early and groundbreaking effort to move politics in a transformative, citizen based, direction.

Part I continues with Chapters 3 and 4. They address the underlying discomfort people have about power and about the tendency of organized power, such as political parties, to veer away from the vision and values that animated them at the start. Chapter 3 sharply contrasts ideas of power as domination (power-over) with ideas of power as transformative energy— the energy of life within each person and that energy, together with others, for cultural and political growth (power-within and power-with). Chapter 4 rather boldly stakes a claim for a new way to balance the organized power of a growing Green Party with a nondirective cultural companion to the Party. Such a companion may be thought of as performing a crucial function: on the one hand interpreting the actions of the Party to the general populace, thereby helping to soften, if not overcome, the anti-political cynicism of the prevailing culture; and on the other hand fearlessly critiquing the Party and its actions in a constructive spirit.

The four chapters of Part I frame the rest of the book. Part II presents a picture of the roadblocks in the present system that stifle answers to problems that scream for attention. Describing the oligarchy that has come to dominate our economics and politics, it also discusses the potential opposition to this domination.

Unfortunately, the potential opposition is still too much wedded to the politics of protest. What is needed instead of protest and/or in addition to protest, goes the argument, is the development of a transformative consciousness and a will to enter the political realm directly. The major parties have both lost their way. They have become encumbrances inhibiting the citizen. Severe problems are trivialized or just plain denied, opportunities are squandered. The situation cries out for new leadership, dedicated to a citizen-centered way of doing politics, and dedicated to policies that nurture and sustain communities, abolish the artificial separation of economics and ecology, and link people with one another across the divides of race, religion, gender, class, sexual orientation, and age.

Parts III and IV describe the efforts of the Greens in the United States to meet this challenge and to organize a social movement, and then also a political party—a party of a different kind. Part III tells the story of movement-building from the beginnings in 1984 to the national Green Gathering of 1991 in Elkins, West Virginia. I have left it pretty much as I wrote it in 1991 (and published in 1992 under the title *The Greens and the Politics of Transformation*).

Part IV goes back briefly to the origins of the Green movement in 1984 and takes the reader forward to the founding years of the Association of State Green Parties (1996-1998). In the Epilogue I underscore a central theme of the book—the stark need for Americans to recover and renew their heritage of political freedom, to break the silence that threatens to smother efforts to transform the political system.

The story I tell in this book is one of evolution, of people feeling their way forward. The Greens did not have all the answers when they began. Indeed they didn't have many answers at all. However, they did formulate what has come to be known as the Ten Key Values. Charlene Spretnak, Mark Satin, and Eleanor McCain initiated a process that led to their formulation and acceptance. Their work has proved a godsend for all the Greens in the United States, of whatever persuasion, in the turbulent years of Green growth and development. The 10 Key Values are cited more than once in the text, but I will state them here as well. They are: Ecological Wisdom, Personal and Social Responsibility, Grass Roots Democracy, Non-Violence, Respect for Diversity, Post-Patriarchal Values, Community Economics, Decentralization, Global Responsibility, and Future Focus (or Sustainable Development).

Both as symbol and as content, the Ten Key Values provided an umbrella under which the Greens could weather the inevitable storms that attend the founding of something new, something so ambitious as a fundamental movement for change and a new, durable, credible, and value-centered political party. Because we were brand new; because we didn't have the answers (nobody could have); because people disagree, especially on the interpretation and application of something as fiercely felt as values; because people have different ideas that need sorting out; and because a new movement attracts not only great talent and wisdom but also people with intense personal agendas, the Greens would take what to some has seemed a lot of time to find their way forward.

Parts III and IV chart that journey. It is both inspiring and bemusing. I have tried to tell the story so that others reading it can learn from it and take heart that however difficult and often treacherous the passage from idea to its actualization, from vision to its implementation, good things can happen, good things can emerge and grow.

The Greens and Internal Conflict

I would add a word or two about conflict. Evolution does not happen without some of it, and as we Greens evolved, we had perforce to experience and deal with the fact that the way forward is often through intense disagreement.

Conflict—it happens to every group and especially to those who care a lot about the world and about the social and political transformation of the world. To head off conflict many groups tighten up and there emerges a central leader or leadership that directs the whole. The leadership exerts the necessary control that presumably will ward off divisive threats from inside and outside the group. This route leads to authoritarian leadership, and it does not really stop internal division. In addition, people fall away and only the hardy and often hardened souls remain who pump one another up with their often one-dimensional loyalty to the cause.

Greens choose a different route. They insist on openness, inclusivity, and democracy. At times their insistence leads to what has been described as "the tyranny of structurelessness," situations in which the practice of total openness can lead to explosions of conflicting and conflicted arguments, recriminations, deeply hurt feelings, and resulting group paralysis.

Yet it is important to realize that the Greens feel that the risk of this happening is worth it, far better than to risk the opposite danger of top down, authoritarian leadership that can so easily come from putting in place control mechanisms designed to protect the group from dangers within and without. They seek a more balanced pathway, but, and this is the vital point, they realize there is no way to arrive at such balance except through accepting the risk posed by being open, being inclusive, and being democratic. It is a matter of learning to do it better by having the experience of it and by using the tools of democracy and the habits and attitudes that go with them.

It is an evolution. Only by being open, by allowing innovation, by respecting, and celebrating, diversity is there hope for the growth—through a process of continuing change and development—of a strong and vigorous group. At any given point in this process, the group facing yet another crisis, there is no certainty, no fore-ordained writ from heaven, that the

5

group will actually survive. Indeed, it may seem at times that one has reached a dead end, the future is hopeless, there is just too much inertia or divisiveness, or both. Too much cantankerousness, pettiness, jealousy, willful ignorance, confusion, and, underneath it all, the seeming intractability of different deeply held views that have hardened into definite positions. But the dreaded moment passes, the crisis resolves itself, the conflicts diminish, or take new forms. New impulses sprout up as in springtime when plants push their way upward through the muddy earth, fresh viewpoints are heard, and the life of the group evolves. There is learning. There is creativity. Strength is developing through this manifold diversity, conflict, and seeming chaos.

Conflict can therefore be a catalyst for forward motion. But it can only be that, or become that, if the fact of conflict is accepted by members of the group. If, however, people think it's a scandal that conflict exists, that things "shouldn't be this way," and that responding to a criticism from a fellow member is just as "bad" as initiating criticism, then a pall settles over the spirits of people, opportunities for clarification and further argument that may lead to greater understanding are lost. But if conflict is accepted, the way is open for dealing with it in a mature and moderating way.

The trouble, of course, is that conflict can get out of hand. People may resort to personal attacks. People may perceive that an attack is personal when it was not meant that way. Or they may feel that a criticism is motivated by malice, or that an action is intended to put them down or leave them out. Retribution follows. Feelings and positions taken get polarized. The atmosphere gets nasty. At that point it takes extraordinary patience and exceptional skills of mediation to help things cool down, to help people step back and recall the key values that brought them together to begin with, and to inch the group along to a new place where they can reconnoitre and regroup. It is especially helpful if the structures in place permit different types of meetings: study groups, caucuses, parallel organizations that each have a different function, autonomous groupings, informal get togethers, and the like; in a word, diverse, differentiated structural patterns.

The story I tell in Parts III and IV is definitely not a tale told as if from Mount Olympus. The person telling it, namely me, was deeply involved in the nitty-gritty of events and actions that constituted the story. So it is a story told from my vantage point as a participant in the action. Once it looked as if an association of state Green Parties, or something like it, could come about, I wanted it to happen, I wanted it very much, and worked hard side by side with many others for its success. This produced an opposition by Greens who did not want an association of state parties, or did not want the kind we wanted, or wanted it to come about in a different way than the way we wanted or thought it could happen. The impact of this criticism and counter-criticism helped to trigger a reevaluation of what should constitute a Green kind of political party rooted in ecological wisdom. The reevaluation has taken the form of such questions as these: Shouldn't we be working towards the kind of party and the kind of structure for the party, that deepens the vision, helps members to relate to one another effectively, and fosters a growing dialog with more and more American citizens?

Thus, since evolution does involve conflict, the fact that the story is also about conflict should not be surprising. What may be surprising is the degree to which the conflict at times took virulent forms—though no more so than in other groups advocating social change that I and others know about. Yet perhaps some may think that Greens would or should be free of the more intense and/or obnoxious forms of infighting. Maybe that is so, and we Greens can and should try to learn from mistakes and blunders that we made in this tumultuous journey towards a strong vigorous movement-based political party. That is partly the reason I am writing about this is some detail.

This account may also be helpful for everyone who cares about working for fundamental social and political change, whether Green or not Green. It offers an opportunity to see how some people have tried to do it, and are trying to do it better. It shows that the problems they encounter are human—all-too-human and yet are also the stuff from which history is made. For, beneath the seeming wrangling, there is an important and yes noble struggle taking place. How do human beings resolve the ancient and perennial tension (some would even call it a contradiction) that seems always to rear its troubled head, between doing things, organizing things, and advocating for them because they seem intrinsically good; and doing, organizing, and advocating because they seem intrinsically effective. That is one way of putting the tension, or contradiction. There are other ways of putting it: the ideal and the real, the vision and its implementation, soul work and strategic work, fundamentalist and realist.

The tension between them is especially felt when it comes to politics, party building, and governing. It doesn't help that the prevailing culture is so deeply alienated from politics and, conversely, that politics as practiced is so removed from the life of the people. The thought of entering the political realm arouses deep and genuine fear of entrapment. It also easily marks those who nevertheless persist in entering the realm as bent on opportunistic self-advancement and of wickedly conniving with the powers-that-be. Such a situation is rich with possibilities for misunderstanding, adopting seemingly intransigent positions for and against "doing politics," and fingering one another's motives. It is also rich with possibilities for dissolving such fixed positions and for transforming both sociocultural and political space and their respective activities. If this book has meaning at all, it is an attempt to show that this transformation is as possible as it is necessary.

These factors enter into the story of the Green evolution in the United States since its founding in 1984. It would not be accurate to say that the story is one of evolving from a movement into a party. Or as if it's a development from idealism to realism, from being "good" to being "effective," etc. That is not what is going on. The journey told in these pages begins with people gathering together in their communities to form small groups that then engage in a variety of different activities and strategies for change. These strategies include electoral politics as one of many, though initially it takes a back seat to other strategies: organizing around particular local issues; study groups on the Ten Key Values; educational outreach projects; life-style changes; and projects aiming at alternative social and economic institutions (barter systems, radio stations, journals, schools, cooperatives). Implicit and explicit in this development is already a debate over the tension, and sometimes seeming contradiction, between the ideal and the real, the vision and its implementation. It's not as if this debate started when party building activity came into greater prominence.

But, for reasons already stated, once party activity and electioneering took hold, the debate intensified. And related structural issues (party organization vis-a-vis social movement structures already in place) began to heat up. Out of this there gradually came into focus the possibility and the need to develop, not just any old party (however "new" it might preen itself to be), but a movement kind of party, what is described in this book as a party of a different kind. Simply put, this means a party in which a high consciousness exists of the need to be grounded in the Green vision and grounded in being effective and participatory. It is a party where a plurality of autonomous structures exist to permit flexibility and side-by-side participation.

This is where things seem to be headed as of this writing in January 1999. With the addition of the California State Green Party in November 1998, as the 24th member, the Association of State Green Parties (ASGP) now embraces almost all of the states that have an up-and-running viable Green Party. Plans are afoot to run a major Presidential campaign in 2000 and this will spark and nurture Green Parties in most of the other states, many of whom already have Green parties in embryo.

Evolution continues. The ASGP's goal is to work towards its own transformation. The 24 state parties that are presently affiliated together in the Association hope and expect to embrace the several other already formed state parties and to embrace Green parties in all the other states as they form and get up to speed. Their input and participation will cause further change and development of appropriate structures. The result will be a fully fledged Green Party of the United States. In recognition of this momentum, the European Federation of Green Parties, in January 1999, announced their decision to recognize the Association of State Green Parties as their partner in the United States. Delegates of the ASGP would be received at the February 1999 Congress of the European Federation in accordance with this decision. There would be meetings at the Congress to develop and adopt a Common Ground statement.

Other possibilities beckon in this evolutionary process. As noted above, a cooperative federation of 30 Green parties has formed in Europe, and similar formations are taking place in Africa and the Americas. A worldwide gathering of Greens is scheduled for the year 2001 in Australia. Globalization of the world's economy by the multinational corporations evokes a need for Green parties worldwide to cooperate on a common approach to a multitude of issues and structural challenges generated by these super-corporations. Sixty-five Green Parties worldwide, including the Association of State Green Parties, cooperated on a joint declaration on climate change in preparation for the Kyoto Conference in December, 1997. It was a first of its kind. As Green parties and their federations evolve, there will be many more instances of such cooperation and worldwide solidarity.

And, finally, in the spirit of evolution, the Green Party only succeeds if it swims in the sea of a developing green culture whose waters flow from a vibrant ecological consciousness. Green culture takes a multitude of forms. Yet I continue to believe, as I have throughout the struggle for a viable Green political structure, that green culture also needs a way to manifest itself organizationally. This is already happening in some form in several states. The Maine Greens, for example, have worked out a theory and practice of "The Triad" in which these separate but related functions coexist: the Green Party, the Katadhin Center for Education and Research, and Direct Action (action around specific issues). This approach is being copied in other states.

I can see down the road, and side by side with the Green Party, one or more institutes, organizations, and annual retreats—or, better still, a confederation of many epicenters, as Ralph Nader would call them, throughout the country—that help nurture the spirit and practice of being Green.

January, 1999
Topsham, Maine

Part I:

Politics: Why Mess With It?

Chapter 1
Ecology and the Tradition of the Free Citizen

"Shine, Perishing Republic!" wrote poet Robinson Jeffers earlier in this century. He foresaw the imminent collapse of the American republic and yet proclaimed its power to renew itself. Today we live in a time of unparalleled crisis for the republic. It seems on track to decline into corporate statism run by an oligarchy whose vision has turned to greed and domination. Yet there are renewing forces. Ecology, for example. Ecology offers a new foundation for a republic of liberty and equality, freedom and order, diversity and unity, justice and compassion, community and peace.

This is a tall claim. But consider that ecology opens up the human mind and spirit to a new and reinvigorating vision of our human place in the world. Implicit in its teachings is an understanding of "the political" that underwrites the best of past traditions and goes a giant step beyond those traditions to locate the human project securely and dynamically in a natural citizen world. It may not be too much to claim that for the first time in human history, we stand at the threshold of a fully citizen politics. We need to learn what it means for us and act to affirm and confirm it.

People are confused and divided. Perhaps fragmented is a more accurate description. The links and channels that are supposed to connect people to their government and to each other, and to connect their government to them, are barely functioning. Politicians take their signals from the entrenched moneyed interests even as their rhetoric expands in the direction of honeyed words to the public that mean less and less. The media itself looks first to the same moneyed interests that own them. Very little real news and genuine commentary about alternatives comes through to the average citizen, even those who are more than a little bit attentive. The two major political parties religiously preserve their monopoly of office, excluding new political voices. They are more willing to serve the special interests than they are to provide real links between government and the people. The people, consequently, by the millions opt out of the political process altogether. Even those who try to stay connected do not often go gladly to the voting booth, but do so holding their nose.

The widespread disgust with politics and government, though it has reached alarming levels in recent decades, is not a new phenomenon. Its sources go back a long way, fed by several powerful cultural streams that have shaped attitudes towards public and political life for centuries, if not millennia. These cultural streams are the Christian tradition, the tradition of rational, *laissez faire* propertarian individualism, Marxism , and anarchism.

13

Each is steeped in a strong ambivalence towards, and in some cases an outright rejection of, political life and government. I call this ambivalence the Great Pejorative.

St. Augustine in the fourth and fifth centuries, perhaps the most articulate and seminal founder of Christian ideas and dogma, stated the matter sharply and brilliantly. The state is evil. It is, he hastened to add, a necessary evil. It is a scourge that God has allowed, even arranged in his providential wisdom, to be inflicted on humankind following the fall of man. Humans wallow in sin. Their recourse is to find community in the City of God, the community of Christians. But Christians are also caught in this life, in the City of Man, and governed by that necessary evil, the State. They can and must, through piety and faith, accept the state's stringencies as God's loving scourge on both the good and the evil. They must obey its laws, and only resist when those laws interdict their worship of God. Thus, in "this life" they must witness for truth and righteousness in personal ways, but they will only find ultimate comfort in the hope and faith of "a life to come" when the City of God will finally triumph over the Devil, over sin, and thus end the ingrained wickedness of the City of Man and its creature the State.

The rational, secular, *laissez faire* tradition was ushered in by the new capitalist middle classes in Europe in the 17th and 18th centuries. It was developed with elan by such thinkers as Hobbes and Locke and Montesquieu, and a little later by Adam Smith. Though less intense than classical Christianity, it is also steeped in a pejorative attitude towards the state and government. The capitalist entrepreneurs were anxious to protect their newly found, newly created, commercial space, the markets for free enterprise freshly carved out of the rebellion against the fettered and declining feudal economy. They were concerned to protect this new space from the still feudal-minded kings and church overlords. But they were equally concerned to protect it from the new state creature they themselves were helping to create, the republican form of government with its representative bodies, a form that had its origins before their time in the late middle ages. They wanted above all to limit government to a certain sphere and within that sphere to balance the various powers of government, in order both to slow it down, and to prevent it from being taken over by any one faction, especially a majority of the people. The bottom line and the message for the future was — in concert with the still influential Christian tradition — that government is not to be trusted, that government is either itself evil or just next door to all manner of perfidy and wickedness.

In the 19th century, new ideas of socialism were hammered into shape by Karl Marx and those who followed him. They viewed the state as nothing but a manipulated superstructure behind which stood the capitalist

ruling class and the forces and modes of production which this class dominated. The proletariat will eventually rise to overthrow the capitalist class,
seize the power of the state, and use the state to achieve a transition to a
new society, whereupon the state will wither away. Though representative
forms of government received grudging acquiescence from some Marxists,
in the main such forms were dismissed as merely bourgeois window-dress-
ing that hid the real power relations of the capitalist hegemony. Thus, here
as well, we find a fundamental fear of, and disrespect for, government and
its works. According to this tradition, reality is imbedded in economic
relations, and political life is just an appendage of the economy. The state
must eventually be abolished, and public life accepted only as it successfully accomplishes "the administration of things."

Anarchist thought and practice also developed rapidly in the 19th century. Though socialist in its economics and its reaction to capitalism, it
identified hierarchy and domination as the core of the human problem.
The quintessential institution that harbors and promotes domination and
hierarchy is the state. The state must be abolished. Nor is representative
government any kind of an answer, for it interposes an alienating power
between persons and the conduct of their mutual affairs. A strict
municipalism (city based sovereignty) and direct democracy at that level is
the preferred and necessary way. Marx, and democratic socialists as well,
are simply wrong in thinking that the state can be used for "good" ends,
and then abolished. The state is inherently a distorted machine for the
purpose of creating and preserving hierarchy and domination. If you think
to use it for worthy goals, it will twist them into their opposite, and you
will be swallowed up.

These four highly articulate and influential traditions have shaped
modern culture and have deeply imbued it with a profound skepticism, if
not cynicism, about government, politics, the state, and public life in general.

There is another tradition, going a long way back, which has viewed
public life, government structures and service, and statecraft as a noble
and life enhancing pursuit. Plato and Aristotle in ancient Athens viewed it
this way, Cicero the same in ancient Rome. Plutarch celebrates political
heroes in the same spirit in his *Lives*. The Magna Carta of 1216 insists on
it. Edmund Burke, the great British defender of the American Revolution,
reveals a similar positive attitude. The founders of the American Republic
strike a similar note, whether it's Citizen Tom Paine; or Jefferson drafting
the Declaration of Independence; or Hamilton, Madison, and Jay, signing
their Federalist Papers with the name Publius.

It's not easy to find a name for this tradition. Some like to call it the
Conservative tradition, though they mean a pre-capitalist, pre-industrial,

15

non-propertarian conservatism. Others hark back to Rome and "*res publica*" and fashion from it the sense of a republican tradition. It's a tradition that emphasizes the dignity and glory of the free citizen; it celebrates the capacity to lay aside narrow interest in favor of an intelligent caring for the whole; it fosters a commitment to open, responsible, and accountable structures of government; and it proclaims the innate satisfactions of public life.

The irony of this tradition is that it has leaned towards aristocracy— towards conservative, or conserving, outlooks and policies. It likes to claim that it is not an aristocracy of birth or of wealth or of honor, but an aristocracy of political excellence that unites savvy, elegance, courage, magnanimity, and concern for the whole. Thus, though it has been a rich and strong source of republican principles and manners, it has not necessarily been hospitable to democracy. Democracy for Plato and Aristotle was associated with the more irresponsible and fractious elements of the population, and this attitude can be found also in Cicero, and, in more muted form, with the founders of the American republic.

But, then, neither has this tradition of the free citizen been necessarily opposed to democracy. Its concern has been to look for and assist in the emergence of citizens, no matter what their origin, who freely and fully accept their responsibility for the whole. Their social and/or economic status is ultimately irrelevant.

Two questions occur: can this tradition be revived and reconstituted in democratic terms? And, can this tradition find renewed strength, and a democratic grounding as well, within an ecological framework? The answer to both questions is Yes!

Seven Ecological Principles*

There are several ecologically derived principles or criteria that together provide a new natural grounding for the tradition of the free citizen, the excellence of public life, and vigorous democracy. I identify seven such principles.

1. Ecology teaches that everything in nature is connected to everything else. Ecology points out that human beings are part of nature. Thus everything in the world that comes as a result of human work is also connected to everything else. One can never do just one thing. Whether one engages in a scientific inquiry, or faces a medical disorder, or encounters a political problem, it is necessary to ask the extra questions of how *this* affects *that*, what more needs to be brought into focus, and whether this or that action will have what sort of consequences. The more we human beings understand this, and learn what it means in everyday life, the closer

---

*The End-note for this chapter references a variety of works that provide a background for this discussion.

we come to that intelligent caring for the whole that is so celebrated in the tradition of the free citizen.

2. Ecology teaches us a love and respect for "all things." No part of the cosmos or of our planet earth, none of the activities we human beings engage in, nor any parts of our bodies and personal life, nor any animals, such as serpents or pigs, are to be marked as evil, or unclean, or inherently corruptible. Ecology directs a caveat to all religions in this regard. Ecology helps us heal the ancient split between "higher" and "lower" things, between soul (or mind) and body, between the "spiritual" and the "carnal," and between the things of "this world" and the "things of heaven."

Res publica (public things), governing and government: these are part of "all things." Ecology, in its emphasis on holistic thinking, in its correlative insistence that everything is connected to everything else, represents a tremendous breakthrough for viewing *res publica* as a natural sphere, a region of real life to be treated the same way as any other sphere of life. Ecology helps us reclaim public life and the terrain of government from the obloquy, shame, misunderstanding, recriminations, irrational projection, that have been heaped upon it by the four traditions identified above. Public life and the spheres of government are a human activity. As an activity it is no better or worse, no richer or poorer, in its qualities or meaning than other seminal human spheres of activity such as the family, or business, or agriculture, the professions, religion, the arts and sciences, or sports.

Indeed, one can well make the argument, as did Aristotle in the first book of his *Politics*—an argument echoed by Hannah Arendt in her famous work written in 1960, *The Human Condition*—that in basic respects public life offers greater scope for the exercise of human capacities for excellence than either private family life or the world of the professions and business.

Confirmed despisers and haters of *res publica* might scoff at this, but government service need not be left to the suave manipulator, the braggart, the visionless technocrat, the combative militant, the informer, the zealot, the seducer, the control freak, the purloiner, the liar, the murderer. Surely we've learned enough about the history of the family or the church or corporate business to know that in these respectable spheres of life the very same syndromes and ingrained behaviors are also rampant! Yet our culture nurses the myopic notion that family life is the fountain of virtue, that business, though it is made of tougher stuff than the family perhaps, is nevertheless efficient and therefore fundamentally honest, etc,. etc.— but that politics and all its works is just plain dirty.

On the contrary! The political terrain, though vulnerable as any terrain to distortion and corruption, is also a terrain for the pursuit of the true, the good, and the beautiful. We can say that without fear of contradiction once we divest ourselves of the Great Pejorative fed to us by past traditions and once we embrace an ecological consciousness which tells us to respect life in all its varied spheres of activity.

This is a major issue. If we humans can learn to apply an ecological consciousness of respect for the political terrain, if we can develop a culture of positive and creative thoughts about that terrain, then we have at long last, in the long and tortuous development of our species, reached the beginning of maturity as a species.

Some, still harboring cynical thoughts, may argue that politics is under the Great Pejorative precisely because it, more than any other sphere of life, is the place where tough decisions get displaced, decisions that would not or could not be made in the spheres of the family, professions, business, sports, and so on. That is why we humans invented this sphere to begin with, the place where conflict in society must ultimately be resolved one way or the other. Because of this, the stakes being invariably very high, and there being no other place to go for a decision, and the abyss of war being the only alternative, the political terrain becomes an intense furnace of conflicting interests, perceptions, and passions; and becomes an inevitable magnet for every manner of skulduggery, underhanded dealing, and arbitrary force, no matter how adroitly such force and fraud may be concealed. In this sense, it may be said, that statecraft, no matter what you might otherwise expect of it, is to a much greater degree than any other sphere, the activity most deeply immersed in ugliness and squalor.

That is a powerful argument. Its very force, however, is drawn from its own implied acknowledgment of the healing and creative functions of the political terrain. It is the only real alternative to warfare invented by human beings, whether that be civil war or war with those on the outside. Not only can and does the political terrain offer scope for healing conflict but it also offers opportunity for creative leaps forward in new policies and new ways to achieve greater democracy, often through the stern discipline of resolving conflict. Though the ugliness is there and often seems to triumph, the terrain itself remains an indispensable and natural realm of the human search for self-improvement and a stable, healthy society.

The political terrain offers instances of stunning breakthroughs. Two stand out in very recent memory: The Solidarity movement's successful effort to bring the Polish Communist regime to a Round Table for talks in the early spring of 1989, an event that triggered a whole new beginning in Polish political and socioeconomic life, and which then in turn led to the fall of the Wall in Germany and throughout eastern Europe in the autumn of that year. Similarly, there was the seemingly miraculous detente in South Africa between the white reactionary government and Nelson Mandela's

African Congress that led directly and peacefully to the emergence of a new constitutional republic in that country.

3. Ecology teaches that the natural relationship between two or more entities is the peer relationship. In instances where the peer relationship is not overtly evident as in parent/child, teacher/student, professional/apprentice, and the like, the goal is to evolve into a peer relationship.

We humans are part of nature. We are not on top. We are not beneath or subordinate, either. We are *with* nature. This fundamental truth has immense meaning and significance for all other relationships. To grasp it, we must turn our mental image away from its millennia-old habit of viewing things from top to bottom, and from bottom to top, and instead develop an image of side-by-side.

Fully adult relationships are interactive on a horizontal plane. This is the posture of true exchange and of dialog. It is also the posture of freedom: freedom for the one, freedom for the other, freedom for every participant. From this is born the very notion and possibility of the free citizen. Ecology teaches us that every being, every person, shares in the posture of side-by-side. By nature, if one may say so, human beings are interactive beings in a side-by-side relationship. Here we find affirmed the notion of the free citizen and the democracy of free citizens. Hitherto, concepts of the free citizen and democracy have been validated by appeals to historical development or to divine revelation or to a higher reason that has extricated itself from mere nature. But with the coming of ecological awareness and wisdom, we must acknowledge that, however helpful these earlier attempts at validation may have been, they are insufficient and weak when seen in the light of what we now know about the processes of nature and our human place within them.

Rudyard Kipling may have had something like this in mind when he wrote "For there is neither East nor West, Border nor Breed nor Birth, when two strong men stand face to face, though they come from the ends of the earth." We must correct for his limiting the encounter to men and we can do so, with his blessing probably, by substituting the word persons for men. His is an arresting image of two persons, both free, both part of nature, both with nature, encountering each other in peace and curiosity, aware of each other's strength, and wanting/willing to find and practice a significant connection. It is more real, I would submit, than Thomas Hobbes' famous insistence on "the war of all against all" in his image of the state of nature.

4. Diversity is a hallmark, perhaps THE hallmark, of nature. Nature is lavish and teems with different life forms. We humans, as one of those life forms, are part of this variety. And within our own species, there is a tremendous diversity.

For much too long we have been in the thrall of cultural, philosophic, and religious forces that have sought to get us to escape this natural diversity, and even our own personal diversity!, in the direction of a more uniform life, and on behalf of so-called higher and more abstract values. Fortunately, there is now at work in the world a growing acknowledgment of natural variety and human diversity. Feminism, multiculturalism, and the movement for an alternative economics have raised powerful critiques, respectively, of the "unitary fallacy" inherent for millennia in patriarchy; of the cultural hegemony and brainwashing embedded in white, Eurocentric world views; and of the mass market society promoted by multinational corporate capitalism which destroys communities and bio-regions and reduces human relations to impersonal, interchangeable monetary values. These movements can find a sure foundation for their critiques in the pronounced emphasis on natural and human diversity that is the hallmark of ecology.

5. Ecology, having brought us human beings to re-enter the world of nature, and in a new way, and having shown us that we humans are not on top, nor on the bottom, tells us that the appropriate scientific and scholarly relationship of subject and object is one of dialog between the observer and the observed. This too has immense implications, not only for science and scholarly work in whatever discipline, but for society and politics as well.

No one observer, no one discipline, no one institute or organization, no one of anything, can claim to see everything about a given object or context or whole. Even multiple takings of the same object by the same observer, as in a series of photographs let's say, will not render that object. Furthermore, each attempt at rendering is itself a function of a relationship at that given time and place between the observer and the observed. Or, to put it more bluntly, the observer partly creates the object (I would say, co-creates the object) through his or her best scientific efforts to describe it. These are the findings, now well attested to by a growing number of scientists and scholars, drawing on the work of post-Newtonian, quantum physics. In this process, respect for the object and a capacity for listening to its responses are at a premium. Indeed, not only is there the need to note carefully its responses, but to understand the object as a self-organized, self-organizing entity. The object thus is not a passive thing, nor only something that is capable of responding, but it has independent agency and moves where it will. *Cooperating* with the object becomes the true scientific posture. It is also the true political posture.

We are thus pushed even more strongly towards diversity, towards peer relationships, and towards dialog. We have ecological grounds for insisting, for the sake of science (and of art and of any human endeavor), on respect for difference, because on it rests the possibility of reaching a better and better understanding of a given object, a given project, a given context, a given whole. The need for input from everyone who is in relation to the object, the project, the context, or the whole is now a necessity, not just a nice thing to do.

Nowhere is this more clearly seen or needed than in the political terrain. Here, in any given political situation, the issues are highly charged and the context of claims needing clarification are highly diverse and complex. Nor is there necessarily one right answer. Often it's a judgment call whether the decision should go this way or that way. The terrain, in other words, is wide open. There is no fixed answer, there is no final authority to appeal to — though many would seek, and have sought, such authority in auguries or religious oracles, or the counsel of elders, or' the fist of the dictator. This being the case, it is essential that the diversity of concerns, of viewpoints, of insights that are inherent and available in the situation be present in the making of the decision. One can see how the political realm is made to order for the free citizen and for the democracy of citizens. It is as if they are made for one another, and ecology has shown us the way.

6. Ecology validates the democracy of diversity, participation, and representation. Governing can now be seen for what it is: a natural activity. To be natural in an ecological sense, the government must be with the people, not on top, not on the bottom. Given the fact of diversity, all contexts, perspectives and concerns that are pertinent to making decisions must be present and/or represented in the governing activity.

Government is not a matter of stable certainties anymore than the society it attempts to govern. Both are always changing; they are always in a dynamic condition. There are links or conduits between society and government that can assist in keeping the connections clear and keeping both government and society connected with each other. These links or conduits are of several kinds, but two in particular are critical because they, in contrast to lobbies and pressure groups, seek to bring a holistic focus to the surge of issues and problems that tend always to overwhelm governments and confuse the people. They are the media and political parties.

The media, when it is doing its job, is appropriately absorbed in the task of providing information and clarification of issues and problems. Political parties go further and, when they are doing their job, pose public policy pathways to the people and, if they find sufficient support among the people for their proposed pathway, they conduct the course of government to those ends.

It is therefore, exceedingly critical for the health of the society and government, and for the republic, that these pathways, and the parties that develop and sustain them, be given full opportunity to emerge, develop, and thrive. In this way, the flux of change is tempered into focussed pathways and is kept fluid.

Political parties provide lateral communication among the people—discussion, debate, dialog—that enables them to think about and form opinions on the desirable direction of public policy. The parties, together with a responsive and responsible press, provide continuing communication—discussion, debate, and dialog—between the governing officials and the people.

At the local level, it is often possible to achieve a degree of direct democracy that is both effective and participatory. There may or may not be need for political parties at this level. The need for them is less since the people can develop direct access to a common dialog via town meetings and direct conversation with governing officials. Yet, it is also the case that most of the people do not spend most of their time on public problems and public discussion; and they have not had an opportunity to hear focussed and holistic arguments about the desirable course of local public policy. Here, again, media can help to inform and clarify, but it may be that parties can show and promote alternative pathways for public choice.

At the more-than-local level, direct democracy is much harder to achieve, though there are intimations that forms of teledemocracy may come into being that will link governing officials directly with the people. However, representative government is still a more practical way of achieving democratic participation in state, regional, national, and international bodies; and it has the additional advantage of providing an opportunity for a full public life for many citizens who have deliberately chosen to pursue a political life; and of providing the general public with such citizens who have so chosen. Once again, however, one perceives the advantages of vigorous political parties, whose internal discipline calls for rotation of party leadership and of candidates for office; and that call for the continuing full development of new perspectives fostered by a direct involvement in the issues of concern to their communities.

One or another form of proportional representation is the best method of assuring representation of the variety of concerns, perspectives, and arguments about the desirable course of public policy. Thus an ecological politics would seem to mandate proportional representation — both in the representative governing bodies and within the political parties themselves.

We've been describing representative government. Mention has also been made of direct democracy, but only briefly. Experimentation with forms of direct democracy should be high on everyone's list of priorities for improving participatory and effective government. Worthy of exploration is the creation of a two-chambered government at the local level. One chamber would be formed by electing representatives in the traditional way. But the other chamber would be composed of delegates from durable nongovernmental organizations. The two chambers would have equal powers, and would together constitute the local government. Joint Committees, as in the U.S. House of Representatives and Senate, would iron out differences. This could go hand-in-hand with traditional annual town meetings.

A two-chambered government of this kind could also be created for state-wide and nation-wide federations of local, bio-regionally defined, communities. In each locale, each local chamber (one of representatives and one of delegates) would select citizens other than themselves from the local population to constitute the governing bodies at the state level and the national level respectively. This two-chambered approach, combining two different ways of effecting participation, could also be adapted for the creation of a planetary federation.

7. Ecology offers us a useful insight concerning change. First, that change is part of the order of things. Change is natural. Second, that change is evolutionary. Applied politically, we may distinguish reform, revolution, and transformation. Reform may be described as doing repairs on a given structure, the aim being to make it work again as it was supposed to. Revolution, on the other hand, may be thought of as taking apart the extant structure, destroying it, and starting over.

Transformation is more like evolution. The idea is to grow beyond the extant structure, to transcend it in some significant way. There are fundamental problems the old structure couldn't or wouldn't solve; or there are new and creative ideas and values that simply could not be accommodated by the extant structure, even if it wanted to. The old is not abolished or wiped away, parts of it, maybe large parts, are used in the new form. Ideas and values that seemed to have a life in the old form are not just abandoned or made a mockery of, but are seen in a new light and may be grafted into the new pattern.

Transformation can go fast or slow. It can be in a great leap or go by gentle increments. Democracy is inherent in transformational development, for dialog among the various participants is of the essence. The processes of transformation are thus nonviolent. Force may be present at times, coercion may appear, but the transforming activity aims at supple, energy-saving, action. Openness, transparency of the transactions, clarity at each step of the way, these are at a premium, for otherwise the situation will probably not really change in the direction of something new but it will relapse once again into the old patterns, or even worse.

For transformation to catch on as a new and ecologically appropriate way for human beings to change and adapt and grow, the structures we invent must more and more be capable of being reinvented. Not that the maintenance of the structure is not important. Not as if the capacity to reproduce what the structure was originally intended to produce is not important (whether that be goods and services, or scholarly work, or policy decisions). But additionally important, and hitherto usually depreciated if indeed it was ever really understood, is the capacity of a structure to reinvent itself in the face of new challenges. As it acquires that capacity, learns how to do it well, it becomes a structure that no longer needs either reform or revolution. What it has discovered and put into practice is on the order of evolution itself, which is self-transforming efficacy and power.

The Party as Transforming Agent

The seven points just made may seem to portray a vision of political life that is far, far from present reality. It is understandable, even inevitable, that it should seem that way. The present reality is of a political system that is running on empty. The people seem very close to giving up on their democracy, such as it has come to be.

Is transformation along the lines indicated above and throughout this book, a possible way to think about the way forward? Or is it too modest a political methodology? Is stronger medicine needed?

I believe that transformation is the way forward. But I have also come to believe that transformation needs a specific agent or vehicle. That vehicle is a political party, and it must be a political party of a different kind.

Throughout the history of the American republic, the political party has been the vehicle through which the body politic and its government have achieved fundamental change when faced by a seeming intractable crisis. The Jeffersonians did a bold thing and entered the political list as a party against the Federalists (braving the widespread criticism that this was fomenting "factional" strife). In the next generation, the Jacksonians swept in from the then "west" and shook up the old established powers of the "east." In the 1850's, with the slavery issue now totally center-stage, the Republican Party was formed and brought Lincoln into the presidency. The Populist movement in the 1890's made great headway as a party but lost their momentum in the election of 1896 when many allied themselves with the old Democratic Party. Franklin Roosevelt's New Deal used that same Democratic Party 36 years later to usher in a kind of "urban revolution" in American politics in response to the crisis of the Great Depression.

In retrospect, FDR should have created a new party. He was hobbled by the Democratic Party during his first two terms. In the decades following WWII, the Democratic Party gradually lost its New Deal elan and its moorings in the people. In the 1980's and 1990's, with the rise of Reaganism and the power of the multinational corporate complex, the Democratic

Party has allowed itself to become captive to much of Reaganism and much of the multinational complex. Any voice it can find for ecology, for democracy, for justice, and for community is tenuous and timid. There exists consequently a great political void. It is time that the void be acknowledged and that moves be made to fill it.

The Green Party, of all the third parties that have emerged in the past decades, is most in tune with ecology and thus also it is the one most aware of and responsive to the fundamental crisis facing the nation and the planet in this era. It has a new vision, rooted in the growing awareness by billions of people around the world that we human beings are part of nature. From that, as I have shown in this chapter, there flows a fundamentally new political culture. This new political culture recalls, and renews, the tradition of the free citizen and it looks forward to a democracy of free citizens. Politics, far from being considered a distortion of the human condition by many traditions of the past, emerges once again as a terrain for free men and women to take action to solve their problems together, to find new answers they would never have thought of otherwise, and to discover opportunities for self and mutual fulfillment.

The Green Party, as it matures and grows, must think through very carefully the role of transformative agent. Its role is that of catalyst, one that assists in the coming to be of a self-transformative system. Its role is not to be the new director of the political process. Once it has accomplished the breakthrough that is needed in order to reach an open and just political system, its job as catalyst is completed. It can then evolve into one of several political parties within a framework of proportional representation.

The Green Party is in a unique position to help the human species discover the full meaning of the free citizen and the democracy of free citizens. Democracy is the practice of free citizenship for everyone. As it is practiced, the need that many people now feel to create Non Governmental Organizations (NGOs) to protest a specific abuse, or to confront a particular injustice, or to fight for rights for a certain group, this will change. The free citizen, deeply aware of interconnections and equally aware of diversity and difference, will seek the sort of vehicle for political answers that offers the most opportunity to find common ground among a variety of concerns and viewpoints.

Thus, though the free citizen, whether as elected official or as member of the body politic, will identify with the specific needs, concerns and causes of the NGOs, he or she will nevertheless also work for answers that go beyond the particular NGOs to embrace a fuller and probably more just solution. These answers are always implicit in the multivarious problems, perspectives, and passions that are present in any given situation. But there needs to be those who look for such answers, sense their presence and potential, and find the skill and dedication to work them up into visible, holistic, and persuasive choices. This is the vocation of the free citizen. Many free citizens, connected together in a political party, a party of the kind that seeks truth and justice, can be the catalyst for a continuing politics of transformation. Nor is their range limited to political parties. They can also find an effective role in institutions of direct democracy. Mention has been made above of a two-chambered approach to government at the local but also at the state, national, and planetary level, whereby one of the chambers would be composed of delegates from durable NGO's in the community. This also would provide scope for action by the free citizen who, though attached to the particular need or issue served by an NGO, would also be a leader of larger views capable of seeing, and acting on, the interconnections with other needs and issues.

The creation of such a chamber, however, will only come about if a political party makes it a matter of urgency. The Green Party would seem to be the logical force to push for this form of direct democracy, and/or for other forms thereof.

The Importance of a Political Ecology

In this chapter, I have traced the outlines of a *political* ecology. Hitherto, the environmental/Green movement has produced several varied and often competing ways of thinking about the world. The leading protagonists are social ecology, deep ecology, eco-feminism, and eco-socialism. Though they have significant differences among themselves, they are all characterized by a troubling absence, to a greater or less degree, of political consciousness; and often by a resistance to developing such a consciousness. They have all been deeply affected by the Great Pejorative. They share the prevailing culture's profound misgivings about the political realm. They concentrate instead on cultural and educational change, life style concerns, alternative social institutions, specific grievances of various segments of the population (problems of labor, the environment, people of color, women, gays and lesbians, senior citizens, and the like), and community-wide issues. But even when, in their organizing, they address the interconnection of the particular issues, and engage in demonstrations, sit-ins, lobbying, and the like, they do not take the next step. They are shy of entering the political realm directly and in a forthright and organized way to do battle with the entrenched political power of the oligarchy and its politicians. They leave the field to the monied, power-driven movers and shakers of public policy. The latter are only too happy to see their potential opposition busying themselves on the fringes of public policy decision making, contenting themselves with loud and brash statements of protest, or immersing themselves in "nonpartisan" good causes. The structures of power are impervious to such fringe activities, and those who command these structures make decisions that inevitably and often irreversibly shape the world.

There is a political ecology, as I have shown. It provides a basis in theory and in our consciousness for a forthright renewal and deepening of the tradition of the free citizen. On that foundation, the peoples of this nation and the peoples of the world will enter the political realm in numbers. They will transform the structures. They will shoulder aside the corrupting forces of domination and greed. They will create the basis for a politics of justice, community, democracy, and ecological survival.

Chapter Two
Ralph Nader and the Transformation of Politics

Ralph Nader's campaign for the presidency of the United States under the Green Party banner in 1996 was a signpost on the way to the transformation of politics. At the root of this transformation is action on behalf of the Ten Key Values of the Green movement. These values have served as both a foundation and a common rallying cry for the Greens of whatever description since 1984, the year the Green Movement/Party was founded in the United States.

The Ten Key values are Ecological Wisdom, Personal and Social Responsibility, Grass Roots Democracy, Nonviolence, Respect for Diversity, Community Economics, Decentralization, Male/Female Equality, Global Responsibility, and Future Focus (or, in the language of the Native American tradition which has strongly influenced the Greens, Thinking to the Seventh Generation).

Four powerful and timely goals inspire Green thinking and action: they are the renewal of democracy, the recovery of justice, the defense and deepening of community life, and the full scale practice of an ecological economics.

For these goals to have a chance at being realized, however, there has to be a profound turning towards a better and different politics. This turning begins and has its being in the reclamation of politics as a truthful, honest, and creative endeavor. It is in this way that Ralph Nader is a harbinger of things to come.

Nader's run, and that of his fearless and caring running mate Winona LaDuke, can and will be seen as a defining moment for Greens, for liberals and progressives, major parties and other third parties. Though on the ballot in only 21 states, he and LaDuke came in fourth behind Clinton, Dole, and Perot. Their 800,000 votes brought them in ahead of the Libertarian, Natural Law and Taxpayers Party candidates. These three parties, though they had the advantage of being on the ballot in 50, 44, and 39 states respectively, yet trailed the Greens.

There are those of the opinion that Ralph's numbers could have been greater. It seemed in the early months of 1996 that with a little bit of money, less absorption by Ralph and his handlers in the niceties of state election laws, and greater concentration by everyone involved in the different and sometimes disparate parts of the overall campaign, that Ralph and Winona could have been on the ballot in over 40 states. They could, in a word, have gained well over five percent of the total vote. As it was, only

7% of the American people even knew that he was running. Suppose that seven times as many, say 50%, would have known that Ralph and Winona were on the ballot? This might well have yielded 5 million votes.

Yet far more important than the numbers at this juncture are several qualitative developments that point to a subtle shift from one political paradigm to another, and this is significant for the future of the Greens and for the future of American politics.

Ralph Nader's entry into electoral politics was a major event. From perennial and internationally acclaimed consumer advocate to political partisan would be a big step for anyone. But for Nader it is a truly giant step given the fact that the numerous organizations he has founded and nurtured over a period of thirty years are nonprofit, nonpartisan organizations depending on the good will of many Democrats and Independents and some Republicans; and depending on the perception among the general citizenry that these organizations, and their founder himself, are above partisan struggle. The aim of these organizations is to further a certain cause, to inform the public, to lobby Congress, to impress the media about that cause. They definitely are not out there stumping for a political party. Furthermore, the air they breathe, the milieu in which they move, is outside the electoral sphere and tends to be fairly skeptical if not cynical about politics.

Why then did Nader defy the odds and habits of a lifetime and get into partisan politics? The answer, quite simply, is to be found in his growing conviction that ordinary people, even those who put more than ordinary effort into civic action, are finding it harder and harder to influence public opinion and public policy development. They are shouldered aside by special interests, especially those organized by major corporations, who buy access to and the loyalty of willing politicians of both major parties. It is a deadly game that multinational megacorporations win most of the time. Their control works its way into communities, schools, the media, philanthropic activities, medical care, sports, and religion. Democracy as a goal and way of life is withering away. The power of people, both as individuals and voluntarily associating together, is diminishing under the impact of a gradually invasive corporate consciousness. Under its influence, citizens learn to spout and tout sacred corporate canons of nature-destroying growth, education as merely training for corporate promotion, and freedom as opportunity to consume. The individual person, whether as householder, worker, student, taxpayer, investor/stockholder, consumer, small businessman and woman, or as citizen is downsized, downgraded, patronized, bullied, made to feel powerless, and made to feel ashamed of any such feelings.

Nader therefore found it necessary to shift gears: to enter the electoral domain of partisan electoral politics and assist in building an alternative political party. Though this realm is dominated by special interests and corporate power, it is still to some degree ruled by the ballot box, and is still regarded by the citizens as presenting the possibility of choice. Nader's message was: go where the lines can be most clearly drawn, go there to fight the hard fight for democracy and the recovery of our freedom. Fight power with new power. Go electoral and build a party that can contest seriously with the two embrittled ones.

So...build a new party, yes! But why the Greens? The answer he has given to me, many of my fellow Greens, and reporters and commentators, goes something like this. The Greens have demonstrated a degree of effective electoral action beyond that of the New Party, the Labor Party, or any other reasonably progressive political force in the country. In addition, they have demonstrated grassroots organizing around community issues and in local electoral campaigns based on a strong emphasis on bottom-up action. Via the Greens, he is able to conduct a campaign that is geared to the local grassroots in which he can be a catalyst, a helper, a guide and not have to play the role of hero on a horse. In his view, this justified his controversial decision to stay within a $5000 spending limit for his entire campaign. This meant that he did not have to make financial reports to the Federal Election Commission, something he wanted very much to avoid. It meant that grassroots, draft-Nader committees in the various states had to raise and spend money on their own. It meant that he could not exercise "control from the top" even if he had wanted to.

But it also meant that the National Draft Nader Clearing House created by Linda Martin and others in Washington D.C. found it extremely difficult to raise money for their operations. The more Nader touted how he was only spending $5000 (from his own resources) the more difficult it became to raise campaign funds for the very separate national draft Nader campaign and for the many draft Nader committees in the various states. Most people did not understand the rigorous nature of this separation, required by FEC rules, between Nader the candidate and the Draft Nader Committees. They each ran as hard a campaign as they could, but were each hobbled by the "separation."

Nader's stated purposes in running, repeated many times, was to help existing state Green parties develop and grow, to foster new state Green parties wherever possible, to push into the national debate the central issues of runaway corporate power and the crisis of democracy, and to send the establishment, especially Bill Clinton and Al Gore, a message that Americans do have a choice beyond Democrat and Republican. These purposes, limited in scope, operationally credible, and strategically inspiring, were all realized to one degree or another. They formed a basis for further political development and growth.

Nader chose not to become a member of the Green Party. This puzzled many Greens, and was resented by some, though as the campaign proceeded, many of those who first opposed him as "not a Green," or as not taking up issues considered important to them, did in the end support and work for his election.

Some Greens and others were dismayed at Nader's caution in getting involved in a range of social issues. Yet he convinced some that the way in which such issues are posed by the media (and often the way they are fought out in society at large) is divisive. It is divisive for a campaign that seeks to focus primary attention on a fundamental issue, runaway corporate power, the decline of democracy, and the evisceration of truth in politics. And it is divisive for the various groups who go to bat for specific causes or groups. They end by competing with one another as pressure groups, wresting small gains from a corrupted system, when they could be associating together, certainly at election time, to find a common political ground to shake and change that corrupted system, and thus improving matters for everyone including themselves. Nader's campaign deserves praise for its gentle attempt to help people see themselves as citizens first.

There is another side to his decision not to become a Green. Just as he was free to choose what part of the Green message to promote, so too were the Green parties free to promulgate their basic message independent of Nader and his own messages. In the end, both learned from each other and the potential for the future is rich. On the one hand, Greens around the country began to focus much of their campaign arguments around Nader's themes of runaway corporate hegemony and the tools of democracy. This bode well because it provided a solid grounding for common action between Nader and the Greens; and it rescued them from the perception (and sometimes the reality) of being "only" an environmental party, in the limited sense in which that word has currency in the conventional media. At the same time, Nader became more aware of the key Green value of ecological wisdom.

For Greens, ecology is not just an add-on to all the other issues, though that is the way the environment is treated by Democrats and Republicans, many liberals and progressives, and new third parties like the New Party. For Greens, ecology is a central factor in all of the issues: whether it's health, the state of our communities, labor practices, problems of our cities, gender and racial issues, and, especially, the structure and operations of the economy and its allocation and treatment of resources. It's not enough to contest and try to overcome the dominance of megacorporations, or to separate them from the pockets of politicians, or even to seek to make them, internally, compatible with democracy, though of course these things are vitally important. But for Greens, it is a blazing necessity that businesses of all kinds, from small to very large, develop a new relationship to nature, one that radically reduces waste, eliminates pollution and ecological degradation, and ends the mindless depletion of natural resources. On this change the fate of humanity depends. Ralph Nader has expressed a greater interest than in the past in learning far more about just what this means for corporate structure and practices, the economy as a whole, and for the way of life of our society.

To recapitulate: three big issues are making their way to center stage and will endure for a long time: (1) runaway corporate power; (2) the recovery of democracy (that includes the restitution of citizen power , community power at home and abroad); and, (3) the rising need to overcome the waste, depletion, and poisoning of nature and its resources. These issues came together politically with the joining of Nader/LaDuke and the Greens. It was a unique and historic union. That it happened is a tribute to Nader and LaDuke and to the Greens, but it is also testimony to the inevitability of the big three issues. Together they are irresistible.

It is anybody's guess whether or not the struggle over these issues will result in creative and timely answers. But the struggle itself will be at center stage. And the Green Party and their candidates will be at the forefront of the struggle in most of the countries of the world. It is happening. It will happen more and more.

Middleburg

A significant step forward was taken just ten days after the Nader/LaDuke campaign came to an end with the 1996 election. The Green Parties of Connecticut and Maine called a meeting in Middleburg, Virginia of Greens, who, in their various states, had been involved in the Nader/LaDuke campaign. The letter calling the meeting specified that, with Nader in attendance, the purpose of the gathering was to explore how and when to form an Association of State Green Parties. Greens from 31 states attended, far more than the organizers had expected. The organizers were Linda Martin of the Virginia Green Party and Director of the Draft Nader Clearing House in Washington D.C., Tom Linzey of the Pennsylvania Green Party and lawyer for the Draft Nader Clearing House, Bert Garskof, representing the Connecticut Green Party, and me on behalf of the Maine Green Party.

The spirit of the meeting was high. Far from considering Nader's showing as something to explain or "put in perspective," the participants recounted the excitement of their campaigns for Nader and for many other candidates for U.S. Senate, Congress, state legislatures, and local town and city offices. They exchanged notes on their struggles for ballot access, fund-raising, media access, and on their success in "getting the message out." The many new Greens who had been drawn into the electoral fight by the Nader/LaDuke run for president seized the chance to get to know the folks they'd been working with in the national Nader Clearing House.

In a roll call of the states on the Saturday night of the conference, Greens from 11 states declared that their parties were ready to join an Association of State Green Parties, and many others declared their intention to work for affiliation of their state parties with such an Association. Some cautioned at the speed at which things were moving. Still others expressed skepticism about going ahead with such an association in the face of opposition from the Greens/Green Party USA (G/GPUSA), an organization dating from 1991. A letter had been circulated by the leadership of G/GPUSA remonstrating against the Middleburg conference and many had been warned by officials of G/GPUSA not to attend. Howie Hawkins, founder of the Left Green Network in 1987 and a leading figure in the G/GPUSA, came to the meeting on Sunday afternoon to try to dissuade participants from creating the association. He was given time to present his views at the close of the conference on Sunday afternoon.

In response to these concerns, several pointed out that the two organizations could coexist. They said that the newly forming Association of State Green Parties aims primarily at fostering and giving a national presence to Green political electoral work, whereas G/GPUSA, though it includes a few state parties, is a membership organization of dues paying locals and individuals, many of whom prefer non-electoral action over that of political electoral action. Several also pointed out that the idea of an association of state Green parties goes back at least to 1992 and that in subsequent years the idea of such an association was approved by several state Green parties. So that, far from this being a sudden new development moving too fast, the idea of an association is now taking a logical next step.

Several voices persisted in pointing out that there is bound to be conflict with G/GPUSA. Some of these voices thought of this as a negative to be avoided if at all possible. Others said that yes there will be conflict, that competition is unavoidable, and that the association should be ready for it and push forward. Still others pointed to the conflicting concepts of unity as a barrier that seemed hard to surmount.

Implicit in these arguments was another that eventually would prove to be very influential if not decisive in the year ahead. Instead of debating the meaning of "unity," and instead of taking sides "for" the party or "for" the movement, this argument simply proposed a national Green party based on statewide Green parties. The assumption here was that each state party has it's own unique way of uniting "party" and "movement," that each state party deserves and requires autonomy in this regard, and that each state party in turn would be based on party locals and/or party/movement locals. In this way, the line would be more and more clearly drawn between a G/GPUSA based on dues-paying locals and individual memberships and an Association of State Green Parties based squarely on state Green parties.

At Middleburg, strong voices could be heard refuting the claim that the meeting, since it was not done under the auspices of the G/GPUSA, was therefore unauthorized and maybe even illegitimate. They pointed to the fact that most state Green parties had chosen not to affiliate with G/GPUSA since its formation in 1991. In addition, the Green gatherings in Albuquerque in 1995 and in Los Angeles in 1996 were planned and conducted outside the "authority" of G/GPUSA. Similarly, the 40 State Green Parties! project in 1995-1996, which sought to inspire the expansion and strengthening of Green parties through a Green presidential campaign, was conducted separately from G/GPUSA. Yet another separate action was the Third Parties '96 project, organized by the Green Politics Network, which sponsored three Green-led national conferences in 1995/96. Its twofold purpose was to stimulate dialog and cooperation among many third parties and to search for a presidential candidate. These efforts converged in the candidacy of Ralph Nader. Finally, in this same vein, when the Green Parties of Maine and Connecticut sent out a call for the Middleburg conference, they did so independently of the G/GPUSA.

The conference passed a provisional set of bylaws. The bylaws provided for a coordinating committee composed of two representatives from each participating state Green Party. The conference laid plans for a meeting of the coordinating committee in early March, 1997. The plans included the hope and expectation that by the year 2000 a fully fledged Green Party federation would come into being.

The Middleburg conference culminated on Sunday with a talk by Ralph Nader. He recalled highlights of his campaign and affirmed his intention to work with the association and with Green Parties. There was also a hint that he might be considering running for the U.S. Senate in Connecticut as a candidate of the Green Party against Senator Dodd in 1998. An air of confidence and bright hopes pervaded the meeting. The delegates were determined to move forward to build a durable and vigorous national Green political party in the United States, one based on grassroots political organizing efforts in all 50 states. It must be a party, they believed, that would be not just a counter force to the Democrats and Republicans but a party of values, of speaking truth, and of spurring continuing dialog among the people, in a word, a party of a different kind.

The presidential campaign of Ralph Nader and Winona LaDuke had been a significant factor, perhaps a *sine qua non*, in bringing the various Green Parties in the many states of the union together at Middleburg. For all who had been engaged for many years in building Green political parties and/or in nurturing the idea of a countrywide association of such parties, or were new to the struggle, Middleburg was a godsend and a watershed. Part IV describes the expansion and further evolution of the Association of State Green Parties.

Five Hurdles Facing the Greens

The path forward for the Greens in the United States has many hurdles in it, some of them covered with thorns. Five hurdles are especially onerous: first, an internal struggle over the form and meaning of a national political party; second, the difficulty of persuading many liberals and progressives to wrench free of their fear of leaving the Democratic Party; third, the slowness of Greens in educating themselves and one another about power and money, and about engagement and transformation; fourth, the rigidity and inertia of established institutions, especially evident in the political sphere; and fifth, as Greens become more successful, the threat of greater and more nasty attacks than hitherto from the established powers.

The internal struggle to create a viable national Green Party has been an important preoccupation almost from the beginning of Green national organizing in St. Paul in 1984. Parts III and IV in this book detail this struggle. Some have lamented that the internal struggle takes away energy of numbers of activists who might otherwise be putting more of that energy and time into their state parties and into creating an effective national party. Yet that energy must be expended. As will become clear in later chapters, a point may be in sight when the fight over what kind of national political organization is appropriate for the Greens will finally be over. Almost all of the states with up-and-running state Green parties have now come together in the Association of State Green Parties (ASGP). As of the December of 1998, this organization is now far along in its transformation into a national Green Party.

The Greens are discovering, through the test of experience, that the best way to achieve an end to the fighting is to pursue a form of organization that encourages diversity, decentralization, individual state party autonomy, and the opportunity in each state to work out its own way of resolving the seeming conflicts between electoral and non-electoral strategies and between "left," "moderate," and "right" ideological residues. These contradictions will recede as Greens learn that there is a way forward that moves beyond the conventional ideological stereotypes of left, moderate, and right. Those who can't or won't learn to move beyond the ideological walls of the old paradigm will continue to voice acrimony and invective. Hopefully, they will be ignored and eventually encouraged to join other groups more hospitable to their ideology and style of polemics.

In any event, the newly minted Association of State Green Parties is now widely regarded by most Greens as a major step towards building a creative form of a national organization.

The second barrier on the road ahead is the continued ambivalence of many progressive-minded voters and leaders about a truly independent alternative politics. Sometimes the ambivalence expresses itself as down-right hostility. Liberals and progressives feel under great pressure from the Democratic Party. They find it hard to break the connection that has long held them in bondage to positions and policies that defy most all the values, goals, and interests dear to them and for which they've fought many a hard fight. They seem not able to realize that their party has turned these values and goals into rhetoric. It is also the case that individual liberals and progressives have found a leadership niche in the Democratic Party. This gives them a measure of power in the party and they will not readily relinquish it.

During October 1996, in the month before the election, the progressive publication *The Nation* carried articles by progressive leaders Jeff Faux, Jim Hightower, Jesse Jackson, and others, calling on *The Nation*'s readership to vote for Clinton and the Democrats. All were significantly silent about Nader and the Greens, even though *The Nation* had earlier run a set of articles on Nader's campaign. When I scanned the articles by Hightower et al. in the midst of my campaign in Maine for the United States Senate, I recalled with bemusement the strong efforts in the fall of 1995 by a group of us connected with the Green Politics Network to enlist progressive leaders to create a "presidential cabinet" as part of our effort to persuade a prominent national figure such as Ralph Nader or Jim Hightower to run for president. We figured that a cluster of articulate leaders supporting a candidate would help spur one of them to run. We eventually hit pay dirt with Ralph Nader. But Hightower, and others like Joel Rogers and Danny Cantor, founders of the New Party, backed away.

This liberal/progressive ambivalence was also manifest in the pro-Clinton stand taken by the Sierra Club and, indeed, by most of the environmental lobbies in Washington D.C. The AFL/CIO strongly campaigned for Clinton and the Democrats. Nor was the Labor Party, fresh from a founding convention in June 1996, willing to bring a voice to bear on behalf of an independent politics.

Arguments have been made excusing the labor unions, including the argument that in the short run the Democrats are the shield that protects labor from the Republicans. A similar argument is made by the environmentalists, and presumably figured in the decision by the Sierra Club nationally to push for Clinton and then to prod state Sierra Clubs, as in Maine, to support losing Democratic candidates like Joe Brennan instead of Greens like myself. The Sierra Club and other established environmental organizations followed a similar tactic in two important Green races in 1997: the run for Congress in New Mexico by Carol Miller in the spring of 1997 and Madelyn Hoffman's bid for governor in New Jersey that fall. They endorsed the Democrat in each case even though each was transparently weak on the environment. The Sierra Club repeated this tactic when they endorsed Phil Maloof, a big business Democrat and no friend of the environment, in a special election for Congress in New Mexico's first Congressional district in June 1998. The man they did not endorse, but should have, was Green Party candidate Bob Anderson. Anderson upset the apple cart of establishment politics by getting 15% of the vote. Maloof lost to a Republican in a district in which the Democrats outnumber Republican voters by 3 to 1. Times they are a'changing but progressive lobbies and leaders continue in the old tracks, wrapping themselves up in the old familiar arguments of loyalty-in-spite-of-all to a moribund Democratic Party.

These losing tactics have been repeated election after election, stretching back decades. Meanwhile, the condition of the poor, of the cities, of people of color, of city and country, of children, of the working man and woman, of the middle class, of labor unions, and of the environment has worsened steadily. Even more ominous is the rising degree to which, in election after election, the megacorporations and the monied interests pour money into the campaigns of both major parties and their candidates. They overwhelm politics and policy making, not only with their money, but with their expertise and their control of the media.

This means that policies aimed at sensible health care for everyone, fundamental tax reform, small business revival, the reconstruction of our cities, the protection of American jobs, support for family and community life, clean air and water, healthy food, and an economy in synch with ecological survival cannot and will not get off the ground. It is for this reason that Ralph Nader focused so hard on the devastating role of large corporations in the body politic: unless and until their stranglehold on our politics and our politicians is broken, nothing serious can be done about our major problems. It is for this reason that I and other Greens running in other states for high office, found ourselves focusing on that fundamental barrier.

But don't many progressives and liberals agree that big corporate money in the pockets of politicians is a tough and all-consuming problem? Yes, yet still they stick with the Democratic Party and seem to think if they hang on long enough they will reform it at last. In the face of decades of greater and greater embroilment of the Democratic Party in the race for money, these hardy but flagellated souls continue to hope and pray for reform. There is irony here and food for thought.

I make two responses to this. The short answer is that Nader's issues of the hypertrophy of corporate power and the perversion of democracy by the monied interests are for him not the goal of his political engagement but are means towards the goals. The goal is to build a political force, free of the Democratic Party, which will compete effectively with the powers-that-be; and correlatively, the goal is to clear the way for the rebirth of citizen self-help in the interest of justice, ecology, community, and democracy. Liberals and progressives who remain locked into the Democratic Party may indeed want to fight corporate abuse of politics and corporate hegemony generally, but by working within the Democratic Party and relying on that party to pursue corrective policies, they render themselves politically ineffective. For Nader and for the Greens the struggle against corporate aggrandizement and creeping tyranny is a strategy towards a larger end; but for many liberals and progressives it becomes merely a tactic within the larger "strategy" of keeping the Democratic Party functioning and in place.

The longer response is as follows. Something else may be going on in the political souls of liberals and progressives, which overrules the distress and repugnance they feel regarding the domination of the Democratic party by big corporate money.

In this book, I have described that "something else" as a protest mentality, or, as I would also describe it: an underdeveloped political consciousness. Liberals and progressives by the millions have grown used to letting others "up there" run the store, reserving to themselves the noble task of criticizing how they run it and/or contenting themselves with lobbying for a variety of causes. They call for this or that structural reform, or policy change, or program for the poor and the needy. Some lobby, some demonstrate and march, some do charity, some push community issues, some work for the election of a Democrat or, in rare cases, a moderate Republican. But the attitude basically guiding the sometimes stupendous amount of energy expended on these things is one of protest, rebellion, anger at how bad things are, wringing of the hands at the latest horror depicted on TV or in the newspapers, and the like.

They stop short of taking responsibility for running the store. Even more, they recoil at the thought of actually transforming the store itself.

It's as if there's an internal trade off in the minds of many liberals and progressives: not for me the kitchen of politics, they're saying. And they add: Yet, since there are these terrible problems, I will work my butt off trying to get those in the kitchen to "do something."

This is halfway politics, or the politics of the underdeveloped political consciousness.

I will put it more sharply. Many liberals and progressives reveal in their behavior a state of mind not unlike that of the unhappy child towards a domineering father. In the classic picture, it's not always the case that the father actually is domineering, he is perceived that way by the child; nor is it always the case that the child is actually a rebellious, stubborn and irresponsible person who can't grow up, though he or she is perceived that way by the father. In the present case, however, that of Washington and all its works vis-a-vis the liberal and the progressive citizen, the reality is one of truly domineering and manipulative leaders facing truly rebellious and protest prone citizens.

The embarrassing secret is that the child-citizen-who-protests actually connives with the father-leader. The child-citizen does so by accepting the power structure as it is. He or she lets that one alone! Too scary perhaps, the father-leader is too powerful, he can't be dislodged or replaced, they feel. It's silly to think you can change the system. We've got to be practical is the rationalization most often heard.

Or, the child-citizen-who-protests fears that a fundamental change, a change that changes how power is distributed and ordered, means being willing to get in there and do it. And that's a no-no. He or she wants to continue protesting, he or she wants "father" to stop being so pompous or thick or manipulative or domineering or unjust, whatever. They want father to be around so that they can continue to kick at him, from the vantage point of non-responsibility—irresponsibility.

But even if, in his or her rebellion, they want "father" to get out of the way (they may want to run for office to replace him, or if their rebellion takes a radical turn, they want "to seize power") they are not equipped to change the nature of the power structure, nor does their underdeveloped political consciousness teach them the way to change it. They vault into the position occupied by "father," but only to step into his shoes. That's not changing the nature of the power structure, it is only using the existing structures of power to promote their (presumably better) policies. As Paulo Freire so urgently and devastatingly put it: the former oppressed become the oppressor in turn.

Can the ambivalence of liberals and progressives be dissolved or at least reduced? I doubt if any amount of preaching will do much to change their political inclinations and actions. But the sustained presence of a clear and determined political alternative to the major parties will gradually help them and persuade them to join in. It is also the case that the politics Greens reveal in their campaigns, their literature, and their day to day responses to issues will have much to do with the willingness of liberals and progressives to make common cause.

The Greens face an arduous challenge. It is to help show the world in word and deed that true responsibility in politics today is a two fold task: contesting for power in a serious, vital, and credible way, AND changing the way power is exercised while doing the contesting.

This leads me to the third thorny barrier on the road the Greens are traveling: getting into mainstream political contests in a spirit of engagement and transformation.

Engagement means getting out of the sandbox of ideological purity and plunging into the task of serious organizing, raising money, and schooling oneself about the nature of power. As Martin Luther King never tired of saying, those who have it will not give it up willingly but need strong pressure applied in nonviolent ways. Among these ways are electoral campaigns, building an alternative party, and once in office acting in a spirit of truthfulness, public dialog, and creativity. Engagement means having a widely shared strategic consciousness that the way forward is to develop momentum from election to election and from small victory to small victory, usually in contests for local and state legislative office, interspersed with campaigns for big key offices like governor, U.S. Senate and the Presidency.

Engagement means finding words and images that communicate effectively the values and concerns of the Greens in the language of the people; it means not talking down; it means finding ways to be and appear to be sincere, reasonable, responsible, down to earth, truthful, and plain spoken. It means being willing to promote yourself and your Green message.

Transformation goes beyond engagement. Transformation means an all out effort to stir people with new ideas and new ways to realize old and shared values. It means using election campaigns for more effective public debates and more serious treatment of the issues than the media now provide. It means using the election campaign to model a new politics rooted in self-help, citizen-to-citizen contact and cooperation. It means spending as little money as possible and only using money that comes from citizens—not from special interests and corporations. It means conveying a message that we citizens together must and can take back the power of our government. This is the kind of message Ralph Nader pioneered in the realm of presidential politics in 1996.

Transformation means overcoming the fear of money and the fear of power. Greens must reach out to the middle class citizen who has some discretionary money but has long since concluded that donating money to politicians for their campaigns is pointless. Greens need to convince them that, first, the government is being stolen right out from under them by politicians who take huge sums from corporate and other special interests; and second, that they should strongly consider donating to the grassroots campaigns of candidates who do not take such money and who pursue a citizen-based politics for justice, ecology, community and democracy.

Transformation means learning to overcome the settled habit of thinking that power is bad. It means looking for ways to change the way power is exercised. This is a huge challenge. Our culture is so deeply embedded in notions of hierarchy, competing to be top dog, and accepting the inevitability of top dogs, that it is hard to argue for, much less model, a peer-based practice of power. Yet that is the way forward for the Greens. Again, Ralph Nader's campaign for the presidency sought to model a relationship between himself and the activists in the states that was based on the self-help and autonomy of the grassroots.

A major step forward for democracy comes when we realize that control from the bottom over the top is almost as dysfunctional as control from the top over the bottom. A more horizontal image, instead of the vertical images that monarchists and populists have been assuming for millennia, must emerge. The horizontal image is that of peer relationships, where top and bottom have both been transcended. This is the "last" transformation, I feel. It is the hardest one, but the most rewarding, and is, in my view, the ultimate test of democracy.

An interesting intimation in that direction was the moment in the Green convention hall in Los Angeles in August 1996 when Ralph Nader entered to accept nomination for President. As he stood at the dais the 600 and more Greens in attendance were standing and shouting in unison "Go Ralph Go!" Suddenly Ralph leaned into the microphone shouting something. The chanting diminished slightly and the Greens heard him singing out: "GoWeGo," with the emphasis on the middle syllable. The audience picked it up and it has become a major Green slogan ever since. The moment is significant: it eloquently says that Greens not only believe in and want participation, but want peer-based participation. It indicates a new direction for politics, breaking the vertical image and reaching for a horizontal image of human relationships.

Finally, transformation means affirming the spirit of freedom in all things natural and historical. Ecological wisdom teaches the world that nature is open, not closed, and the determinisms often attributed to nature and/or history are nothing but constructions of human ideologies wrought in the face of seeming fate, destiny and intractable "reality." Greens see in nature, and thus also in history, the reality and promise of new possibilities. Their hope for a better future is not a matter of wishing but is rooted in knowledge of nature's ways. These ways combine the assimilation of old patterns as preparation for creative leaps into the future. There is a wildness at the heart of things that Greens respect and that gives them the heart to carry on in spite of seeming routinization and constraint, and in the face of the always abundant voices of cynicism and despair.

A fourth hurdle on the road Greens travel is the rigidity of the institutions of an overripe industrial society. The political sphere is especially obnoxious in this regard. The monopoly on politics by the two major parties is so great that waves of third party activity in the United States in the last two decades have been beaten back and beaten down. Highly restrictive ballot access laws; ingrained media favoritism to the established parties, to wealthy individuals, and to incumbents; a first-past-the-post system of choosing and electing candidates—these are just some of the ways in which the political system obstructs change and transformation. Greens need to focus far greater attention on practical strategies to open up the system. One such strategy is to pursue with vigor a change to proportional representation, which almost every democracy in the world now has. In order to accomplish this more quickly, Greens need to build coalitions with other third parties, state-by-state and nationally.

The Third Parties '96 project conceived and sponsored by members of the Green Politics network, drew together a wide spectrum of parties to produce a Common Ground Declaration. The first of seventeen major propositions in the Declaration was to declare strong support for a system of proportional representation. Greens and other parties are fortunate that a strong organization has formed to promote and educate people about proportional representation. It is the Center for Voting and Democracy, headquartered in Washington, D.C., whose director is the vibrant and hard working Rob Richie.

A fifth hurdle for Greens on their way forward is the rising resistance of the old guard of entrenched corporate power and corporate mind-set. As Greens grow in outreach and in numbers, the resistance will not only increase but will turn nasty. Greens need to think about ways to deal with the resistance and especially with the nastiness. Decentralized organization is a necessity in this regard as well as a desirable political direction. The dispersion of leaders and leadership makes it much more difficult for the established and increasingly nervous political and economic powers to hunt, blunt, divide and destroy. But Greens must never underestimate the power and resourcefulness of the established oligarchy to invent yet more ingenious ways to divide and conquer.

It's critical for Greens to leave aside their egos, for it's through the manipulation of egos that the corporate media and the so-called intelligence agencies are often able to disrupt and derail social and political movements.

Furthermore, Greens need to learn a lot more about the meaning and applications of nonviolence. Their objective is to convince increasing numbers of citizens to look for, find, and join the struggle for democracy, ecology, justice, and community. Greens need to learn how to take the brickbats of disinformation and ugly half-truths hurled at them, turn them against the perpetrators, and put the message they seek to present to the people in language, both verbal and body language, that seeks higher ground.

Greens also need to promote and create support groups among themselves. They need to make it known to people in their communities that such groups exist as safety zones and healing places for anyone who is politically and/or physically assaulted for their struggles on behalf of democracy, ecology, justice, and community.

I've used the image of a road the Green Party is traversing. Yet sometimes it feels less like a road than a trackless frontier. Frustration and sadness alternate with high hopes and the satisfaction that comes when you know you've won a victory, however small or large, that can lead to a better life for everyone on this planet. As we make the frontier crossing, we might learn from the trek the Mormons took westward. All along the way, they thought about those who would follow. They left measurements, signs, directions, bridges. It is not enough to just make the journey—we must make it easier for those who follow.

The call to action is ever more clear and compelling. No one can slough it off. None should be denied the opportunity to join the struggle. But there must always be respect for each person's integrity of choice. We live in a time in the course of events, human and natural, when choice seems ever more rare and yet ever more necessary. Greens must touch the hearts and minds of people with the ecstasy of freedom. The freedom to choose.

Chapter 3
Power and Its Discontents

A disinclination to seek power or have anything to do with politics may at first sight seem unbelievable and even perverse-especially on the part of those who seem in every way to have a strong political consciousness and a marked capacity for leadership. Your usual man of the world, including your typical oligarch, would certainly snort in cynical laughter at the very idea that someone with "fire in the belly" would voluntarily renounce the struggle for power. In their world, to their way of thinking, no one and nobody does nothing for nothing, surely not regarding matters of power.

"Men of the world," including the oligarchs, have considerable difficulty truly comprehending people like Ghandi or Martin Luther King or Sister Teresa or Vaclav Havel. Actually, they mostly only pretend to comprehend them. They make them over into papier-mâché "heroes" with the help of their advertising machines. Indeed, insofar as they laud such people at all, it is for what looks to them like the exercise of power. Trying to put it in their terms (and they never permit themselves to question those terms), they brand what they see as "spiritual" or "psychological" power, using these otherwise excellent words in a lame way. They attribute this power to a "charismatic personality."

Their unspoken assumption about the nature of power is never questioned. They think of it as a force exercised by someone over someone else. Their political scientists describe power as the ability to get the other person(s) to do something they would not otherwise have done. Many of these scholars, therefore, when they describe "charismatic" figures, lump Ghandi and King and others like them together with Napoleon and Stalin and Hitler, since, so claim the "value free" scholars, these leaders have in common the ability to exercise a seemingly intangible and inexplicable "spiritual" power over the masses. This comparison is true only in the formal sense, they hasten to add, not wanting to offend the sensibilities of us mere laymen, but it is clear from their writing that for them the formal connection is the crucial criterion of objective scholarship.

Indeed, a key reason many good people want nothing to do with power is precisely because the oligarchy and the scholarly tribes they keep in their stables have defined power as "power-over" and because these same good people—accepting that power means this—rise up in reaction against it, resolving henceforth to renounce power altogether. They are mistaken and foolish in accepting the oligarchy's definition. Neither Ghandi nor

King nor Sister Teresa nor Havel made such a mistake.

Power may indeed be corrupted into its merely instrumental aspects and become "power over," degenerating inevitably into domination. But power has a different meaning from that given it by the oligarchy and their paid scholars. It is more usefully understood in three closely related ways: as power from within (expressive energy); as the power of a centered self which is conscious of itself (dignity); and as power with others towards common ends (mutual energy in community).

Power as expressive energy has its source in the life-principle in which every person participates. The life-principle expresses itself in and through the whole body/self that constitutes an individual. So that this first, expressive element—the erotic element as Audre Lorde describes it; or the body-subject as Maurice Merleau-Ponty perceives it—puts the individual self, which is much larger than the ego, in immediate contact with a force greater than itself but including itself. [1] By its power, this expressive, erotic energy enables and indeed pushes each individual body/self towards an immediate identification with all life and with each and every particular manifestation of life. This is what the Greens have in mind when they speak of ecological wisdom as the source of a Green consciousness.

Power as dignity is the sense of existential pride of each individual body/self, protective of its own boundaries and capable of exulting in the life force within itself. It has been confused with the narrow concept of ego advanced by thinkers from Hobbes to Freud. But the ego is only part of the self. The self includes other states of consciousness extending inwards towards the source of the body's self's existence and outwards towards other particular beings.

Power as mutual energy in community is power with others for commonly negotiated purposes. "Power-with" is a natural and social power embracing individuals together in many intricate patterns of partnership. [2] Conflict is not assumed to be out of this picture at all. It is brought within the range of expected behavior. The participants, through action together, deal with the conflict as a natural and surpassable phenomenon. Actions that look like instances of "power-over" are either distortions of what should be happening, and must be dealt with as such and not rationalized into institutional hierarchies; or must be seen as part of the necessarily untidy process of mutual working out of the conflict.

To explain the latter, it may happen, as it does in the best of relationships, that one partner in a mutual undertaking (a household, a friendship, a writing project, or any one of many different business or professional or political ventures) may at a given moment feel put upon by the others, may feel that he or she is carrying more of the load than is fair, or is being treated with less than respect, or is shortchanged when it comes to sharing the benefits. What has happened is either a distortion of "power-with" into "power-over," in which case the structure and process of the relationship must be questioned and corrected; or what has happened is that a short-term imbalance has occurred which can be lived with and sorted out gradually. Of course, if the short-term imbalance persists (one person always winds up doing the dishes, an example that is meant literally as well as symbolically), then the situation is, once again, one of distortion, must be subjected to structural and procedural scrutiny, and must be transformed towards a situation of "power-with."

It must be emphasized that the three elements of power are interrelated and form a whole in each body/self and between all body/ selves. In a context and institutional milieu in which "power-with" is the ongoing regime, "power- over" is at the best eliminated or, short of that, has severe limits placed upon its manifestations.

The search for a new approach to the definition and meaning of power is a crucial part of the Green vision and program. The contributions of feminism and Native American traditions have been and remain the most important sources and backup for this part of the Green vision. Feminist authors have for over two decades conducted a fundamental critique of "power-over" behavior and concepts, which they rightly perceive as the hallmark of masculine-dominated thinking. Some, however, seem to have done so in the name of abolishing all power, making a mistake similar to many utopian and romantic male thinkers. But most have seen that the problem is not one of whether there should be power in the world, but what its true nature is and how it can be manifested creatively.

It is because of this new definition of power that the Greens are beginning to engage willingly and deliberately in actions that contest with the oligarchy for power. This represents a critical shift in the thinking and attitudes of the potential opposition and heralds a growing resolution in the grassroots "not to take it any more," but to organize into an effective alternative power.

However, there is more to it than that. Having a better definition is important, very important. But many still hang back. They have seen two opposite dangers engulf movements for fundamental change in the 20th century. The one is the politics of vanguardism and the other is the equally disturbing phenomenon of co-optation and sellout.

Vanguardism did not die with Lenin and Trotsky and Stalin, unfortunately, or with the earlier Jacobins of the French Revolution and their many heirs. It seems to be like a cat with nine lives. It erupts whenever and wherever leaders come forward to foist their own narrow definition on what the movement of the day is and means, and, armed with The Word, form a tight organization. In the name of The Word (ultra-Left or ultra-Right) couched in flaming abstract rhetoric, and in the name of the need for tough action now, they do battle with everyone who "deviates" from their correct political line, trying to rouse "the masses" to support this or that action. Nothing ever happens with most of these eruptions, they come and go, but all together they take away an enormous amount of energy from the overall movement for change. They also turn off many who might have given balanced and inspired leadership. And, worse and worse, they force those who do persist in trying to give balanced leadership in the spirit of "power-with," into expending frustrating amounts of energy and time trying to heal the divisions and confusion such vanguardism generates far and wide. It is no wonder that there are those who feel that vanguardism and its "heroes" are put up to it by the oligarch's intelligence agencies, even though in most cases this is not true. Yet those same intelligence agencies must be hard put not to give them covert support and not to laugh uproariously and sardonically at the antics of the vanguards.

Soft vanguardism is also fairly prevalent: the deformation of popular protest movements into domination by a few activists. Much of their behavior is similar to the hard vanguards: the preaching of The Word, the line that everyone is supposed to mouth and not deviate from, the gearing up for action now to win this victory, the perpetual calls for money to support the organization. It is an additional factor in persuading potential oppositionists to stay clear of politics.

An opposite phenomenon is the tragic story, repeated over and over, of the co-optation of successful individuals and movements. Indeed, one of the reasons vanguardism continues to exist with its almost paranoid insistence on the purity of doctrine and on having nothing to do with those who won't accept every jot and tittle, is precisely the continued slippage of those who start strong in opposing the way things are into a gradual and eventually total accommodation with the powers-that-be.

Many potential oppositionists are lost through co-optation, but what is not sufficiently realized is the impact this has on so many others who might otherwise have taken up political struggle. The latter are turned off by the change in so many who, having as individuals gone into politics, or as leaders of groups gone forward to battle for their cause, simply wilted in the glare of their own success. They've seen them gradually and subtly shift away from a clear politics of and for the people into earnest manipulators doing the bidding, and often the dirty work, of the masters of money and power. Or short of that, the once-upon-a-time heroes have become stereotypical "liberals" protecting, and being protected in, their niche within the masters' system of money and power. They do some "good" there, they may prevent even worse things from happening, but they also, by acting as a kind of shield, prevent ordinary citizens from seeing the true perversity of that system. And, most disturbing of all, they teach many to shun politics. A friend of the author, and a once promising potential activist, told of a man he had previously known as a serious up-and-coming political leader. He had just met him, after many years, in the halls of the state legislature. The now self-assured politician hurriedly shook hands with him. He wore, said the friend ruefully, the telltale "glazed look of the true politician"!

Whole groups and movements have played that role throughout the 20th century. What happened, and happens, to them was chronicled, analyzed, and prophetically anticipated earlier in this century by Robert Michels.[3]   He called the phenomenon "the iron law of oligarchy." His object of study was European socialist movements and parties. He argued that once they got access to the halls of political power, several related things occurred: gradually the parliamentary wing of the party/movement came to dominate, the policies of the party/movement shifted more and more to an accommodation with the prevailing system, and the internal organization became more and more top-down and hierarchical.

Examples, since the time Michels wrote, are many and sobering: the British Labor Party; the American labor movement in most cases, though with some signal exceptions; many social democratic parties in Europe and Latin America. References are limited only to those movements and parties that were intent on alternative system-changing programs and were serious about taking responsibility for leadership.

Those who have hitherto rejected politics from choice do, however, in most cases, have a strong sense of caring for the whole and an equally strong sense that action for the whole needs to be on a basis of power-with and not power-over. These are profound political sentiments and are badly needed by the body politic. How, then, can such spirits who are turned off to politics-as-usual be won back to doing politics? Nothing short of a program of renewal that calls for the transformation of relationships in family, economy, and government in the direction of mutuality, give and take or, to use the terminology already introduced, power-with. On this basis, with this vision, many who are now turned off may indeed get into "it" with vigor.

A companion feature of a new politics is the requirement for nonviolence. In the struggle between an opposition and the powers-that-be, a commitment to nonviolence enjoins a commitment to political solutions and not to force or fraud or both. That is, neither power-over nor manipulation. Though power-over and manipulation are the typical methods of the oligarchy, these cannot be the "weapons" of the opposition. The opposition's strength is the insistence that genuine political negotiation must be sought.

Both Ghandi and Martin Luther King argued for the transformation of the system they opposed. They argued that this transformation is a superior and necessary thing for both the powerful and the powerless, for both the privileged and those who suffer because of that privilege, for both the leaders of the status quo and for the opponents of the status quo. The assumption is that there is room in a new situation, one that transcends the old situation, for everyone.

This runs counter to the tendency hitherto of those engaged in political conflict to demonize the other, with the result that both sides sink to the same level of force and fraud. It can be seen from this how valuable to the powerless is the insistence on nonviolence, because it contains the common ground of genuine political negotiation. Nonviolence carries within itself the very principle of mutuality that a creative opposition to the system demands of the system. It is an irresistible force in spite of all the physical violence and mental manipulation perpetrated by the extended monopolies of power.

So a new politics does not trade on "enemies." It resists such demonization. But it also for that very reason strongly insists that both defenders and opponents of the status quo must focus clearly and directly on the vision and values and program for social, ecological, and political renewal. It is only through a focus on renewal that there can come ultimate reconciliation and a better life. In a transformed society, where mutuality prevails, those who are now grossly wealthy, morally pinched in their privilege, and condemned to using power-over to preserve their domination will have a much richer and satisfying life.

This kind of politics can succeed! It can appeal as none other to a rebirth of spirit and to the hundreds and thousands of those who at present are hiding their light under a bushel. Jesus complained in his day of so many good people doing just that, of hiding their light. Hiding of the light is probably a prime factor in why so many civilizations have perished. Good people must stop hiding their light, lift up their eyes, see the imperative need, and take bold, confident steps.

Chapter 4
Culture and Political Action

Will the Green Party in the United States fulfill the aspirations of its founders? Will it develop and deepen into a party that truly lives up to and sustains its vision? Will it do so even if and when it enters office in a big way, not only in various states but also in the nation at large? There is an undertow in politics, even at its best. It pulls parties and politicians away from their convictions, away from truth seeking and truth speaking, away from serving the people in a genuine and down-to-earth spirit, and away from persevering in the continuing search for common ground. Why should it be different with the Greens?

There are several reasons for thinking that the Green Party in the United States will not easily go down the pathway of opportunism and failed expectations. I will briefly describe these reasons and then argue, however, that in addition the Green Party needs help in the form of an active cultural and educational force side by side with itself, what I call a cultural companion.

Internal Supports Fend Off Opportunism

First, the Greens have struggled fiercely with one another over issues of principled action and compromise during the decade and a half since their founding and they have learned from it. Secondly, the Ten Key Values have acquired a deep and powerful hold on the consciousness of Greens. These values are more than a symbol, more than a burble of rhetoric, more than a convenient litany. They are values the Greens have been trying to live. This has deeply molded the party's spirit and resolve.

Thirdly, the struggle that new and small parties have in the United States to win elections and put candidates in office is not an easy one. It is a trial as by fire and may forge a sturdy spirit of conviction if, as now seems likely, the Green parties are here to stay and will continue growing. Ballot access laws are stacked against third parties in virtually every state. The winner-take-all system means that even getting double digits in the vote, something American Greens have done repeatedly, does not yield them any representation in government. By contrast, Greens in most other countries of the world, where they enjoy a proportional representation system of voting, are able to place people in office, even though they regularly receive no more than 5 to 10 percent of the vote. This is an intensely frustrating situation for U.S. Greens, yet, if they persevere, and by doing so win the confidence of more and more voters, they will not only gain office on a regular basis, but will have developed through hard times the discipline and dedication that goes hand in hand with deep commitment to their origins and their values.

A fourth reason stems from what would seem to be an important task for the anarchist-leaning Left Greens, as well as the nonpolitical life-style Greens. They maintain a continuing barrage of criticism of the eco-political Greens and of the party they have built. This critique, sometimes gratuitous, often harsh, has nevertheless had a sobering impact and helps to keep attention focussed on the dangers of accommodation.

A fifth reason is that the Greens are informed by values and not by doctrine or fixed ideological principles. Their view of life is already tuned towards flexible response to diverse contexts and situations. They are not in the Puritan or Jesuit tradition of fixed certainties. Greens believe in evolution and this means, in the realm of political and moral action, both a steady attention to the vision of what is right and a readiness to work with people and the diverse situations of their lives in a spirit of give and take. For them, therefore, there is not this yawning gap between theory and practice, principle and action, vision and daily life as is adumbrated in the philosophies and theologies of the past.

A sixth reason is the nature of ecology itself. Ecology goes well beyond environmentalism in that it goes to the roots of the human condition. The ecological disruption which the planet has suffered will not be satisfied with band aids, nor even with solutions to particular problems that leave the social and political structure intact that produced those problems in the first place. It is not too much to say that nature now insists on fundamental change in our human economic, social, and political arrangements. We humans are challenged, perhaps more powerfully than by anything else in our past, to reach and sustain a politics of transformation. This is a powerful inducement and support for sustaining the vision of the Green Party. Thus the crisis has both an inspiring and a seasoning impact on the everyday politics of the Green Party. It will continue to have such an impact for some time to come, the reason being that the encounter of society with the ecological crisis will last a long time.

These are all good reasons for thinking that the Green Party will definitely develop and deepen into a party of a different kind, one that not easily goes back on itself or loses its elan. Nevertheless, it is my belief, one shared by many Greens, that something more is needed — a force, a presence. I think of it as a cultural companion.

What Is Needed in Addition and Why?

What sort of companion? One who is a friend. A strong friend, standing side by side with the party, organized separately in its own way and on its own terms, and able to be both critical and supportive. A friend who is not afraid to call a spade a spade. A friend who understands the moods and

51

frailties of the party, does not turn tail when serious mistakes are made that bring down denunciations and scorn from the established powers; nor rushes in to blast the mistake-makers. A friend who maintains a steady constructive voice that urges the party to look at itself with unfailing humor, genuine pride, and critical understanding. A friend who is able in a helpful, nonpartisan, spirit to examine, from an ecological standpoint, the issues and claims brought forth by Green party candidates and office holders—to explore them, develop them, and find ways to educate the general public about them. In this way, an ecological consciousness can grow among the people. This will help in the evolution of a cultural milieu that is more and more aware of the importance and nature of Green Party ideas and stands.

To be sure, other parties, large and small, do conduct a critique of the Green Party—by their very presence and their competitive politics. However, their criticism is necessarily partisan, delivered with an edge, and can too easily be dismissed by the Green Party as negative propaganda.

But, granted that the party needs something more, why think of it as an organization? Why not let it be the general voice of a growing green culture? Books, clubs, journals, radio shows, environmental studies departments, think tanks, nongovernmental organizations, environmentally conscious small businesses, and a gradually evolving change in consumer choices and habits, all of these and more constitute a milieu that both supports and critiques an emerging Green Party. Why need more?

A pertinent answer is that the sectors of an emerging green culture and the many nongovernmental organizations (NGOs) that are active on behalf of its concerns, are fragmented and often self-absorbed. They don't, perhaps they can't, develop a sustained and credible critique that could be helpful to a political party. Green culture is politically immature. It reflects more than a little the general culture's particularism, specialization, and narcissism. More problematic still is the apolitical, even anti-political, sensibility which it shares to a degree with the general culture. Indeed, the emerging green culture is, if anything, even more alienated from politics than the general culture. It exudes a righteous reaction to the world of politics and politicians so that within its circles, it is often considered chic to be anti-politics. The counterculture often give itself airs that it is "above" politics, even though even a casual glance at the strife, bickering, and chicaneries that go on in their own organizations and social circles reveal a "political" condition not any different from what they claim the world of political affairs to be.

Nor are the NGO's especially equipped to provide the holistic, vision-conscious, and friendly but critical support we are seeking for the Green Party. They each have their own fish to fry. They are usually immersed in one particular cause. They compete for tax-free gifts with other NGOs.

The fact that they are tax-exempt makes them pull their punches again and again, so as not to offend the powers-that-be. Their Boards are often studded with members of the corporate oligarchy. Their outlook is often limited to getting specific gains in a narrow sector. Though they are part of the solution, they are also very much part of the problem. In any case, they are not made of the sort of stuff from which might come steady, valuable, holistic political criticism and guidance.

There is a double need here. On the one hand, the world of politics requires a focussed and sustained cultural critique to infuse and inspire its demoralized and de-spiritualized domain; and on the other hand, the cultural milieu, including the developing green culture, is desperately in need of a fundamental corrective for its de-politicized, irresponsible, and often thoughtless dismissal of politics.

These two worlds are moving on separate tracks. It is a desperate situation. It is a situation made to order for the rule of an entrenched money-fixated oligarchy and its multinational super corporate machine. The oligarchy fattens on the failure of the culture to overcome its fragmentation and its steadfast refusal to confront the problem of power. They dominate the Republican and Democratic parties, whose demoralized condition makes their politicians easy marks for the lure of money and personal prestige. It is a situation classically programmed for the breakdown of civilization, which also now means the destruction of our planet.

Defining the Concept More Carefully

Can we define more carefully the role we want the party's companion to fulfill? Not a think tank. Not a church. Not a Green-style Rotary Club. Not a good government institute. Not a Green college or university. Not the free press. Not even the alternative media. Many of these have elements we are looking for. Some of them have made historic efforts to be THE balance wheel to organized political power. One thinks of the Catholic Church during the Middle Ages. Or the Communist Party in Soviet-style regimes. Or the Free Press in modern democracies. They have all been failures.

Both the medieval Church and the modern Communist Party, in their respective roles, came to dominate the State behind the scenes. This "hidden" monopoly decided who was to have power, how it was to be exercised, for what, and for whom and against whom.

As for the Free Press, it has been highly touted as the bastion of a free, literate and politically aware populace and of a counter-force to Government and State. Its failure is twofold. It affects an unbiased, neutral stance "above" the political strife; it consequently gives as much weight to voices and forces that harm the planet and people as to voices and forces that defend, restore and enhance the planet and people. Secondly, the free press has come under the control of a moneyed few to such a degree that a mere handful of powerful corporations dominate what is written, how it is written, and for what purpose it is written. Both of these conditions can also be attributed to contemporary universities and colleges. Their self-proclaimed historic mission to seek truth, and to speak it to the world, has faltered in the face of corporate and government money; and it is also deeply undermined, if not wholly ruined, by a technocratic fact/value dichotomy that eviscerates values in the interest of so-called "facts," and makes academia a place of self-censorship for both faculty and students.

In our search for a cultural companion to the Green Party, we are not looking for a Green University nor a Green Press nor yet a Green Think Tank. These are useful institutions, no doubt, but something is needed in addition. In our search we must keep one thing clearly and deeply in mind. What was it that past historical examples (the medieval Church, the Communist Party, the Free Press) were supposed to accomplish in relation to political power and government? The answer I would give is that they were supposed to provide some form of steady and responsible critique of the exercise of power combined with, and in the light of, a clear exposition of the critical policy issues of the day.

The companion we seek for the Green Party (and for the political process of which it is a part) is a cultural agency or force that will — in the context of the real-world actions of the Green Party and the extant political process — do two kinds of things. It will study in a nonpartisan spirit the issues and ideas that emerge in the political encounters of Green Parties, candidates, and office holders; it will discuss and publicize the results of this on-going examination. Secondly, at a deeper level, it will also conduct a steady exploration of the interconnections of the world of the spirit and the spirit of the world.

Such a companion thrusts aside the assumption that these things are separate, that one gives to Caesar the things that are Caesar's and to God the things that are God's. Instead it operates on the assumption that worldly and unworldly things are connected, are interrelated, and cannot be thought of and treated as if they were in totally separate compartments. Though they have been and perhaps always will be in a state of tension with each other, the relationship must nevertheless be explained, explored, examined, clarified; and this must be done on a continuing basis. A cultural companion of the kind we are considering here also thrusts aside the opposite assumption that these things of matter and spirit are identical, as if one can apply a set of truths or a settled dogma to the actions of worldly politics that will "reconcile" the dilemmas and contradictions. Again, our companion must be of a kind who understands that the Church in the past, as well as the Communist Party, made the huge mistake of thinking that they possessed "the truth" and that it was their solemn duty to instruct governments and political powers in that truth. Consequently, both the Church and the Communist party got embroiled in the political game and were thoroughly corrupted by the very power they had been commissioned to critique.

Obviously one is dealing here with a difficult, a very difficult and even dangerous, problem. How can human beings interrelate these two seemingly antithetical worlds, the mundane world of everyday power politics and that other world, equally everyday, that speaks to and of the spirit of truth and goodness and beauty?

It seems clear that if we were to be successful in finding a suitable cultural companion to a political party, that companion would not itself exercise any political or governmental power. At the most, it's function would be consultative. It's influence would be in terms of ideas, questions, and recommendations. The strength of that influence would be directly related to the wisdom, sincerity, astuteness, and steady self-critical balance of those who together constitute the cultural companion.

Giving the Concept Institutional Form

What institutional form might we give the cultural companion? One suggestion is for the Greens throughout the United States, who have organized, or are involved in, local study groups, educational foundations, culturally concerned bodies that speak to the common good, and so forth, to encourage these groups to conduct, on an ongoing basis, two different but related activities. The one activity would be to hold periodic public Forums in their communities. These Forums would take up for discussion and close examination issues and ideas that are raised in Green political campaigns and by Green office holders. The other activity would be to create Eco-Storefronts in their communities. These Eco-Storefronts would be places where the general public could get information about the Greens and their issues. The Storefronts would not be partisan Green offices, but fully autonomous and available for people to come in and browse and for eco-activists to meet and discuss issues popular in the community and the wider culture. The Eco-Storefronts would be in close contact with the public Forums.

One could imagine that over time these local community activities by Greens and Green-minded people would form links across regions and across the country as a whole. Perhaps an annual conference would evolve that would draw people active in public Forums and Eco-Storefronts. The conference would be an opportunity for the participants to share perspectives and experiences that are pertinent to issues of ecological and social justice, quality of life, democracy, and political transformation. The conferences could develop a regular relationship with the Green Party. It might issue periodic assessments and recommendations to the Party. There would be a continuing rotation of people attending the annual national conferences. In this way, there would be continuing and organic grassroots input into the thinking and recommendations of the annual conference, and it could thus grow into a strong and helpful position vis-a-vis the Green Party. It could become a low-key but effective balance wheel for the Green Party on the one hand and an effective interpreter of the Green Party to the developing green culture on the other.

We recall that Greens in this country began in 1984 with local groups, the Ten Key Values, and a Clearing House in Kansas City. After a few years, there were several hundred local groups throughout the country, all in contact with Dee Berry, the Clearing House Coordinator during those important founding and nurturing years. Greens then began to create state Green Parties, and eventually these parties created the Association of State Green Parties. Most of the local groups joined in the endeavor to form state parties and a national Green Party. The intent is to be and become a party of a different kind. In this, they combine civic action and electoral action, local issue-campaigns and candidate campaigns, single issue causes whether global, national, regional, state, or local as well as educational and political advocacy for coherent and credible platforms.

However, the earlier local group emphasis on studying and exploring the meaning and applicability of the Ten Key Values has tended to diminish. The proposal I am making here for a cultural companion is to root the composition and activity of such a companion in the thinking and experience of activities like a periodic public Forum and Eco-Storefronts, for these would have a broad cultural and educational concern for transformation. They would of course appeal to activist Greens to engage in study and exploration in addition to their activism, but the group would also be open to others who are not activist in issue-campaigns and/or electoral work. The local activities would be a continuing source of new thinking, critical thinking, and creative ideas. These could be, and would be, very useful to local and state Party bodies and, via an annual conference, equally useful and important to the national Green Party.

It is my conjecture and belief that in no area would a cultural companion be more important or useful than in the age-old, difficult, and dangerous question of the relation of spirit and matter, principle and practice, body and soul.

Spirit, divorced from matter, is reckless and inopportune. Matter, uninspired by spirit, is dull, routine, and inescapably bureaucratic. Or put it this way: body and soul need each other in order to fulfill each other. Similarly, the body politic is not just about the calculations of power and interest; nor is the soul-food or culture we create just about ideas or about the good, the true, and the beautiful. The body politic and the culture need each other to fulfill each other. Yet they have become estranged from each other and both are stunted as a result.

Green philosophy has made strides in its thinking about how to lessen the gap between body and soul, between body politic and the life of the spirit, between strategic calculation and intrinsic values. The Greens have successfully built the foundation for an American Green Party. The Association of State Green Parties is well on the road to becoming a fully-fledged national Green Party. Greens also need now to pay close attention to the cultural side and how to give a growing green political culture greater focus and meaning.

Part II

Dealing With Domination:
The Limits of Protest

Chapter 5
Revolutionary Ferment

In the beginning, according to the book of Genesis in the Jewish and Christian Bibles, God created the earth and its creatures and crowned the creation with the fashioning of a man, Adam, who named all the creatures in the world. God then created Eve. One notices the gender hierarchy in this account and the power of naming.

Names are used to define the way things are. In an age of technological development like our own, the power of those on top of the heap is magnified and amplified throughout society because of their control of highly sophisticated print and broadcast media technologies. This gives them enormous power, through the use of naming, to define things as they see them. They are then also in a position to distort, misinform and generally obfuscate public debate on any issue. A singularly bemusing instance was the success of Ronald Reagan and the right wing, and of George Bush in his campaign against Michael Dukakis in 1988, in hanging the word "liberal" around the necks of their opposition. From being an honorable word, as in "liberal education," and a word associated with the great American liberal tradition, it became an epithet to put down welfare advocates and people "soft" on crime. In both cases, it also became a way of telegraphing a racist message to the American white middle class without appearing to do so.

A similar process has taken place with the word "revolution." The founders of the nation had little problem with it and Jefferson thought it would be a good idea to have one every twenty years. But in recent decades, both the anticommunist crusades and the growing might of corporate wealth, following its temporary setback in the halcyon days of the New Deal, have combined to help right wing pundits, scholars and politicians create a verbal climate of fear of anything that smacks of radical politics. Part of their propaganda has included attributing to the American people a penchant for conservative views and conservative politics.

If what is meant by conservative is a love of one's land, a passion for community, a decent respect for one's own rights and a willingness to give the other guy the benefit of the doubt, then, yes, the American people are conservative. But if what is meant is that they will not take up arms against a sea of troubles, will not rise up to defend those rights and those communities, then Americans emphatically are not conservative.

The right wing, with the tacit and not so tacit complicity of scared liberals and Democrats, has pulled the wool over many a person's eyes.

They have conned the omnipresent media, with the latter's cheerful cooperation, into believing their lies about the American people.

This book heralds the coming of a renewed revolutionary period in American life and is a call to assist in its coming. A revolution in the way government is run and in who runs it. A revolution in the way business conducts itself and in whose interest. A revolution in how people live and to what end.

This book is also a primer in what revolution means. It defies the easy use of the word to cover the same old thing, as when Richard Nixon announced a revolution for America at his second inaugural, or when the big foundations pushed the so-called Green Revolution on Third World agriculture in the '60s and '70s. This book also defies the notion of revolution as a bloody affair led by a heroic vanguard at the barricades. We have had enough of these two twentieth century failures. The East/West and Left/Right dichotomies are defunct.

Revolution means a turning. A turning in people's hearts and minds, in the way public and private affairs are conducted, in ownership patterns, in the structures of decisionmaking, and in the attitudes of people making those decisions in family, education, business and government.

Today, what would that turning be? From what to what? A turning away from the politics of nostalgia and institutionalized greed; away from an existence dominated by corporations; and away from a life of waste, macho-posturing and mutual fear. A turning to a life-in-community that is rooted in the land (a sense of place) and in the spirit of liberty; to a life of conservation, caring and cooperation; to multiple forms of ownership featuring small and middling firms; and to a politics of confidence and inclusivity led by many people who together take active responsibility for the sustainability of their communities.

Revolution has been mistakenly thought of as a sudden breach with everything in the past and as something that will happen "someday." The first American revolution surely was not like that. It did not happen overnight. It started happening before it "happened." Many things led up to it that prepared the way for it to happen. Many stupid actions by the King of England and his government, matched at times by a stubborn truculence on the part of the colonists, pushed otherwise loyal, solid subjects of the King into determined resistance.

Their resistance was not a gentle affair of ringing rhetoric followed by tepid changes in business as usual. Nor was their resistance born out of the desire to replace the system from top to bottom and start over. It was rooted in a rising conviction that they were not going to be pushed around any longer. This conviction in turn deepened into a reflection about the nature of government and the relations of human beings to one another and to their land and communities. As this fresh thinking took hold, and as the king nevertheless persisted in having his way, and only his way, the struggle was joined.

Initially, the Committees of Correspondence intended and practiced nonviolence. The arts of political organizing and debate were employed to seek a fair solution that would guarantee the colonies their rights and due representation and would still leave the king with certain rights. However, shots were fired and the issue was settled on the battlefield.

The revolutionary spirit did not die with the victories at Saratoga and Yorktown. Again and again, the same determination not to be pushed around by remote and manipulative power, or pushed around by public or private monopolists, has come radically to the fore, all fueled by an ingenious mix of idealism and self-interested anger. Almost always it has been accompanied by fresh thinking concerning the nature of government, the right relations among human beings, and their relation to the land and their communities. It happened in the 1820s and 1830s in the revolt of the then western farmers against the eastern establishment. It happened with the great Abolition and Underground Railway movements, out of which was born the Republican Party. This culminated in a protracted civil war whose radical aims came to include the freeing of millions of slaves. Again, it happened in the first feminist campaign for equal rights that paralleled the antislavery movement and that extended into the 20th century with the gaining of the right to vote for women. It happened in the era of the populists around the turn of the century and in the progressive movement that lasted into the 20s. It happened in the labor struggles starting in the 1880s and ending in the triumphs of the New Deal. Again it happened in the civil rights movement, in the antipoverty movement, and the student movement of the 1960s. And yet again in the second great feminist rebellion that began in the 1970s.

Today, as we exit the 1990s, it is happening once again. The ferment that began in the 1960s and 1970s on behalf of African Americans, Hispanic Americans and Native Americans, of women, of gays and lesbians, and of students is still simmering and growing deeper and stronger. Along with this, and often interrelated with this, a revolutionary spirit has been fermenting for a quarter of a century around and about the condition of the environment. At its core is the perception that nature is sick and tired of being pushed around and that people are suffering terribly because of it. People are beginning to see and feel that nature is not something "out there" foreign to us and to which we can do most anything we please. It is increasingly felt as a force near us, around us, and even within us which in some fundamental way is us. If nature is us, and is being pushed around, then it is also very much we who are being pushed around, and we who are helping ourselves be pushed around. It is a lesson that has been discovered and often learned the hard way by each of thousands of grassroots groups that have come and gone to do battle to defend their community from yet more pollution and disfigurement.

As the environment becomes a household word, a change is beginning to introduce itself into the hearts and minds of people long accustomed to thinking of nature as a set of external powers to be captured, mastered, and subordinated to human desires. In this old view, so hardened it has seemed impossible to change, technology unfortunately came to be seen as the key instrument in subduing nature, and not as a tool to enhance the quality of all life, including human life. Technology came to be widely, even rapturously, embraced as the one answer to toilsome labor, and then to labor itself. It came to be seen as the one answer to the search for an easy, happy life through ever more consumer goods. It was embraced as the answer to problems of distance between human beings through instant communication and ever faster modes of travel. Eventually, technology came to be seen as the answer to problems created by technology itself, the ultimate "technical fix."

Corporations were invented and came to be thought of as the master deployers of technology, this prized key to abundance and control. Corporations grew into huge organizations fostered by laws and Supreme Court opinions that endowed them with the rights of persons, and fueled by an appeal to "the bottom line" of ever greater profits. They thrust ever newer technologies indiscriminately upon an awestruck public. Corporations, the bigger the better, have in effect been given license to produce, produce, and produce without stint or stopping. This has meant, in practice, license to extract, extract, and extract from nature without giving back, and license to pollute, pollute, and pollute. Cleaning up the mess after the fact was eventually granted as a privilege to the public to pay for and administer. For decades into the industrial revolution, none but a prescient few thought much about the consequences, and when dire results of the flagrant misuse of technologies were pointed out, the corporations, with the apparent acquiescence of the people, tended to shrug them aside and get on with business as usual.

Acquiescence to the reigning ideology of "more is better, bigger is better, and to hell with the consequences" is shifting. Questions are being asked. Resistance to the effects and consequences of investment decisions is rising. True, people for the most part do not connect those effects with the fact that investment decisions have been made by flesh-and-blood people in real boardrooms in real buildings not very far way. Also true, even though many people may half suspect that this is so, they do not feel able enough or confident enough to blow the whistle and demand an accounting. Yet, the number of whistle blowers increases. And, most important, there is more room now for those voices to be heard which for decades, especially since the publication of Rachel Carson's *Silent Spring* in the early '60s, have been warning of disaster and calling for a halt to the endless plundering of the planet.

But the plundering goes on. Just as King George III refused to alter his policies of squeezing the colonies, so too do those in charge of investment decisions, both in the corporations and in high government circles, refuse to alter their policies of squeezing the environment. And just as King George III refused to listen to charges of arbitrary rule, so too do the big investors and their backers refuse to hear charges of their own unaccountability. They have become adept, far more so than was King George, in cloaking their real actions with rhetoric shamelessly borrowed from their opponents. Behind this carefully constructed facade, they continue to plunder. And those who are willing to believe in all this, as if it were real, disarm themselves and thereby contribute to the plundering.

The issue of the environment, deeply etched now in the consciousness of millions, behaves in a manner similar to revolutionary surges in our past. It arouses that sense of not taking it anymore, that enough is enough, and that we're sick and tired of being pushed around. The farmers in Kansas in the days of the populist revolt began to shout that it's time "to raise less corn and more hell!" More people are getting to that point once again.

And along with the action comes again the demand for fresh thinking. Why can't something important be done? Where's the bottleneck? What or who is holding it back? Can individuals do anything? What is necessary to get a hold on the crisis? Supposing things could be turned around, how can that be done? What kind of a society should we be thinking about? What might our life be like if we can get past all these crises? How can a new attitude toward nature, which we are beginning to absorb and understand, be applied to the economy, to education, to government, and to the family? The range of questions provoked by a revolutionary spirit is broad. People are asking themselves these questions today, as only they do in times of revolution, and it is one more indication of the likely depth and progress of this revolution.

An ecological consciousness introduces a renewed respect for revolution. It reinforces a Jeffersonian concept of revolution as against either an industrial capitalist concept or a Marxist concept. Industrial capitalism, taking a *laissez faire* approach to growth, argues that "the market knows best." What they presumably mean by "the market" is the pushing and hauling of ever larger corporations to produce, distribute, and make profits. In their view of evolution, adapted in a distorted way from Darwin as "the struggle of the fittest," things even out over the long haul. Sure, Flint, Michigan, may be devastated by this pushing and hauling (GM moving its plants to Mexico), but that's life, and people need to get used to scrambling, moving elsewhere, competing with others for the jobs and the goods. In this way, though there is much jostling and suffering, there is also much mobility, new and better production, and progress. Sure, we run out of certain resources, and gradually oil will cost more, and maybe eventually even run out. But by that time, science will have figured out alternative resources and the market will dictate when and how they will be phased in.

The irony of this *laissez faire* doctrine is that it is touted as if it were conservative, but in its essence and its consequence it is a profoundly radical script, radical in the sense of extreme. The corporate, *laissez faire* movement of capital has almost always meant a radical, extreme disruption of the lives of people.

Marxism has been extreme in an opposite direction. Instead of *laissez faire* and markets, it would have us rely, first, on getting government control of the capital created by the corporations, and then reconstructing it and planning economic and social development from the center. After this has taken effect and people's attitudes and habits have also undergone change, or have been changed, in accordance with a new collective life, the need for coercive state power would vanish and, under the guidance of efficient administration, the people would spontaneously lead socially satisfying and productive lives. In this model, human intervention into the otherwise evolutionary flow of life reaches an intense degree; but once again, just as in the case of the model of *laissez faire*, the impact on the lives of people is extreme. Nor is there any indication as to how those who administer the planned society will do it noncoercively or with wisdom. Nor is there any indication that they will not, in attempting to change human behavior, reach into the subjective and psychic realms of human beings to alter them in accordance with their "humanist" pretensions.

An ecological consciousness steers decisively beyond these models. It understands the relation between the human and the natural as one of co-evolution. *Laissez faire* is part of it, but only part of it. Planning is part of it, but only part of it. Or, another way of putting it: We acknowledge and respect the nature of which we are a part. We are in no way separate from nature. We perceive that this nature is not closed but is open to new possibilities, and we recognize that to be thus part of nature is also to be open to, and to act upon, new possibilities. We participate in our own natural growth. We participate not as passengers along for the ride, going with the flow; we participate not as an engineer remaking the world into some image of our own human contrivance. We don't push the water, but we also do not just let it carry us hither and yon. We participate both by actively assimilating the evolution of things in and around us and by being creative within the matrix of that assimilation. The whole is a process of coevolution.

Another important word in this transaction that combines assimilation and creation is "feedback." Life is a negotiated dance: we are part and parcel of the dance. We relax into it. We learn from the movements we and our partners make and turn creative, now leading the dance into new movements. We assimilate the new movements, letting ourselves get the hang of it, and then we may be ready for more learning and more creativity. We unite action and reflection, doing and learning, we find a rhythm, we learn balance, we learn to avoid extremes. We feel fully the life within us and about us. In more and more situations of life, we discover both how to redress the imbalances, now leaning to one side now to the other, and also how to move beyond the balances already struck.

It is easy to see the application of this to the concept of revolution. No sharp and heroic breaks, please; no sudden closing down of the shop and starting up a new one somewhere. Such an extreme only succeeds in bringing Peter in by the back door when he has been thrust out of the front door. Nothing really changes. Only Thermidor happens, the word used to describe how when the bully has been bullied out of the government, a new bully rises to replace him. After the Czar, Stalin.

No namby-pamby actions that merely flirt with change, either, please. As if in the dance we go with the way it's going and make no move to enhance it or to try something new. Boring. And suppose, as is often the case, the dance is lopsided. Suppose it is badly structured and the people in the dance are full of problems that mirror and reproduce the awkward movements and structure of the dance. Time then for revolutionary action: we do lean to one side, and maybe follow this up by leaning to the other side, and then once again lean to the former side, striving for a new dynamic and harmonious equilibrium. We strive for balance. Not the balance between the mutually awkward distortions of the dancers—that would be mere management, a merely mechanistic project—but a new balance that both alters the structure of the dance and edges us into a new creative mutuality.

That is the challenge of a coevolutionary revolution. Its best historical example goes back to Jefferson. It is much in keeping with our new ecological understanding of the movements of nature. Social science has been married for too long to the *laissez faire* and Marxist views of evolution and revolution. It itself needs to undergo a process of revolution and in so doing assist the social, economic, and political transformation of society.

Chapter 6
Parties Without Vision, Government Without Trust

Successful government requires a degree of trust between leaders and the general citizen body. It also requires a capacity for decisive action on critical root problems by those who lead. And it requires a steady opportunity for alternative voices to be heard in the councils of state. One may go further and say, as did the founders of the American Republic, that successful government also requires that alternative voices have a full opportunity to seek and share power at all levels of government.

Measured by these minimal standards of successful government, politics in the United States is failing. An abyss of mistrust and underlying fear separates the leaders from the led. Each seldom encounters the other in relaxed settings of give and take. Each is therefore deprived of learning anything important from the other. Accountability is eroded and corruption festers like an incurable disease through all the echelons of leadership, especially at the top.

The leaders are for the most part attached to, and often deeply beholden to, a narrow stratum of moneyed oligarchs. This fact, or rather the innermost workings of this fact, must nevertheless be concealed as much as possible because the official rhetoric proclaims America to be the world's greatest democracy. This profound disjunction between the appearance and the reality casts an awkward pall over the doings of government and gives it an air of inauthenticity, even hypocrisy and bad faith.

Just as damaging, leaders regularly place means over ends. Indeed, they make the means their end and then deny or "forget" that this has happened. Leaders are disproportionately drawn from those occupations in society that are most deeply distorted by compulsions to subordinate the ends to the means, occupations such as big business, mass media, sales, corporate law, banking, large universities, advertising, and movies. Therefore, it's imperative that an alternative politics emerge, based on a broad Green-centered social movement, to shift public priorities and leadership into transformative channels.

Many people in the United States have decided not to participate in electoral politics at all. It constitutes absolutely no part of their thinking or of their everyday life. Most of the rest of the population who do participate in some fashion do so only to the extent of going to the voting booths from time to time, doing some jury service when they're not able to get out of it, signing a petition now and then, or, after having their arm twisted, attending a coffee for a candidate arranged by a friend. Only a tiny number are involved in a serious way in politics and many of these get caught up in campaigns because they happen to know someone who knows someone who is running for office. For the great majority of the registered voters, politics is something of a spectator sport.

Yet politics goes on. It is not as if nobody is doing it, or that what they are doing is not unutterably significant, or that vast sums are not being spent in the process of doing it. The anomaly, and the irony, is that we have a system of government in which people who are in the government are forced constitutionally to go "before the people" on a regular basis in order to stay in office; but at the same time they either feel they do not need very much serious citizen attention, or they do not want it. In either case, they surely do not get it.

Public officials therefore do their work in a kind of vacuum. They try to fill the vacuum through whirlwind exposures to the public: pre-announced meetings with constituents to hear grievances and give general and often meaningless reassurances; gladhand tours through factories, business offices, and downtown streets; photo opportunities (on a boat in Boston harbor, on horseback in California); press conferences at major airports; command performances at carefully selected sites, including White House press conferences; and, mostly, carefully packaged commercials on TV. It is "mass" politics, commercial politics, image politics.

But this kind of politics remains a critical matter even though it looks like a circus. Government couldn't go on unless it were done. Or unless the Constitution were finally changed to fit the new realities and no one was required to run for office anymore. That might be a boon, say some, though not very loudly and usually in private places, fearing an "image" backlash. What they mean is that the present mode of getting and keeping people in office is mostly a sham anyway. And it is extremely dangerous for the public good.

The election campaigns are largely meaningless as far as getting a general policy direction from the people is concerned. Once in office, those elected have virtually no guidance coming from the people, no basis for a prudential assessment of a given problem drawn from what the people think should be done. Yet somehow they must contrive to make it appear that the actions they take and the policies they pursue are consonant with the desires of the great masses. If they don't, competitors for their jobs are ready and waiting to use their apparent betrayals against them.

So election campaigns are exercises in make-believe, in phony images. Yet it is a real world that confronts public officials once in office. It peremptorily demands from them decisions of one kind or another on many complex and difficult issues. The buck stops here, as a hard-nosed president once said. All the conflicts that were displaced from somewhere else come here and shout for attention and resolution. The ship of state, the public weal, the interests of the whole, the common good, whatever one chooses to call those realities of public life demand judgment and decision.

The folks "up there" in office have got to respond to dangers near and far, if only for their own protection and the protection and enhancement of their immediate circles, their lives and their interests. A few among them actually have both the largeness of vision and the brains to think beyond their own narrow interest and sincerely want to make informed decisions for the general interest.

The result is that the workaday leaders in office make decisions with one part of themselves and with the other part carefully work out a way to "sell" it to the great masses. In doing so, they are constantly exposed to the assiduous journalist who, for whatever reason, wants a glittering story and is willing to risk a lot to get that special angle, not really caring about the consequences of his or her story for a carefully wrought policy or a still pending case. Always, as well, politicians are exposed to other politicians who play only to the masses: the demagogues for whom reality is only the game of mirrors, who don't really care about policy as such, and who are adept at willful distortion and mass manipulation. And always they are exposed to the crank, the maverick, the zealot who, filled with self-importance for their narrow cause, will stop at nothing to discredit, defame, and defrock.

That is the situation, and while most political scientists and analysts will privately agree, they think it impolitic actually to come out and say so. The public well-being is thus in danger from mismanagement, corruption, and failure of policy. Small wonder that the problems pile up: the debt, foreign trade, foreign military adventures, AIDS, drugs, lawlessness, TV, pornography, racial oppression, health, jobs, global warming, a thinning ozone layer, energy supplies, deforestation, to name some at random. And worst of all, a permanent accountability crisis and therewith a constant hemorrhaging of public confidence on which the whole system is still supposed to depend.

Small wonder that a growing number of people conclude that democracy is dead, or ought to be. For the sake of effective governance, for the sake of the salvation of the country, they argue, let's just own up to the fact that democracy cannot work. Let's tear down the facade of rule by the people, a mirage of idealists from a simpler age, put an elite in charge, and give them the room and the authority to rule unencumbered by the paraphernalia of "popular consent." Before offering a different opinion and suggesting a way forward that is both democratic and responsible to the general interest, it is necessary to point out a limitation in the analysis just made. It focuses only on the problem of the vacuum that exists between office holder and citizen. It does not focus on a companion feature of the political landscape: the fact that office holders by and large respond to a tune not coming from the people at large but from some few with immense resources of money and power. This necessarily puts the office holder and would-be office holder in an embarrassing relationship with mass appeals, clever packaging, the whirlwind exposures mentioned above, and so forth.

True enough, lines of communication between leaders and led are so lengthy, so tenuous, so easily obscured, so bureaucratic, and the people are so often not wanting to be bothered, that leaders tend to settle for evasive language and mass appeals to stretch across the vast communication gap between them and the people. But this tendency is intensified, and to a degree even caused, by the leaders' dependence on and identification with a moneyed, oligarchic elite. The decisions they make in office are almost never against the interest of this elite and most often are calculated to protect and enhance that interest. It becomes a necessary part of successful politics to make decisions favorable, or at the very least not unfavorable, to this small power elite, and at the same time to whip up the rhetoric to assure everyone and themselves that what they are doing is on behalf of the great masses. This charade is the dirty secret of both Republican and Democrat party politics, but especially of the Democrats because they pretend, more than the Republicans, to be the party of the people.

There is a way forward, but it is surely not an easy one. The way forward must deal both with the vacuum between leader and led and with the interlocking problem of the "invisible" domination at the top by the corporate-based moneyed elite. Attempted solutions that concentrate on only one of these, or even which emphasize only one while keeping the other "in mind," are inadequate. Both, fully and together, must be joined in the struggle for change. Otherwise, there is a tendency to frame the problem in either a reformist or a pseudorevolutionary way.

The reformist usually concentrates on the problem of the vacuum and demands greater access and accountability. But he or she ignores the fact that the system is in a way very functional. It permits leaders a kind of indirect or borrowed legitimacy from the people in spite of all the clever packaging and the lying. The packaging and the lying help the leaders, especially Democrats, to solve the embarrassment factor. Forcing them to be genuinely accountable sounds fine in theory, and indeed is fine, but is without realism or sincere understanding of their predicament. They serve a different and dominating master, but are trying nevertheless to preserve a relationship, however remote and false, with the people. It is therefore necessary to deal with the whole problem if one is critical of this reformist behavior, as one should be, and if one is going to push for genuine accountability. The whole problem necessarily includes the need to deal decisively at the same time with the fact that our present leadership's real masters are the oligarchs who provide the money to run and remain in office. This money—the big money, the money necessary to win—does not come from the people, although when you stop and think about it, it probably is their money!

The pseudorevolutionary, who attacks the problem of the moneyed elite running the show behind the rhetoric of democracy, tends to be insensitive to the accountability gap. He or she may not have thought very much about the problems of government per se; that is, in a context irrespective of class or race or gender or any other kind of special privilege that puts some in position of power and others not.

Just abolishing any such privileged position does not yield an answer to the problem of accountability. In a world, let's say of the future, where no special privilege of this kind could become the basis for visible or invisible domination, there would still exist the problem of the relation between the leader and the led. It is a question of the relation between a people at large and those from among them who, for whatever reason and on whatever terms, are given a responsibility to take action and make decisions on behalf of commonly perceived matters of importance. This seemingly abstract but fundamental theoretical issue leads to the third feature of the present political landscape: the way in which politics is practiced and what we are to think of the fact that so few people are seriously engaged in politics.

Let's start by looking again at what was said above about the fact that so few people actually participate nowadays in politics, or that so few people give others' political work serious attention. Surely this is a scandal. It is an indictment of the present system of doing politics. Yet a low number of people engaged in political work is not by itself necessarily unnatural, unhealthy, or preventable. This is underscored, for example, by the fact that many Greens who are presently engaged in political work would rather not be doing it. They would rather be engaged in another kind of work: farming, carpentering, teaching, nursing, doctoring, engineering, artwork, parenting, and the list can go on and on. They are willing, in spite of their attraction to other pursuits, to put a disproportionate amount of their time and energy into political work because they are worried about the planet, about their communities, and that others who should be doing a responsible job in office are not doing it.

It is unlikely that in any society, under fairly stable and normal conditions, one would find more than say 5 to 7 percent of the people willingly and naturally interested in serious political work. Their attentive public would also be a small though significant number, say another 12 to 18 percent. Maybe even the low figures are too high. Adding the two groups together, one sees that in approximate terms, no more than 17 to 25 percent of the population have a degree of feeling for politics.

Some may leap to say at this point that surely in times of crisis, especially protracted crises such as now, those figures certainly rise. This is doubtful, because though on the one hand more people are concerned and get drawn in, many others who had been concerned are alienated and become apathetic or destructive. These assessments are gloomy only to people who have an exaggerated and distorted image in their heads about politics and people, pro or con. An ingrained myth from the past, aided and abetted by generations of modern liberal scholars, journalists, and politicians, has it that government by the people means that every person, no matter who, must be involved in public affairs on a steady basis.[1] Failing that, there must be something wrong with government by the people. The early democratic theorists tended to think of it in those terms. Their critics, who called themselves revisionists, also thought of it in similar terms, thinking that therefore we should settle for some retrenchment of democracy. And the critics of these critics, in turn, the antirevisionists and protagonists for a full participatory democracy, have also thought of it in these terms.

The equation of "real" democracy with perpetual participation by all is now a kind of conventional wisdom among liberal-minded scholars and large numbers of the attentive public. The conventional wisdom does not ask the decisive practical question: if everybody is working at politics all or most of the time, when will the work of the family, the school and the productive economy be done, and who will do it? In other words, politics not only appeals to a relatively small number in the general population, but politics is also to some important degree a specialized activity. Just as any of the professions, such as parenting or teaching or engineering or running a business.

True political work is a special kind of specialization: it specializes not in a particular aspect of society's activities such as parenting or teaching or running a business, etc., but in the general workings of society as a whole. It cares about the whole: it itself does not do the work of parenting, teaching, engineering, or running a business, but it assists and facilitates the work of these activities, and it mediates the conflicts emanating from all of these activities. Some people are good at this sort of thing. Others are not as good at it. A good society with a good politics offers opportunity for participation in political work to all who are good at it: it does not shut out those who are good at it just because of their class or race or gender or sexual preference or religion or wealth or of any other politically irrelevant consideration.

Conversely, a good society with a good politics tends to discourage those from participation in political work who, though they may have talents that seem to fit in with what politics does, are much better advised to use those talents in a different activity. Without being necessarily invidious, one can think of movie stars in this regard, or businessmen, or charismatic religious leaders, or lawyers. It is not as if people from such professions shouldn't do political work, but they shouldn't do it in terms their professions have taught them. The talents they've trained for and used in doing movies, running a business, being a minister, priest or rabbi, or doing legal work for corporations are not as such adequate for political work and may even be inappropriate. If they can adapt those talents in a genuine political direction, or better still if they can discipline, and even abandon, the talents they have been used to, they stand a much better chance of doing well in political work.

There is this further vital consideration: modern society and culture has been inundated by an egoist mentality trained to think technically and instrumentally.[2] A fundamental source and spawning ground of this mentality is monopolizing capitalism with its dual fixation on profits and technique, the ruthless search for profits-above-all between aggressive, monopolizing firms which grow bigger and bigger over time, killing or absorbing smaller competitors; and the technical rationalization of work processes within the ever enlarging firm. These fixations have placed a premium on ego narrowly defined, and a premium on the ego equipped with an instrumental logic that always puts questions of means to an end above the analysis of ends themselves. This reaches a point where the fixation with means becomes itself the end. Occupations in the world of big business, corporate law, banking, advertising and sales, as well as occupations in media work, public relations and popular movie making are especially susceptible to this instrumentalizing bias. But all other spheres of life have felt the effects of this bias including especially the universities, hospitals, and the big publishing houses.

Nor, of course has politics escaped. Politics has been saturated with the instrumentalizing bias even though, with the exception of the home and spheres of friendship, it may be said to be the sphere par excellence of a natural concern for ends, for the common good, for the care of the whole. Recruitment for politics has more and more come from precisely those occupations and spheres of life that are most distorted by the instrumentalizing bias to a point where a virtual revolving door exists throughout government: government officials, elected and appointed, go back and forth between jobs in government, big business, large and/or prestigious law firms, banks, universities, media, and the like.

No doubt about it: democracy does mean the enfranchisement of every person. No one should be excluded from the vote or from the opportunity to participate in the political process, however minimally, however maximally. The argument just made is that political work is a serious activity of society. It is a specialized activity of a certain kind. It requires a substantial degree of time and energy and commitment. The number of people who have a feeling for it is naturally small. A good society with a good politics would strive to place in public office only those with a genuine feeling for political work who exhibit the capacity to inspire public trust, are good at mediating conflicts, and care about the whole.

To sum up: not only is the gap between leaders and led enormous and trust of leadership waning in the United States; not only does the system cater to just a very few with money and power; but, in addition, the wrong sort of people for the most part are running it. The people in it, no matter their personal decency, are there because they were not the wrong gender, the wrong class, the wrong race, and because they were not people with a bare-bones bank account or no bank account at all. This does not make them "wrong," but they constitute an exclusive club and have a vested interest in maintaining the exclusivity.

Furthermore: those at the top of the political hierarchies have risen to the top because in most cases they exhibited not a care for the whole, but a facility in a kit full of instrumental and technical talents learned in selling products, running a business for maximum profit, doing legal work for corporations and the like. The derangement of public life forces the selection of instrumental and technical types of people into political work who have psyches undisciplined by wisdom. They in turn further intensify the impersonal, ego-driven instrumentalization of public life. This constitutes the real, fundamental, corruption of modern politics. It is a pseudopolitics which they pursue, however much personal decency they possess and may from time to time still exhibit.

So, the way forward is to consider whether, and how, a relatively small number of people—-inspired by a new wisdom rooted in an understanding of ecology and democracy, and motivated to do serious political work— can move together effectively and arouse the serious attention of a sufficient number of other people, say a number four or five times their own, so that together they become a compelling force for a political alternative. One need not belabor this, but it is extremely important, both for the political activists and their immediate and potential supporters, that they free themselves from the widely held illusion that political parties and political movements have, or must have, hundreds of thousands, even millions of members and active supporters. The reality is very different. A small number of people did it in Eastern Europe, for example; a small number did it in the American Revolution, or any revolution one can point to.

What makes the difference is not numbers as such, but a shared vision rooted in the major historic challenges of an epoch, effective organization, trusted leaders, a capacity for inclusivity, a respect for both wisdom and competence, and creative energies coming up from the wellsprings of society. The appropriate question, therefore, is not "How can an alternative leadership emerge and gain power in the United States" but, "Why hasn't this already happened?"

Chapter 7
Oligarchy USA: A Breed Apart

The book of Daniel in the Jewish and Christian Bibles tells many favorite stories, especially Daniel in the lion's den. Lesser known perhaps, but chillingly told, is the story of the impending destruction of the ruling house of Babylon. The incumbent Belshazzar is giving a sumptuous feast. Suddenly, in the middle of the wassail and gaiety, the shape of a hand appears out of nowhere and writes on the wall: Mene, Mene, Tekel, Upharsin. The terrified king demands that someone be found to explain the words. Daniel is brought in and interprets the handwriting: "You have been weighed in the balance and found wanting," he intones. That same night, so goes the biblical account, Belshazzar loses his throne and the kingdom.

Something of this sort might well be spoken to the ruling circles of American society today. The handwriting is on the wall, if they would but lift their eyes to see it, or get a Daniel to take the scales from their eyes so they could see it. They have squandered incredible resources and wealth. They have wrung these resources viciously from a generous earth, from defenseless Third World populations, and from the unremitting toil of scores of millions of their fellow citizens. Their aggressive performance is becoming less and less competent, less and less adaptive to vastly changing conditions, and less and less just.

Still, it is extraordinarily important to judge carefully the competence, the adaptiveness, and the justice of their rule. The strategy of those who oppose them, in the interest of finding an adequate and just solution to the contemporary crisis, hangs partly on such a careful judgment. The powers-that-be are not an ossified and entrenched ruling class on the order say of those who dominated the dying days of Russia's Czarist regime. Nor are they to be likened to the tyrannical and cultish crowd that Hitler led in Germany following the first world war of this century. They are blander, more sophisticated, more resourceful, more flexible, less arbitrary— though some of their hangers on are sufficiently sinister to make the wise shudder.

Questions must be put to them. Are they any longer able to mind the store? Do they have the wit to respect the limits of power and nature? Do they reveal an instinct for the care of the whole? Are they good models for the rest of society, for young people growing up? Are they as concerned to be good and to do justice as they are to appear to be good and appear to do justice? Do they adequately comprehend new conditions? Does their vision extend to all parts of society, or only to those of their own set? Do they think ahead further than the next election or the next report of earnings?

These are questions a person would and should ask of any leadership group in any society. A peculiar impoverishment of the discipline of political science is that it no longer asks these questions. The controllers of the mass media are likewise tongue-tied in this regard. Denial that these questions are pertinent and the simultaneous suppression of that denial are a major characteristic of academic institutions and of those entrusted with the arts and powers of communication. They behave more like sycophants of power and privilege than serious critics. Even their efforts at exposure in most cases extend only to the personal foibles and faults of this or that business leader or government official. Their investigative reports seem to go in depth into this or that mismanagement: but there is no considered or holistic critique of the structures and modes of power that such mismanagement reflects. There is an eerie silence about the interrelated structures of money, power, and ideology that together shape and constitute the ruling strata of American society. Instead, these institutions of academia and dominant media, presumably blessed with responsibility to and for the truth, daily reinforce the blase assumption that we all live in a democracy in which the people's voice really counts, in an economy in which the market is free and consumers have unlimited and qualitative choice, and in a society in which there is far more equality than inequality. On the other hand, this blase assumption is daily battered by a stream of particular news items, individual (and carefully separate) government reports, and books that tell quite a different story. It is a story of immense disparity of wealth, colossal concentrations of economic power in a few hands, and a political system in which the old structures of constitutional rule established by the founders are being eroded. The erosion goes on day by day under the impact of an imperial presidency, a fragmented Congress, an inertial bureaucracy, and a growing disinclination of people to bother with the political process at all.

The cover story and the hidden one are so at odds that politics itself has become a school for permanent schizophrenia. A kind of mass numbing has taken place.[1] People solemnly and regularly genuflect at the symbols that represent the cover story and yet daily encounter in their lives constant and disturbing refutations of the cover story. This cannot go on.

Ancient writers, in contrast to the vast majority of modern day political scientists and media moguls, did manage to ask the tough questions and apply accurate criteria to the political systems of their day. Aristotle, in many ways the founder of scientific method, undertook an exhaustive study of the political systems in the Mediterranean. With the help of his students, he studied over 140 of them. He summed up what he learned in several writings, the most comprehensive of which appears in Books 3 to 6 of his *Politics*. He classified systems both in terms of their stability and their goodness, or lack thereof. Their stability had a lot to do with whether they used power wisely, and their goodness was measured in accordance with whether they acted on behalf of the interest of the whole. In addition, Aristotle applied three interwoven criteria to any political system: how it distributed the leading offices; what social force in society was preeminent; and what was the way of life (we might say values or mind-set) of this preeminent force.

Accordingly, Aristotle identified monarchy, aristocracy, democracy, oligarchy, polity (also translated as mixed regime), and tyranny. Of these, aristocracy, for example, was the rule of the few whose merit was their proven virtue (political as well as moral excellence) in ruling for the good of the whole. Aristotle liked this one best, but it is hard to come by, as he ruefully admits. It also excludes a lot of people from rule who might well resent their exclusion, and for that reason Aristotle felt that democracy made a valid point in its insistence that the common person (though still excluding women and slaves) should have a part in ruling.

Aristotle readily acknowledged that oligarchy made a good claim to have the rule. Oligarchic leaders have in common with those of an aristocracy that they are few (and thus more decisive than the democratic many), and they insistently point to their wealth, their property, as evidence of their right to rule. They argue, he sympathetically notes, that they have the most to lose from bad rule; and that, because of their wealth, they provide most for the defense and order of society. Aristotle defined oligarchy as the rule of the rich who tend to be relatively few in number.

At the same time, however, Aristotle distrusted their capacity for rule because of their tendency to have contempt for the masses, their greed for ever more wealth which obscured their ability to rule on behalf of the interest of the whole, and because they inevitably saw to it that their children would inherit their money. Over time, their rule thus would turn into a closed dynasty. Oligarchic rule would eventually degenerate into tyranny, which, whether the tyrant be one, few, or many, means arbitrary rule, the sowing of mistrust and alienation throughout the society, and thus a growing isolation of people from each other. In the end, Aristotle, though he saw aristocracy as the best (if you could get it), felt that a mixed regime (the polity) was preferable, a system that balances the needs and rights of the rich and the poor, although it only works if it is based on a numerous and politically vigorous middle class.

It seems pretty clear that, in Aristotle's terms, the American founders created what he would have called a mixed regime, or polity, balancing the needs and rights of the rich, the poor, and the middle class. However, equally clear, the carefully constructed constitutional system they founded has in the past century and especially since WWII gradually turned into an entrenched oligarchy, with disturbing intimations of tyranny.

There is no concern here to demonstrate the logical purity or ultimate truth of the preceding paragraph. Most of the people who read this book "know this already." It's no news to them. And those who, upon reading the book, are skeptical or even hostile to the thesis are not going to be convinced by the marshalling of fact upon fact, argument upon argument, to validate it. For that matter, many scholars have already done this in the past.[2] The trouble with attempts to validate such an obvious thesis is that the validations are often put in terms of absolutes. Books written to prove the existence and dominance of an "elite," and books written to disprove it, both genuflect to a presumed canon of science that any fact or phenomenon that doesn't fit the thesis may be seized upon as proof that the thesis is false. People do vote, not every rich man is a ruthless capitalist and some indeed support causes contrary to the interests of the rich, labor unions have substantial power, polls indicate support for capitalism from large segments of the underclasses, government does many things that can't be explained in terms of subordination to the wealthy, etc., etc. Such facts, that seem to run counter to the thesis of "a ruling class" or a "power elite," are decisive only if one has already accepted the notion that something is not true unless and until it cannot be falsified by any particular fact. This is a distorted application of a scientific doctrine of nonfalsifiability. There is another, counter to that, which insists that the exception proves the rule.

Even more pertinent is the need to get away from an either/or logic that seems to underline the debate over whether or not there is a ruling class: both the left scholars who propound the thesis and the capitalist scholars who attack it are caught up in this either/or logic. Ralph Milliband, a British left scholar, labors strenuously to explain all the possible exceptions of the sort mentioned just above in order to fit them into the thesis.[3]

But is there any need to do this? The left (and the right) should look again at their way of thinking about life and about history. They might discover how deterministic they've become. No "historical epoch" is uniform. Cross currents abound. Legacies from the past, structured in the life of the people as residues, are still vigorous and play a powerful nostalgic role. Intimations of a new way of life, a new epoch, grow and gather strength even in the face of a dominating stratum in society. No ruling class is monolithic, therefore, as if everyone in it must be assumed to conform to the prevailing norms it sets for society. No proletariat class is monolithic as if everyone in that class must be assumed either to be opposed to the ruling class or brainwashed by them. The same applies to the middle class: they surely are not monolithic, nor is it necessary to squeeze every last one of them into the rigid and simplistic either/or categories of conventional left/right thinking. Far better to abandon its outmoded logic; far better to apply a both/and logic which is able to sort out the differences and the similarities.

It is both the case that an oligarchy rules the United States and that, as in all societies, remnants of a long-ago past and intimations of alternative futures are jostling with the powers-that-be for a hearing and for power. This is a natural model, an ecological and Green model, for understanding the flow of history. It is a vital point, because action and strategy for change flow from it, just as they do from the either/or and left/right model which it replaces.

The earlier disclaimer about proving the thesis that an oligarchy, with tendencies to tyranny, rules the United States can now more clearly be seen as a deliberate refusal to get snared in a tired and tiresome debate. It is better to pose the issue as follows: how are we to think about the oligarchy? The answer, which needs amplification, is that we must avoid simplistic putdowns and pejoratives of the powers-that-be; must avoid putting up impenetrable barriers between the good guys and the bad guys. This on the one hand. And on the other, we must be clear that the way forward is by forging, shaping, helping to grow a social movement and a related political party to confront their power. The posture of confrontation we need to adopt is not one of proving them wrong and "us" right, but by pointing to a transformed society that transcends both them and us, by working for it and being willing to fight for it. "As I would not be a slave, so would I not be a master," said Lincoln. Or to paraphrase the forgotten side of Marx: beyond the world of the proletariat versus the boss lies a better arrangement of equals at work. This of course means an outer and an inner change for both boss and proletariat, for both master and slave. This is a Green message, not populist nor liberal nor Marxist nor conservative. But Green.

Analyzing the Oligarchy

In the interest of thinking about the oligarchy in realistic ways and reminding ourselves of the depth of the problem they pose for society, the chapter turns to an explication of the bases of their rule and domination.

Notice was made above of Aristotle's three criteria for describing any type of rule: first, an ordering of public offices; second, the nature of the social force that is preeminent in society and government; and, third, their way of life, or mind-set. As we do this, we keep in mind the questions any person would or should ask of any ruling group: Are they competent? Are they just? Are their strengths relevant to new conditions?

First, the ordering of offices: The constitutional order created by the founders, and creatively modified in favor of greater democracy by later generations, has shifted markedly in a hierarchical and centralized direction in the past several decades. In spite of the rhetoric of successive presidents to the contrary (when they were candidates), the centralized bureaucracy in Washington has continually increased in size and in its capacity to invade the life of the average citizen.[4]

Within the bureaucracy, the powers and structures of the military have mushroomed, as have also those of the secret police. Congress has continued to lose ground overall to the office of the president, and the system has veered away from the careful balance between them intended by the founders. The 535 senators and representatives are daily pressured by 6,953 lobbyists, many of them highly skilled lawyers, former congressmen, and generally much better paid than they.[5] They are continually having to beg, borrow and steal for money for the next election. Many senators have to raise $12,000 to $20,000 per week while in office to build up a sufficient campaign fund for the next election. Money comes, not from the generality of people, but from the rich. A 1980 survey showed that less than 7% of the population made direct campaign contributions to political candidates. Since most of these are very small, the big ones have a big impact.[6]

Each important vote that a congressperson makes, and most votes are important to some one or other of a rich contributor, is watched with care by wealthy individuals and/or well-heeled Political Action Committees (PACs). So sedulous and artful has this game become that Congress has grown into a kind of closed club of incumbents who regularly succeed themselves in office. Since only the rich or those with access to money from the rich can win elections, Congress is becoming a true reflection of the oligarchy as a whole. Some persons of political responsibility to the more general interest still persist or still try to fight their way in, but they are the exceptions that prove the rule.

The presidency, from being once thought of as a kind of fatherly monarch above the fray, and then being thought of as a tribune of the people, has more and more adopted the trappings of imperial monarchy and has become the tool of oligarchic power and greed. The presidency's power in foreign affairs, its power to give and withhold favors, and its control of information and thereby its power over the media have combined to place it above and beyond accountability. Not that the incumbents don't have to sweat for it, but they now dominate the levers of power to a degree even

George III would have found awesome. And, lest we forget, it was because of George's arbitrary exercise of power that the revolution to create a truly constitutional government was launched.

The high officers of the executive branch now exercise enormous powers that the president, though he has appointed them, can barely oversee, much less control. Contrariwise, a slick holder of the office of president can use the widespread presumption of a sprawling bureaucracy to absolve himself from responsibility for controversial actions that top bureaucrats are said to have taken on their own initiative.

See here the steady leaking away of accountability. Washington, the center of the oligarchy's vast empire, seems paradoxically devoid of power. Political scientists write naive books claiming that basically the system is self-perpetuating or "out of control" and that no one is any longer in charge. Thus, no one is any longer "to blame" for anything, and life in Washington just happily blunders along. Presumably, no one then needs to pay much attention to it. Such naivete is an additional smokescreen behind which real people in real offices in high places do make decisions deeply affecting the fate of each American and the entire world. They should be accountable for this, but they aren't.

There is still turnover in the presidential offices, of a sort. But the men (and by far most are men) who occupy them are overwhelmingly recruited from the ranks of the oligarchy and overwhelmingly share their point of view. Reshuffling of the same people, a kind of musical chairs, takes place regularly, and it almost doesn't matter whether they are Republicans or Democrats. There is also the famous phenomenon of the revolving doors through which people move easily from top positions in business, law firms, banks, university, and the media to government and back again, and then back yet again.

A kind of folksy and exclusive club, a pool of "the best and the brightest"[7] exists from which new presidents draw their team. It is the oligarchy's answer to the nomenklatura system which has been in vogue in Communist countries. Nomenklatura refers to the list of acceptable candidates, kept by high Communist party officials, from which vacancies are filled in all important positions in the entire society: government, economy, education and institutions of culture. The revolution in Eastern Europe, which rapidly spread to the USSR, finally focused its anger and its attack on the nomenklatura system. Similarly, in the United States, healthy change cannot take place and relevant policies put in place unless and until our "invisible" nomenklatura is dissolved.

Continuing for a moment to look at the "ordering of offices," one must not overlook two critical "extra-governmental" institutions: the so-called fourth estate (the media) and the political parties. Jesse Jackson has expressed his frustration more than once with what he describes as a small group of Washington news personalities who control much of the access to political talk shows. "They are each other's guests," he has said. "There is a group of about 15 through which most information is strained."[8] Media reflects the overall economy in many ways, but especially in the degree to which it has become centralized and concentrated in fewer and fewer hands.[9] This is just as true of broadcast media as it is of print. Competition takes the form of an intense game of trying to get as many consumers as possible to watch, or read, one's media product. The product itself, designed presumably for people with very short attention spans and minimal imagination or intelligence or judgment, varies very little from station to station, from newspaper to newspaper. There is considerable attempt at marginal differentiation: the personality of the anchorman, the particular spin given to this or that personality in the news, the choice of this or that story to embellish the product so as to entertain the consumer more effectively. But the news and the backgrounders remain stolidly bland. Certain other shows on TV or an exposé in the newspaper, on the other hand, go to the opposite extreme of digging for dirt, oversimplifying a problem, and having the net effect, not of enlightening the viewer or reader, but of deepening their cynicism. Actually, since the aim is to entertain, to get the attention of the consumer, nothing very substantive is heard or learned by the citizen.

The mainstream media, whom Ralph Nader has accurately dubbed the "corporate media," has moved beyond shame into shameless purveying to "the masses" the pablum they, "the masses," are then (falsely) said to demand of the media as the price of listening and reading. In this, the media does a job for the oligarchy: numbing the intelligence of the people even while addicting them to the simplistic fare they receive. The fourth estate, even in its moments of "investigative reporting" and in-depth inquiries into problems of the day, almost never probes into the whys and wherefores of those problems. If they were to do so, they would offend seriously the hand that feeds them. The mainstream media gets $70 billion annually from corporate sponsors.[10]

In sum, the fourth estate has abdicated its role of critical responsibility. The people, the society, and the earth are the losers. So are the oligarchy, however, for they also tend to believe what their media feeds the people.

Political parties are not effective in providing channels of communication and two-way debate between governors and governed. Controlled for the most part by the oligarchy, both parties together speak to and for the top 20% of the people, though some would argue that it's only the top 5%. Only during election campaigns do they refurbish their rhetoric and sound as if they might be capable of standing for the general interest instead of the interest of the few. But once the elections are over, they return to the familiar paths of elite rule and intra-elite communication.

These two vital extragovernmental institutions, the press and the major political parties, should have been avenues through which the oligarchy's overweening power could have been modified. But those hopes have varnished in recent decades as they have come under the domination of the economic and political power of a homogenous capitalist minority.

Second: the social force that is preeminent in society. Wealth based on capital is the major characteristic and driving energy of the dominant social force in the United States. The accumulation of capital and its concentration in the hands of a few is what they are about.

The Center for Popular Economics in 1987 described the potential for economic control by just a very few families. In 1984, the richest 400 people and 77 families directly owned assets worth about $181 billion. Two assumptions may be made: first, individuals can borrow an amount of money equivalent to their assets. Second, because a corporation's stock is usually divided among many shareholders, any one who owns 15% of the total stock of a company can pretty well control management decisions. If the above-mentioned 400 people and 77 families borrowed an amount equal to what they directly owned, they could invest $362 billion dollars. If they bought 15% of the stock of as many large corporations as possible, they could then control about $2.4 trillion dollars of productive assets. Such a sum amounts to about 42% of the privately owned factories and equipment in the United States.[11]

A financial survey by the Federal Reserve Bank in 1983 showed that the top 2% of income recipients owned 50% of all stocks and 39% of all bonds. The top 2% of all wealth holders owned 54% of all net financial assets. On the other hand, more than half of all families either had no financial assets or owed more than they owned.[12]

Related figures show that 44% of the American people have no income from property at all. Another 54% get less than $10,000 per year from their property. It is the wealthy 2% who get more than $10,000 per year from their property, who in a word may be said to own the country.[13] Concentration of capital is increasing: assets owned by the top 100 industrial firms in 1961 was 44% of the total assets owned by nonfinancial corporations. In 1970 this figure had risen to 51%; and by 1984 to 61%.[14]

It is also an old story that in the so-called free market economy of the United States, a few large firms dominate each industry. In heavy electrical equipment, for example, General Electric and Westinghouse call the tune; in computers it's IBM; in military aircraft, truly competitive bidding can never take place because Boeing, McDonnell-Douglas, and Lockheed rule the roost. In 1983, the top ten commercial banks held 34% of all bank assets.[15]

In addition, most of the largest corporations in the world have operations in more than one country and are for that reason often called multinationals. This gives them great bargaining power in their dealings with local employees and host countries. In some important respects, they are almost nations unto themselves. The worldwide sales of these global behemoths exceed by many times the gross domestic product of many small countries. For one example, Exxon had sales of $113 billion in 1981; Nicaragua, Zimbabwe and the Philippines together had a gross domestic product in the same year of $42.4 billion dollars.[16] It is no exaggeration to say that between 5 and 10 percent of the population of the United States own and/or control most of the economy of the country. Through the multinationals, and in concert with their opposite numbers in other industrial countries, they own and/or control most of the economies of the world. Thomas Dye has, for example, estimated that 3,500 corporate leaders in business, banking and insurance, many of whom sit on several corporate boards, control the bulk of the economy of the United States.[17]

The annual income of the country's top chief executives is flagrantly high even if they were doing a good job—goodness here includes being responsible to the common good commensurate with their power. Forbes magazine, in the spring of 1990, did a survey of executive compensation in 20 industries. Eleven of the 20 industries had median compensation of more than $1 million per annum. Median is the level at which half the executives earn more and half earn less. Perhaps the most disturbing figure in the survey is the one that shows that health-care CEOs are the most highly paid of all: the median compensation is $1,420,000. This may be seen side by side with the fact that 37 million Americans are uninsured; and that insurance rates for most of those who are insured have risen enormously.[18] Other figures, though varying in the amount of compensation claimed for the corporate elite, show a similar picture. For example, data presented in the "Proceedings of the American Economic Association" in May 1989, show that in 1987 the average compensation for the chief executive of large corporations was more than $2 million. Between 1960 and 1987, in the United States, the gap between the pay of such a wealthy person and the average factory worker increased from 41 times as much pay for the CEO compared to the factory worker to 93 times as much— more than double. In the same period, the pay of the CEO leaped to 72 times that of an average schoolteacher, from 38 times as much in 1960.

The Oligarchy's Belief-system

Yet the power of the oligarchy is not fully understood until one applies Aristotle's third criterion: the way of life, or mind-set. The members of the oligarchy, no matter how they fight one another, are united on some very basic understandings of life. A core understanding is what they call individualism and self-fulfillment. The term is actually inappropriate. A more accurate term might be ego maximizing, or ego accumulation, or ego autonomy. A still more accurate term would be the "the striving of the thinking ego." Thinking ego derives from the famous *cogito ergo sum* ("I think, therefore I am") of the French philosopher Rene Descartes writing at the dawn of the industrial era when much of the philosophic spadework for the new capitalist/industrial era was being done.

Ego, heroically sovereign and alone, separate from nature and from others, but united with the power of mental calculation, is the foundation stone of the industrial and capitalist philosophy of life. The philosophy of thinking ego was eagerly embraced by the rising new men of industry and has come to be an embedded—and an unexamined—assumption of their inheritors, the contemporary oligarchy. By "autonomous ego" is meant the right, and the duty, to compete with all others in pursuit of power and wealth; and by "thinking" they mean the ability to figure out how best to get from one point to the next. Some call it the rationality of calculation; others prefer to call it instrumental rationality. A further manifestation of this type of rationality is the passionate drive for the efficient control of all factors in a situation, a drive that leads to hierarchic patterns of organization and the solution of problems through managerial manipulation.

A second core understanding is a deep belief in what the oligarchy trumpets as "the market." But again this is an inappropriate term. What the oligarchy has in mind is the circulation and accumulation of commodity values, expressed in terms of an abstract representation of a good or a service, i.e., money. Aristotle warned against the degeneration that occurs when the medium that is used to achieve the exchange of goods and services (money) becomes itself the goal of the actors who participate in the exchange.[19] Then, as Marx (who later analyzed this phenomenon more precisely) points out, the aim of production becomes no longer the manufacturing and crafting of end-use values but the making of commodity values (that is, exchange values).[20] A good or service in the form of commodity is not valued for what it is and can do for human beings, but for what it brings in the form of money. Marx called this "commodity fetishism."

True enough, some goods do happen to serve useful ends in this process, though many do not, but that is not the purpose of a commodity-oriented, profit-centered system. Aristotle warned that putting instrumental values ahead of end-use values leads to the substitution of the former for the latter. It brings to the fore a type of human being whose character is indubitably shaped by this substitution. After a century or more of full-blown industrial capitalism, one may go even further and say that not only does the economy serve instrumental values primarily, but that this substitution of means for ends, and the pursuit of the means as if they were the ends, has seeped into and overwhelmed all other spheres of life from the family to the school to the media and government.[21]

Gripped by the ideology of commodity production, the ruling oligarchy wrenches free of nature, free of society, free of moral restraint, free of leadership responsibility, free of "womanly" sensibilities. It uses up the resources of nature without thought for the future. It pollutes nature to a point of irreversible calamity. It abuses the bodies and souls of billions of people around the world, starting with the citizens of their own society. They are, in objective terms, the most ruthless, extremist, and ideologically motivated class in the history of the world. Since in subjective terms they are continually surprised by the consequences of their actions, innocently unaware of what they are doing, claiming decency and good intentions, they also then become one of the most dangerous classes in history, dangerous to themselves, to everyone else, and to the planet. In her portrait of a rich man, owner of a far-flung candy empire, racist autocrat of his household, outwardly decent, inwardly torn by fears and prejudice, Toni Morrison acidly exclaims: "Is there anything more loathsome than a willfully innocent man?"[22]

A third core understanding of the oligarchy is its tendency to elevate macho values above those of caring and social responsibility. The ego dynamism of industrial man (the gender connection is deliberately made) has wreaked havoc on the older concept of the father. The latter, though a tough patriarch, still had a sense of caring for the whole. The new man that rose to power with the decline of the old aristocracy, admired, even envied, the old patriarch his supposed aggressive powers; but under the impact of ego-centered values, that older sense of social responsibility declined and dissolved. The result has been a kind of hyperaggressiveness, often hidden under a mask of polite sophistication, that characterizes the men of power in the modern industrial world. Their macho understanding of the world makes them also admiring of military power, or say that their incapacity to understand "needs," only "means," removes from their minds a context of wholeness and contextual responsibility within which their lunge for mastery might otherwise be modulated, if not contained. Unfortunately, the great promise of commerce, that it would soften manners and work for peace, touted by 18th century thinkers such as

Montesquieu and Kant, has, under the impact of the ideology of commodity production, proved to have the opposite effect.

A fourth core understanding that is characteristic of the oligarchy is to think of connections between things and between people in formal, abstract terms. It is not as if the industrial mentality did not provide for a general moral and political framework within which ego-maximizing would and could go on, The market was itself supposed to provide, through a hidden hand embedded in the competitive play of forces, a certain equilibrium. In addition, certain formal rules, regulations and procedures have been devised to keep the competitive game in bounds and on course. In politics, it's legal norms that attracts the oligarchy. Given their instrumental lawyer's bias, they love to pursue linear causes and effects that can be generalized to more and more instances of "the same thing." Also, theories of a group process in politics and government are widely disseminated, which, like the market in the economy, is supposed to achieve equilibrium through the interplay of competing forces. In ethics, it's objective "rules of the game" with which they are comfortable. In philosophy, it's the niceties of logic that compel their attention. In social relations, it's behavioral uniformities that are looked for. And so on.

Thus, real relationships between things and between peoples are obscure to the oligarchs and their followers. Contexts and situations may be acknowledged, but thinking contextually, thinking situationally, is hard for them. They are quick to assign the pejoratives of sentimental or emotional or intuitive or womanish to anything that looks like an appeal to the deeper context of a given problem, to holistic thinking, to intrinsic values, or to concrete relationships of one thing with another, of one person with another.

A Breed Apart

This portrait of a ruling class could go on for many more pages. Finer lines could be drawn, certain arguments extended, but for the purposes here, there is enough to ask if the oligarchy is really suited to the great task at hand. That task, after all, is to stop the butchery of the earth and to learn how to cooperate with nature; to discover together with women on an equal footing, with all people of color and with working people, a society in which a mosaic of races, cultural groups, and a variety of life forms can interact and flourish; and to redistribute economic and political ownership and power throughout society. These tasks are critical. The civilization to which the oligarchy itself pays lip service will not survive unless these tasks are accomplished.

The oligarchy is not equipped for this. They have a far too privileged position in offices of governmental power, and this makes them blind to their own responsibility. They are far too rich and lead such incredibly opulent life-styles that it makes them unaware of what life is like for 99% of the human race. Their economic power is so great that of them it can be said that "though power corrupts, absolute power corrupts absolutely." Their own self-advertised strengths tell against them: their vaunted belief in male autonomy, in the virtues of independence, and in being separate, lonely heroes facing the world. Merrill Lynch—one of their most prestigious firms, an icon of Wall Street and industrial capitalism—ran a brilliantly executed advertisement in the '80s that featured the catch phrase, "A Breed Apart."

"A Breed Apart" is a fitting accolade for the entire oligarchic stratum. They do not inspire the world with confidence that they, who are so apart—apart from nature and from others—can provide the creative, responsive and responsible leadership in these new times. It is a capacity for interaction and mutual responsibility, and for an intelligence based on that, that is needed now for survival. Such a capacity doesn't spring up at a moment's notice. What is first of all necessary is a deep perception, indeed a conviction, that new qualities are needed. Precisely this perception is not forthcoming from them. They continue to charge forth in terms of the strengths and values (autonomy, instrumental rationality, macho self-importance) which they are used to. They are like a Goliath strutting about trying to convince the world that they are still the best and the brightest.

Consequently, how would they respond to the following ten requirements for business and government (assuming they could be convinced to listen to them)? The list of ten is taken from an editorial in *Multinational Monitor* for March 1990. The demands are fairly modest, but they do cut to the core of the ecological problems facing the planet and the United States.

The ten requirements are: Ban all hazardous waste exports. Mandate recycling for paper, glass, and plastic. Exempt environmental protection and health and safety laws from the General Agreements on Tariffs and Trade and other trade accords so that they will not be overturned as nontariff trade barriers. Stop all pesticide use and make a transition to organic farming techniques. Expand governmental cost-benefit analyses to include the environmental impact of products and projects so that agencies no longer make choices without taking into account the full costs associated with their decisions. Build and maintain mass transit systems; stop the tax subsidies going to individual auto transport. Close all nuclear plants and institute a national energy policy centered on solar energy and conservation. Ban all nonessential use of plastic and asbestos. Stop all production of chloroflurocarbons (CFCs). Require environmental impact statements for private ventures.

These policies are pertinent to only one field. A similar list could be drawn up for multicultural policies, the male/female impasse, and issues of democracy. But the oligarchy can't and won't get on with it. They are too stuck in their power, their privilege, and their old way of thinking. Or, if they do grudgingly and slowly initiate changes, they will do so only under duress and then with much back pedaling and undermining of the efforts being made.

One may well ask, why bother with them at all? Better to get them out. The problem is that they are deeply entrenched, politically, economically and culturally. Can they be shaken up sufficiently so that they can and will change profoundly? There is little evidence they have such a capacity, though many are trying to learn a little. Much is asked of them of course: not only a change of heart. That might come fairly easy. But a change of mind and mind-set, that is much harder. A willingness to give up a substantial measure of their power, political and economic: this is the hardest of all, especially for them since they value their money and their power above all.

The record of the oligarchy in almost every area of life today is replete with failure, greed and perverse priorities. Even after thirty years of clear warning not to depend on Middle East oil, the oligarchy still has no policy in place to reduce and replace that dependency, but has in fact increased it! They have no program that can shift the economy over to nonpolluting renewable energy sources. This is a stupefying failure and interlocks with failure to curb seriously the carbon emissions that will warm the earth disastrously, the failure to preserve forests, protect soil resources, radically reduce the production and emission of CFCs, or deal with the mounting mountains of waste, much of it toxic. Always avid for the technical fix, because that is what their mind-set leads them to dream of, they are incapable of developing a comprehensive approach for these interwoven problems and are incapable of identifying and getting popular support for policies that implement a comprehensive approach.

In seemingly smaller things, their ineptness, matched by their greed, is also apparent. The savings and loan debacle, that inflicts over $500 billion on the taxpayer for decades to come, is truly a scandal of the oligarchy. The rich and the powerful of all echelons and of both parties were in it up to their eyeballs, to a point where those "responsible" to do something about the mess were themselves the ones "responsible" for it.[23] The military-industrial complex, the oligarchy's classic creature, has milked and bilked the taxpayer for decades; and, again, the people regularly called upon to examine and do something about the mess are as regularly the ones who have aided and abetted, and long profited from, the growth and good health of the "complex."

How could it be otherwise? The oligarchy is that kind of a force in society. It rules, it controls, and it tries to punish and purge its own ... or pretends to. One sees a striking example of the latter in such famous cases as those of Oliver North. Or in less reported cases such as that of former Attorney General Edwin Meese III who was awarded by a federal court almost a half-million dollars for the legal fees he incurred when he was the subject of an independent prosecutor's investigation. That investigation concerned charges that Meese had illegally helped the Wedtech Corporation of the Bronx obtain a military contract. At the end of that inquiry, the independent prosecutor reported that he had found potential tax violations, but that he would decline to prosecute them, saying they were insignificant.[24] For contrast, one might note an item that the *New York Times* put right next to the Meese story. It reported that the Internal Revenue Service had been demanding about $90,000 from Mitch Snyder, one of the nation's leading advocates for the homeless, when he was found hanged in a suicide in Washington the previous week.[25]

Newspapers provide a continuing parade of items that reveal failure of policy, personal greed, pusillanimous leadership, and misplaced priorities. A random selection during a recent period reports that the national debt tripled in one decade to over $3 trillion and rises by $200 billion per year, and that the interest on the debt was itself $170 billion, paid, of course, to the members of the oligarchy; that the Department of Housing and Urban Development diverted millions of dollars intended for the homeless into the pockets of rich Republicans; that the Pentagon admits that the Star Wars program will never be able to protect the nation from nuclear attack even though they have already spent $21 billion on that program since 1984, and continue to spend on it; that the U.S. intelligence services were wrong in assuming that the Soviets could mount an invasion of Europe in 10 to 14 days, that the real number was more like 33 to 40 days, and that the difference rendered unnecessary huge investments that were made in troops and equipment; that the Pentagon is pressing ahead with a $4 billion electronic radar-jamming device that has failed crucial tests on fighter planes it is designed to protect; that more than $130 billion, 23 percent of U.S. health care spending, goes to managers, administrators, insurers, marketers, lawyers and other paper-pushers compared to only 13 percent in Canada; and that few of the 65,000 toxic chemicals listed by the EPA are tested for neurotoxic effects, yet the agency's request for $1.5 million to do more testing was denied by the Office of Management and Budget.

It is quite right and appropriate to say that it is the oligarchy who must be held responsible, rigorously responsible, for these failures and lapses and perverse priorities. They have the wealth and power and have provided the leadership. It happens, to paraphrase their own "great communicator" Ronald Reagan, on their watch.

Thus, they are the problem, culturally, economically, and politically. Not the minorities (as they call other people of color), not the women, the drug culture, the lesbians and gays, the secular humanists. Not the workers. Not the consumers. Not the people. But the oligarchy: they are the problem. As much for themselves as for the rest of us.

Opposition to them must be at once tough and understanding. This is a hard thing to achieve. Moralism is not a useful response. Something like a clinical attitude would be more helpful, in an older sense of the word which means being both objective and caring. This is said not to deny feelings of outrage and anger. But it is said to season the outrage and anger with a deeper consciousness and responsibility. Otherwise, we may just repeat the impotent moralism of the past which shakes the fist at daddy, with the implied demand, and childish assumption, that "he" put things right.

"We" must put things right. Not excluding members of the oligarchy from the "we." It's a political consciousness, beyond moralism and protest, that must get born among people in all sections of society, including members of the oligarchy. It's doubtful that the oligarchy as a whole will change, or change in sufficient degree, or change in time. So they must be pushed to change through the nonviolent marshaling of cultural, economic, and political power that will get them, as individuals, either to adapt profoundly or to stand aside so that others can get on with the task. What is required is a social movement and a political party rooted in that movement that can marshal such multifaceted power. A Green movement/party is, at this historic moment, in this ecologically critical moment, in a position to make that happen. At any point in this process, the oligarchy must be invited to join the task. We must do just as our opposite numbers did in Eastern Europe. If, as a result of pushing, the oligarchy does not budge, or tries through soft measures of seeming compromise to co-opt us, we must not go away or give in. We must keep the faith with the planet and each other and push forward firmly until we achieve what we have set out to do.

Chapter 8
From Protest to Transformation

Greens find themselves in a historic moment. Visions of the world rooted in Marx and industrial class struggle are fading. Visions of the world rooted in anticommunism are also fading. The Cold War has been declared over and the USSR is undergoing immense changes. Containment of Soviet power and communist ideology has been the keystone of United States government policy at home and abroad since WWII. Anticommunism has served as a point of departure for conservative, liberal, and social democratic thinking for at least half a century. But it can no longer be a successful rallying cry for colossal war budgets and military intervention around the globe. It can no longer serve as an effective rationale for suppression of activism at home. Nor can it be the clinching argument liberals and social democrats have often used to persuade the rich to go along with welfare state doles. Something else will have to be put in its place by the oligarchs, whether they are self-styled realists or self-styled humanitarians.

What might it be? Some would promote capitalist consumerism run by the big corporations and making the whole world safe for that. This might work. It's doubtful, however, if many people would be moved by it. Nor would the world environment survive the full-scale planetary corporate capitalist onslaught this vision would entail.

A more sophisticated version of the same thing would be to take a basically corporate consumerist approach, but coat it generously with a carefully constructed ideology touting traditional values, religious indoctrination, environmental regulation, and the need for continued military policing abroad, primarily in the Third World. Environmental regulation would consist of technical and bureaucratic efforts to control the worst excesses of capitalist production and would earnestly seek to permanently adjust the general population to bad water, air, food and overall living conditions.

This too might work, but it is fraught with severe problems. It is an authoritarian solution and difficult to make it seem even remotely democratic to the consciousness of many people. Nor would most members of the oligarchy, who are very secular in their outlook, feel comfortable having to kowtow in public to the newly minted religious opium of the masses. In addition, the fabricated ideology would be indelibly Eurocentric and inherently sexist so that as a vision it could not find ready acceptance among most people of the world or of the demographically changing American society. Furthermore, it is dubious if anyone in society, ruler or ruled, would put up with a permanently second- or third-rate environment. True, the rich might be able to get clean water and air and good food, but at great financial and social cost. Finally, who is to know if nature would not continue to fight back hard and nullify even this qualified exploitation of its resources?

The oligarchy cannot escape nature or history. Both demand of the oligarchy that they make a profound turning: a turning towards democracy in family, business and politics, towards multicultural consciousness and society, and towards an ecologically sustainable economy. The shrewder and more imaginative wits among them may well wish to do this, but they are outnumbered and are much too timid.

The time is ripe for a Green movement and a Green Party, unfettered by the baggage of Left and Right ideologies, to articulate a vision and a strategy for democracy, multicultural society, and ecological sustainability. A strong Green movement/party can pose new options. This could galvanize the many separate social forces who are opposed to the status quo, and opposed to oligarchic domination, into making common cause together. It could draw creative energies from all sections of society to focus on a new beginning. It might even successfully pull the oligarchy away from plans and policies that lead to authoritarian solutions, ethnocentrism and environmental disaster. Barring that, it could successfully blunt the oligarchy's power, so that dominated people are protected, promising economic and social projects are supported, and the environment is given a chance to recuperate itself. This would at least avert crisis for the time being and provide space and time for new solutions to emerge and grow.

For any or all of that to happen, it is imperative that those seeking change stop for a moment and recollect what it means to be political. This is first of all a question of consciousness, not of specific actions. Any action undertaken with a political consciousness, no matter how small or how ambitious, is what the present situation calls for. But action, and any thinking that goes with it, which is undertaken without political consciousness, no matter how exciting or seemingly successful, tends simply to regurgitate the status quo.

A person is not on the road to political consciousness until he or she truly encounters the issues of domination and exploitation in themselves, in their relations with others, and in the society at large. Political consciousness does not grow and take off within such a person until he or she truly encounters the fundamental source of present day domination and exploitation in the supremacy of the oligarchy. That supremacy reaches into all spheres: economic, political, and cultural.

The one characteristic of contemporary American action for change which most inhibits the birth and flowering of a political consciousness is its immersion in a protest mentality. Protest assumes, often unconsciously, that someone in charge can do something about a problem and/or should have done something about it. This is not an inappropriate response to problems if the society and its government is still accountable to some mutually understood and accepted standard. But there is no accountability and no mutually understood and accepted standard when the society is dominated by giant impersonal corporations that exercise arbitrary power, and when government has the latter's interest primarily at heart. In that context, which is our context today, protest, though often full of pathos, is inappropriate and politically inept. Yet this is where much if not most activism in the United States is still stuck.

Some historical background may help to situate how the protest mentality came to be.

Industrial urbanized capitalism began to replace agrarian society in the United States following the end of the Civil War in 1865. The populist movement of the late 19th century had a robust political consciousness, but was rooted in, and largely tied to, a declining agrarian population. There emerged then the urban Left, inspired by socialism and the ideas of class struggle, and it became a major source of opposition during the early decades of the 20th century. It too was rooted in a strong political consciousness. But Left politics began to take a turn for the worse following World War II.

The oligarchy was high in the saddle, and getting higher. Their industrial machine, based on outrageously cheap oil (two dollars a barrel), spewed forth the products of what was called affluence[1] to a middle class avid for things. Never mind that a few generations of people in one country squandered in reckless haste the stored solar energy that had taken nature millions of years to accumulate. Never mind that in their thoughtless lust for more, these few generations polluted the waters and land and air of the planet to a point where it is now seriously at risk as a place of habitation for humans and for most other species. The oligarchy, presiding over this cosmic debacle, airily dismissed the lone voices crying halt! And almost nobody listened or cared.

The Left, with its Marxist and socialist antecedents, gradually lost its cutting edge and its confidence. The proletariat that was supposed to get worse off and more and more numerous, were getting "better off" and relatively diminishing in numbers. More and more people thought of themselves as middle class, and already by 1950 the number of white collar, or service jobs outnumbered blue collar, or mining and manufacturing jobs. The trend has been increasing ever since. Labor union membership declined to a point where only one in five workers belonged to a union. Their bargaining position faltered even as the union leadership in many cases became a self-selected and permanent caste at the top. This development was aided and abetted by the powers-that-be in the corporations. The industrial class analysis of the system, applicable to an earlier era, began to break down under new conditions.

Either not daring, or not inclined, to question the goals of unlimited and indiscriminate production and consumption, the Left turned to issues of distribution and access, and away from the more fundamental problems of production and the underlying, but still relatively unseen, rape of nature that the oligarchs were orchestrating. The Left often even acknowledged that the problem of production had been basically solved by capitalism. That industrial capitalism knew how to "deliver the goods" became almost a piece of conventional wisdom in progressive circles in the '50s and '60s. Socialists continued to call for the nationalization of industry, under which presumably the forces of production would be in even better condition to spew forth the things of affluence, but the calls had less and less conviction.

The Left took up the causes qua causes: blacks, Native Americans, Hispanics, women, gays and lesbians, and the poor. Too often they took them up only as instances of people being left out of the middle-class affluence; and as people being kept out of the political system and the opportunity it presumably gives people to fight for middle class affluence for themselves. In addition, the Left scored the powers-that-be for not treating the left-out and the kept-out with the respect due them for their potential to become part of the middle class.

Eventually, environmental issues and the peace movement were also included in the list of acceptable causes, but they have never been very easily assimilated into this picture of people knocking on the doors of the system to be let in to join the fun and the decision making. How does one let nature in, or nonviolence in, without questioning "the fun"—or questioning the structure of decision making and top-down patterns of authority? So, environmental and peace concerns for two decades have been treated as add-ons, as "Oh yes, and then there are the environmental causes; and, of course, the peace people, let's add them to the list."

Some on the Left looked deeper, especially artists who warned of the devastating cultural effects of affluent living. The Situationist movement from the late '50s to the early '70s daringly and provocatively revealed the creeping emotional passivity of modern life, the spectatoritis of millions, the loss of inner values.[2] But such manifestations of cultural concern became split off from others on the Left, and the latter in turn divided up into factions and separate academic schools. Many became social democrats and sought a niche in the Democratic Party. Others, concerned for purity of principles, crept away into elaborate and sophisticated groups of Marxist cognoscenti, an academic Marxism "far from the madding crowd." Still others, open to change and searching for further adaptations of the Marxist tradition, became lone voices for a return to fundamental and creative questions.

The net effect has been not only to marginalize the Left but to marginalize what had been a source of fundamental criticism. What was left (pun intended) was a watered-down Marxist humanism which increasingly based itself on a synthetic effort to add up all the causes and make out of them a new tapestry of opposition to the powers-that-be.

In one sense, this is not a stupid idea. But it is insufficient. It panders to all the causes as if the goal of the cause is beyond criticism and the only thing required of the cause is to join in with enough of the others to form coalition after coalition to shake this or that concession from the system. As argued throughout this book, such tactics may get something shaken down (or made to trickle down), but it does little or nothing to combat the steady erosion of the basics of life and livelihood that affects every person, whether a member of a cause or not.

Yet, Left activists and the leaders of causes have continued with this kind of politics, which is rightly called the politics of protest. It fits in very much with one of the unfortunate legacies of the '60s: the making of extreme demands on the system in strident language, peppering one's rhetoric with anticapitalist abstractions, and invariably either losing, or settling for small, piecemeal gains. Both psychologically and politically, such a posture reveals a lack of confidence and a lack of willingness to take responsibility for running the store. It suggests an attitude toward authority much like that of an angry child who suddenly one day rebels against the perceived authority of the parent. The child demands that the parent do something or get out of the way. He or she has not yet reached a mature decision to let the parent know that it is time for the nature of the relationship to change fundamentally. Nor is there in this a willingness to shoulder and share responsibility for how things are to be done. Nor does it show much of a will and willingness to get in there and do it. In a nutshell, this is what was wrong with the '60s. The politics of protest was endemically and even ineradicably immature.

Nor did the Marxism that seemed to give some intellectual ballast to the young Turks of that era help at all in this regard. Marx is notorious for his failure, his own declared refusal, to provide any sort of a worked-out alternative program as a basis for action. He was worried about being "utopian." But, more importantly, he had disarmed himself from making a serious political analysis, including a discussion of the nature of the government of the future, by adopting an economic determinism that saw government and politics as merely epiphenomena of economic forces and economic organization. Actually, and ironically, the absence of a seriously meant alternative political program in Marx and Marxism produced the opposite of what he intended. Visionary pronouncements came to be made in his name in the '60s, too: much intellectual moonshine but very little in the way of practical steps to a better world. It was easier, and more fun, to shake the fist at the system and attack the symptoms of its manipulative and impersonal rule.

The Left has put a heavy emphasis on issues concerning the distribution of wealth and on issues of who owns what. But they have pushed into the background issues concerning the creation of wealth. The creation of wealth is now coming more and more onto center stage for those who want to change the system. The pollution and degradation of ecosystems and human life and the wanton extraction from nature characteristic of industrial capitalism and industrial communism make us realize that our very livelihoods are hanging as by a thread. Society must discover better ways to create wealth. But a fixation on patterns of mal-distribution and a tendency to attack existing patterns of ownership without showing ways to create wealth more effectively has the effect of deepening a mentality of protest. The general populace gets the strong impression that those calling for basic change are not "on top of it" when it comes to producing the goods. This perception increases people's willingness to put up with the system, no matter how flawed it is. This is especially the case since appeals to a better distribution of the pie seem to imply an ever greater hardship for the middle class. In this context the protest, however sincere and justified, still comes off as irresponsible and immature.

The legacy of immaturity, of proneness to protest, continued into the '90s. It has become the acceptable method of doing politics by people who might otherwise together truly change things. It is subtly encouraged by the politicians who find it a useful method to know where the shoe is pinching in an otherwise passive and politically inarticulate populace. They can then promise and reward, now this, now that group, with small favors and play successfully the game of divide and conquer. Even the more obstreperous and forceful groups are kept in line, though often not without considerable manipulation.

Protest, initially attractive as it may be to those who want to get involved, is a dead end. Of itself, it merely helps to keep the system going. The Greens are the harbingers of a new, more seasoned politics. Hopefully, they will also be its practitioners. They turn away from protest to concerted action through sustained organization for the transformation of

society and its politics. They directly challenge the industrial mode of
production, whether run by comrades or capitalists. It is a task that has
been dropped or weakly conducted by the Left. But they do so, not only on
the Left's ground of unjust increment (surplus capital) and the inefficien-
cies of corporate competition, but on the equally serious grounds of the
industrial capitalist system's inherent incompatibility with nature and its
inherent intensification of human rapacity and greed.

The latter critique dares to enter a field the Left tended to soft-pedal:
the personal responsibility of citizens, in their role as consumers of capitalist production, for the degenerating state of the world. Greens insist on
the need to critique our attitudes and life-styles and to resist the intense
propaganda barrage of the advertisers to consume and waste. What lies
behind this change from the Left, of course, is a rejection of the latter's
naive assumption that once objective conditions change, people will be
good. So-called objective and so-called subjective factors interrelate con-
tinuously and fundamentally. A narrow economic and "objective" critique,
or a narrowly cultural and "subjective" critique, are equally inadequate.
The cultural and economic critiques cry out to be supplemented by and
woven together by a political critique.

The Greens challenge activists to graduate from fractured protest and
its negative posture to a proactive and positive affirmation of the need for
an alternative program for society and an alternative leadership. Greens
will join in and support protests conducted by groups fighting for their
rights. But they will do so in order to draw the attention of these groups
away from just wanting something from the system to the need for thinking more deeply about the implications of their action. Greens urge them
to consider how much more effective they could be if they joined in with
many others to combat the same corporate foes and their government allies
on behalf of a transformed society. Only in this way can their actual needs
and wants ever be satisfied. This is the real work, and though much harder
than protesting, it is far more satisfying.

Greens are a catalyst for the coming into being of a broad and sweep-
ing movement for transformation. Such a movement is centered on the
idea of community and has many parts. At least nine are critical. They are
listed here in no intended order of importance.

First is educational work. This includes public forums on key issues,
public rallies, study groups, and alternative education projects like the Green
College. It also includes transformative caucuses within the social science
disciplines, such as the organized section on Ecology and Transformational Politics within the American Political Science Association; and, in
an informal but significant way, it includes aspects of interdisciplinary

studies at colleges and universities.[3]

Second is building alternative institutions such as self-help economic experiments at local and regional levels, alternative style business firms, and alternative life-style associations and neighborhoods.

Third is direct action such as demonstrations and civil disobedience.

Fourth is Green party work: electoral and parliamentary action.

Fifth is citizen action: not only Green-inspired lobbying but also the lobbying carried on by thousands of kindred organizations and groups for causes that relate to Green concerns.

Sixth is multicultural work and the formation, for example, of multicultural learning circles among activists and concerned citizens.

Seventh are special caucuses for young people, and organizations of students such as the Students for Environmental Action Coalition (SEAC).

Eighth is alternative journalism, the hundreds and thousands of magazines, journals, newsletters, and books that are produced by thousands of people with a broadly Green commitment and read by millions.

And ninth is the exploring of vision and values, as for example Green spirituality, and the development of linkages with churches and religious bodies.

One of the earliest Green formations in the United States occurred in Maine in January 1984 when several activists in the environmental, peace and alternative economics movement in Maine met to form a Maine Green party/movement. In the spring of 1984, the first North American Bioregional Congress was held in Missouri. From that Congress came the impetus to hold a meeting to bring into being a national Green organization. This took place the following August in St. Paul. How it has evolved is the guiding theme in the succeeding chapters.

Greens have sought to go beyond the politics of protest. They have sought to be a catalyst for the birth of a powerful social movement and a powerful political party. Greens have come to see that protest groups come and go for the most part. Protest groups usually have an intense trajectory, springing up suddenly in response to a need, led by one or two individuals who do incredible amounts of work, and who are, relative to the group, given much power. Too much, usually, and many in the group notice it. But this is justified because things have got to get done. And, besides, the actions taken have a known beginning and end, and once the end comes, the group fragments, often in spite of the efforts of the leader(s) to keep it going, and eventually it disappears. Other groups come forward and the same trajectory repeats itself.

Protest groups may, however, last much longer in some cases. They settle down to push for their cause. Organizationally, they change from the heady days of their beginning into fairly "normal" patterns of internal hierarchy. A leader may become the leader. Policy then tends to come from the top down and the group is identified more and more with him or her. Or the leader may be rotated and much day-to-day work is done by a paid staff, headed often by a manager. A board meets from time to time. There may be sustained tension between board and manager and leader. Or, the leader position is subsumed wholly within the board, and then there is often tension, sometimes bitter struggles, between board and manager. In many cases, the manager, if he or she is alert and works at "board politics," will be able to prevail in most disputes.

In these cases of group longevity, the once-upon-a-time participating members have become the rank and file. They are now only fitfully in touch with what is going on. Power and responsibility, have shifted upwards. If in addition, the people at the top conduct strong direct mail campaigns, they become also financially independent of any base they may once have been beholden to. Meanwhile, being well established, the boards and managers and/or leaders form lateral relations with the people at the top of similar groups and with people in government and business with whom they contest. But the contest is about "practical" adjustments in the way things are done. There is not much time, energy, or focus expended on changing the oligarchic system from within, much less from without.

Building an alternative politics with an alternative program which aims at transformation of the system must begin in the consciousness of trying to avoid the above protest-oriented scenario. The task is both to build for durability and to build for internal democracy. It helps to have a conviction that the end is deeply conditioned by your means, if not indeed created out of your means. Greens recall the words of A.J. Muste, the labor organizer and voice for peace, who poignantly observed: "There is no way to peace. Peace is the way." Or, to put the challenge of organizing for transformation in different words, the way you organize yourselves should be in a manner that prefigures the kind of society you say you want to bring into being. That is a profound challenge, and most Greens perceive it and accept it. This is the meaning of their concern about any appearance of hierarchy in their organizational structures and practice; their emphasis on seeking consensus as a method of arriving at decisions; their interest in issues of process; and their determination to base their regional and interregional networks on the primacy and authority of grassroots groups.

How this affects the scope and conduct of leadership is hotly debated among the Greens. Similarly debated is how this affects the capacity of regional and interregional networks to function successfully, how this affects their ability to work with other groups, and how this affects their overall capacity as Greens to become a catalyst for transformation of society.

Yet, once the decision is made to act to change the status quo fundamentally, then such questions are vital. Any person, any group, must ask these questions. For how else will society, and the people in it who perceive and know the mistakes of the past, avoid making those mistakes again? Democracy means democracy and it starts and is nourished in the souls of people where they live and where they act for change.

It happens among activists that these values are asserted as something necessary and good for society "in the future" or "when the revolution comes." Or these values are paid homage to in brochures, speeches, lectures and articles as being very important in the here and now, but they are only lukewarmly practiced, if at all, within the group seeking change. How serious are such groups and such movements? What credibility can they have with society, with others, or with themselves?

There is thus an enormous difference in thinking about change and in working for it when you move from protest to transformation. It is new sets of relationships you are building. Indeed, it is an institution you are building, a new institution, even if it seems initially just a small group of people meeting to study Green programs and Green values, or if it seems just another group fighting for their favorite cause. Greens are here to stay. They are building new patterns of relationships and they are seeking to be catalysts for transformation. Both the actions they take together in the world, acting upon that world, and the way they relate to one another within their organizations are equally critical to success. This is not pressure-group work anymore, though it may include work that seems like it. It is instead revolutionary work. And that makes all the difference.

A political consciousness in situations of great injustice and incompetence includes at least the following elements. It begins with a clear sorting out and identification of what it is that pinches one's own soul and body. There ensues an effort to identify the sources of alienation and oppression, both in the outer world and in yourself. This is followed by a will to strike out against injustice and incompetence in the world "out there" and not to spare yourself in that equation, meaning that you also become critical of your own hangups and your own failure in the past to respond to injustice and incompetence.

Action follows. You engage by yourself or with others to demand that the immediate, or overtly obvious, injustice or stupid policy be corrected and you take appropriate action to follow up on that demand. Within you there dawns an awareness, then a growing conviction, that the injustice or the incompetence, which you have experienced is part of a larger structure of injustice and incompetence. Your will is accordingly honed to fight to change that. You experience a desire to join with others whose anger stems from other experiences than your own, but which are now seen to be related to your own. You and they now organize for a common political struggle against the ever more widely perceived systemic injustice and incompetence. This goes hand-in-hand with a rising commitment, shared by more and more people, to find, build up and nurture into being new and renewed structures of culture, economy and government for a transformed society.

Revolution is not a tea party. Neither, however, is it a blood bath. It is of the stuff of life, not of death. There come times in a people's life when revolution calls. At no time is a political sensibility more necessary: else the ferment and the struggle will either flicker and die or it will get twisted into forms of violence. In either case decay sets in. We face a great and grave challenge. We must meet the challenge with grace and poise. It is not only the matter of the revolution that matters. It is the spirit thereof. A political sensibility without a natural spiritual foundation is incomplete. Yet with equal force it can be said that a spiritual sensibility without a political foundation is also incomplete.

Part III

Green Movement

Chapter 9
Quest for Community*

Ralph Nader has been quoted as saying that "if all the different issue groups represent seeds on a desert, I want a third party to irrigate the desert."[1] In response to the question whether a third party is possible today, he went on to say, "Sure it's doable, but you need 1,000 grassroots organizers full-time. That is the hidden chip. The Citizens' Party got 225,000 votes, and they didn't even have two organizers. You need 1,000 organizers."

Ralph Nader is probably about right as far as the numbers go, 1,000 organizers, and as far as the commitment of each goes. The Greens ask some further questions. How are organizers to be found in such numbers? How are they sustained once they appear? How can we be sure that they do not turn into a special elite? A further question that goes to the heart of strategy is: should all organizers be party organizers or should they be distributed among different activities of the overall movement? If the latter, how can they be connected effectively so there is some common motion in the same general direction?

The Greens, by and large, are not averse to a national political strategy if it grows out of and supports grassroots institutions and grassroots political capability. Some Greens, however, do express an intrinsic distaste for getting into "that mess" of national politics in any way, ever. In any case, as far as electoral action is concerned, local and state efforts must have priority. Without experience gained at the local level in many parts of the country, any effort to engage in presidential politics, for example, would be premature. That sentiment was expressed in a takeoff on a familiar Green slogan by the Kansas City Greens in late 1989 when they exclaimed, "Think globally. Party locally!"

Greens need to think hard about the conditions for the successful emergence of a new political force that is locally based and can and does gradually mount a serious attack on entrenched national political power. What is the relation between local, state, and national networks of political activists on the one hand and on the other hand the grassroots idea and ideal which the Greens talk about so much? Or, supposing that a vigorous grassroots organized Green presence is established in many, many locales, even much beyond the 300 at present, what relationship should evolve between those in the local grassroots group who have elections and party on their mind and those who are much more interested in all the other facets of overall movement work? The answers would seem to be that the

*This chapter and the next three chapters are preserved as written in midyear 1991.

emphasis on grassroots has to be more than just a strategy. There must be something about the idea and ideal of grassroots that makes it a goal worthwhile for its own sake. Producing activists who become good organizers in and through electoral campaigns is fine. But they need to be sustained over time. They can't exist as if "up in the air." Likewise, they will not remain Green for long, either in their respect for good process or in their politics if, being "up in the air," they form a new technical elite unrelated to the grassroots—unrelated to one another except insofar as their narrowly understood political skills bring them together. This is where Nader's concept of 1,000 organizers needs to be examined carefully and put into a context.

That context for the Greens is community. In fact, there is a sense in which Greens can speak of "community within the community." Their struggles to foster community among the people in their local areas (for example, health clinics, municipal power facilities, local assembles, home rule, multicultural learning circles) must be matched by the formation of community among themselves.

Thus, conducting electoral campaigns must be seen and accomplished by Greens in the context of fostering "community in the community": community for everyone in society through many kinds of actions, and community among the Green activists themselves starting right away. From this basis, a strong, durable electoral effort can take off, grow and prevail, whether locally, statewide, or nationally. The Greens will have woven an organic web of support, and of mutual responsibility, for those who enter the always perilous seas of electoral politics. Seen in this way, "grassroots" is both an end in itself and a strategic basis for an alternative political force.

Many have criticized the Greens in the United States for being slow. Slow to get in there and do it. Slow to organize. Slow to develop a political message and direction. But the Greens have sought to get back to the basics of sound organizing. The more they have done this, the more they perceive the need to build from the ground up and the more they perceive that the ground one stands on must be worth standing on for its own sake. This takes time.

Many critics also have in their mind's eye a model of action derived from protest and pressure group activity. That is a misleading model. Building for a revolution, especially a revolution that is transformative and nonviolent, one that strives for internal democracy within the movement as well as democracy in society, is a wholly different matter and requires new models. These are not discovered or applied overnight. Still, there is ground for impatience! Seven years after an initial national organizing meeting in St. Paul in the summer of 1984, the Greens were still a

small and insignificant group of mostly middle-class whites, with a sprin-
kling of other people of color, scattered in small groups around the country. They had not yet fully developed a fund-raising arm, they had con-
sumed much energy in a seemingly arcane dispute over whether to be more
"social" or "deep" in their understanding of ecology, and their regional
and interregional (their word for national) organization was weak even by
standards of confederation. And, most trying of all to those Greens who
saw the vacuum of vision and direction in the upper regions of mainstream
politics, the Greens seemed so tied up in awkward structures of their own
making, and so hesitant in their gestures towards political engagement,
that the prospects for a successful Green politics seemed to be fading away.

Yet, looked at from the bottom up rather than only from the top down,
it was at least arguable that the Greens had planted the seeds and saplings
of their movement carefully among the grassroots throughout the country
and that these seeds and saplings would grow into sturdy, enduring and
powerful movement bodies, including Green Party formations, in the '90s.

Out of the meeting in St. Paul came a new name, plans for a central
Clearing House, and a document entitled "Ten Key Values."

The Greens adopted the name Committees of Correspondence, a term
used by dissenting church groups in England after the Reformation. It was
of course also the name of the network set up by rebellious Town Meetings
to exchange views and coordinate the political action that led to the American Revolution. The rebels closely followed the advice given to Benjamin
Franklin and others by the Penacook and Iroquois confederacies to have a
movement grounded in and controlled by strong local units.[2]

Efforts to locate the Clearing House in St. Paul faltered, but a group
in Kansas City volunteered to establish it there, and by 1985 it began to
function in earnest. It had minimal funds and, at the beginning, minimally defined tasks. An Interregional Committee (IC as it came to be
called) was formed to oversee the Clearing House and to be a low-key
facilitator of local, interlocal and interregional development. It was composed of two representatives from each of as many Green regional organizations as formed throughout the country. In the beginning, there were no
more than seven or eight regions, more or less bio-regionally defined. By
the end of 1989, their number had grown to 36.

Regions were episodic in sending their delegates. As a result, conti-
nuity and momentum were hard to sustain. Locals who hosted the many
delegates for an IC meeting, providing bed and board and travel logistics
that stretched their limited resources, got "burned out" and stopped sending delegates to the succeeding meetings. Always there was criticism at
how the meetings were conducted and at the perceived difficulty in getting

the IC to take action. The perception tended to forget that the IC had been deliberately set up in a manner that prevented it from taking very much action at all. So the IC came to be blamed by critics and locals across the Green political spectrum for sins which it couldn't help committing. The expectations the Greens had of the IC led to making demands on the body that it was not constructed to fulfill.

At the Ann Arbor IC meeting in June 1990, the delegates worried over the failures and generated a new enthusiasm to revise the structures and functions of the IC. Plans were made to expand its power and functions and to reduce the number of regions, thus reducing the number of people having to travel great distances to make decisions. Proposals for change were brought to the third National Green Gathering in Boulder, Colorado, in September. The locally based delegates at this meeting, there to ratify a three-years-in-the-making Green Program for the '90s, were sounded out on the desirability and feasibility of substantive structural changes in the national organization. Strong support for such a move was evident and an ad hoc Working Group was elected to create a comprehensive proposal. This group met in Kansas City in late November 1990.

The salient features of their proposal to the participating Green locals included: change the name of the overall organization from Green Committees of Correspondence to The Greens; reduce the number of regions to 11; have one representative from each of the regions sit on a Green Council (formerly the Interregional Committee); create a Coordinating Committee of seven members to guide the ongoing operations of the Green Clearing House and related Working Groups and to speak out on the issues of the day; establish an annual Green Gathering of delegates from each of the Green locals; create a mediation committee; and reserve 11 slots (additional to the 11 representatives of the regions) on the Green Council for Green Party organizations. These proposals were voted on by Green locals in April 1991 and, with one exception, were approved by over 90% of those participating. The proposal to divide the Green Council into two kinds of delegates, those representing party bodies and those representing regionally organized locals, was narrowly defeated.

The Ten Key Values that came out of the St. Paul meeting in 1984 swiftly became a symbol and source of unity for Greens throughout the country. Expanding on the four pillars of the Green movement in West Germany (Ecological Wisdom, Social Responsibility, Nonviolence, and Grassroots Democracy), the USA Greens added "Personal" to the second pillar's call for Social Responsibility and identified six more values as preeminent in defining Green politics. These six are: Community Economics, Respect for Diversity, Post-Patriarchal Values, Decentralization, Global Responsibility, and Future Focus/Sustainability.

With the Ten Key Values in hand and with a fledgling regional and interregional structure in place, the Greens turned their primary attention to building their base: local Green groups in as many local and regional areas as possible became their overriding goal. They began with about 25 such groups, mainly in New England and northern California. During 1985, the number grew to about 50, in the next year to about 80, then to 150 by 1987. By the time of the Eugene, Oregon, national program gathering in June 1989 there were about 200 groups, with at least one in almost every state; and by the fall of 1990, the figure had reached nearly 300.

The Green objective was, and continues to be, to seed communities of community-minded people everywhere, groups that are open in spirit and in membership to anyone, that mix business with pleasure, and mix social life and politics. It is hoped they will study and take long views about politics and social change, seek to show through their actions on particular, seemingly short term issues both the interrelationship of one issue with all others and the need to find comprehensive solutions. For example, it is not enough just to halt a mass burn garbage incinerator; nor is it enough to recycle and compost; nor yet to get consumers more conscious of ways to classify, reuse, and reduce their waste. Equally, if not more, important is to get business and industry to reduce radically the type of manufacture and marketing that results in waste. Understood and applied in this comprehensive way, the garbage question is seen to be part and parcel of consumption issues and production methods and ties in with the overall goal of a sustainable society.

Thus, the Green goal is to strive to be far more than a pressure group, and far more than an electoral group aiming to put people in office. Pressure politics and running candidates are part of Green action, but Green action and the meaning of being Green is not limited to those activities.

Greens, coming together and growing, together as a community, are called to be a multifaceted, multi-issue and multistrategy force for transformative change in their communities, and then regionally, interregionally and globally as well. They seek to engage in more than one type of action over a period of time, though some groups will favor one type over another most of the time. The types of action include: educational work such as forums on public issues; citizen action (whistleblowing, lobbying, referenda); multicultural work (helping with others to build bridges across groups and movements); alternative economics and institution building (starting a mutual self-help system, planting gardens in abandoned city lots); direct action (demonstrations, Street fairs, and civil disobedience); electoral action (running candidates); and self-study. The last named is often the favored initial activity of most groups. Once sufficiently familiar with the roots and scope of the Green movement and Green vision, and once feeling

111

sufficiently comfortable with one another, groups will take on one or more of the other types of action.

Doing an action to accomplish this or that short-term goal or developing a more comprehensive analysis or program for the future are, to be sure, of critical importance to the Greens. But to them it is equally important to foster community among themselves and indeed among all activists who are engaged in a variety of activities relating to the Green vision of democracy, ecology, and multicultural society. Greens are beginning to realize the critical importance of developing a wide open and firmly grounded organization and the skills that go along with that kind of organization building. This especially is where they differ so profoundly from pressure groups, cause-related groups, and conventional political parties. Greens are, in effect, trying to "grow" new institutions at the heart of which is the idea of community.

Greens apply their idea of community in the first place to local, physical space, to habitat. This bio-regional concept lies at the core of their insistence on the crucial importance of habitat, a sense of place. Furthermore, the idea of community applies to regional and interregional, and then also international groups of activists who participate together in meetings and via multiple forms of electronic technologies, such as fax machines, modems, videotapes, and the telephone.

Their goal for themselves, and for the society at large, is to develop and enliven the interrelations among people and between people and nature, so that community can serve three vital needs: first, offer the best protection there is against tyranny and exploitation and against the atomistic loneliness of the industrial and capitalist concept of life; an opportunity for personal growth and happiness; and, a reality much missed and abused by an industrial, capitalist machine, restoration of the human interrelationship with the land, with habitat, with nature.

The Green inspiration is that by spreading the idea of community throughout society, and by modeling that idea in many ways, society will develop the power to resist tyranny, exploitation, and the separation from nature which the present system daily reproduces; and that, from this as a base, a political force can and will emerge to contest with the powers-that-be.

Their local groups are in one important sense living laboratories of a public meaning of community. People with diverse experience and often very different backgrounds come together not for "their thing" but for a more common and commonly arrived at "thing," expressed as values and principles and concepts, expressed as tapestries of interests, and expressed as a common program for action in society. This is close to a much older meaning of politics, and since the whole of this new group endeavor is also to infuse everything with a renewed sense of the human relation to nature, one can say with some confidence that though old-fashioned, these groups are also bearing a meaning and a message that is very new. They represent an awakening of a new political sensibility. The key is community and its organic ties to nature and to democracy.

It would be Pollyanna to report, much less expect, that this vision of community is being realized by Green locals. Many problems daily frustrate the effort to do so. Six are singled out here for attention: a fuzzy picture of the idea of community in people's heads; reevaluation of male/female relationships and of old gender identified roles within the group; the relative absence of other people of color in almost all local Green groups; decision rules and leadership; the kind of issues a local Green group should focus on; and the slow growth of a distinctly political consciousness.

A major pressure comes from false expectations of community on the part of people who are attracted to the Greens. This is completely understandable because the culture in which we are reared is seriously deficient in the understanding and practice of community. Not infrequently, longings for a new perfect harmony constitute the ground of these expectations. They push the local group towards a family-ness, a clubiness, which may be high on congeniality when it works, but also turns easily into a new exclusivity. Differences are muted when they shouldn't be, conflict is assumed to have been transcended when it hasn't been, and the member finds it necessary either to conform, lapse into passivity, or get out.

But, most often, the family-ness doesn't work even though the expectation that there "ought to be" perfect harmony still animates the members. The famous double bind ensues: there is not supposed to be conflict but, scandal of scandals, there is.

A contrary set of problems stems from an opposite tendency: to see community only as a place, or vehicle, for people to get together to accomplish objective goals. A take-charge mentality asserts itself, one which is impatient with questions of process and almost contemptuous of the need to deal with interpersonal relations. It persistently calls on the members to submerge their personal difficulties and get on with the action. Though there is merit in this tendency, the professionalization of the movement and of community is inherent within it. Conflict is projected outwards. Internal conflict is either denied or is increasingly channeled through bureaucratic fail-safe procedures.

Both of these ways of living the action of the group prevent the real conflict that exists from being dealt with creatively. They also prevent the differences which form the ground of conflict from becoming energy for forward motion.

Community, thus, is neither a family-type nor a professional type organization. It is neither a relationship of intimacy merely, though closeness is important; nor a relationship of objective doing of tasks merely, though action to some purpose is equally critical. Community is of the order of a public relationship and a public action. It is intimate in one sense and professional in another. It is intimacy with a dash of the professional; or it is professional with a dash of intimacy. Some lean in one direction, others in the other direction. But if each spins off from the other, community ceases to be, a public is lost, and the group or society at large goes the way of a closed tribe or, on the other hand, a closed bureaucracy.

The problem is not with the people in conflict, not in the first or basic sense. The problem is an immature concept of community which people carry around in their heads derived from the dominant culture. Community is not the same as a family or any other kind of personal, intimate relationship. Nor is it a set of objective relations that can be formalized and put in a code. Community, to put it quite starkly, is a place where "others" meet. They meet because they have larger, wider purposes, and broader interests in view than an intimate relationship on the one hand or than a set of specific objectives on the other hand. People in community are "others" to one another: not only physically and mentally, but sociologically, economically, politically, even spiritually. They come together, yes. They will stay together, partly because their differences from one another, or rather the distortions that derive from those differences, diminish in some degree; but partly also because their differences do not disappear and stay intact.

Differences are the source of energy and new ideas! They must be preserved! The goal is not uniformity, nor is it congeniality. It is co-unity based on respect for difference, based also on common values, and based on doing common tasks. For that to happen, members would need to acknowledge first of all that conflict is natural. With that firmly in mind, they then need to have recourse to the arts of interpersonal, mediatory skills (which includes the exploration of values), to the arts of interphilosophical discourse, and to the arts of interpolitical negotiation. And they have to be aware that this is all perfectly O. K. Some Green groups have met and surmounted the challenge posed by people's immature and/or professionalized expectations of "community."

Some have not. Most remain in a fuzzy state on these issues, lurching from one side to the other, now reveling in seeming congeniality, but then bursting at the seams with intense interpersonal conflict and charges of inaction; now seeming to move along smoothly to accomplish decisive action in their areas, but then stymied into inaction by quarrels over process.

The relations between men and women in the local groups can also get strained, sometimes very badly. This, too, is understandable, given the crisis proportions of the male/female alienations and confrontations in the wider society from which the members come, coupled with the value intention of the Greens to change deeply the prevailing character of male/ female relationships. Women are often the ones who perforce have to raise these issues in the local group since men often don't see them or don't see them as having a top priority. This adds to the strain, since women become frustrated and resentful and men quickly sound defensive and behave as if they were surprised.

The issues are familiar ones: women often feel that men dominate the discussions, no matter what the issue. Often they can't get themselves heard; and when they do, what they say is not given the weight it deserves. Often the issue taken up for discussion is not as close to women's own experience as it is to the men in the group who have a long tradition behind them of male assurance when talking about the "problems of the world." Furthermore, male habits of talking, and talking much, overwhelm the meeting, so that even the best discussion facilitation can't seem to find the right balance.

Often a point is reached where the women will insist that the group deal with these distortions and the word often used to describe them is "process." Women contend that the men in the group are not aware of their own overly "masculine" style of speaking and behaving, that the meetings are exercises in old modes of domination, and that they, the women, feel stifled. There may, and often does, ensue a special meeting, or a weekend retreat, and out of this a sharper awareness of these sources of conflict and alienation, though it may have to be repeated in the not too distant future. It may happen that men will begin to meet together to discuss relationships and women will meet together to develop greater political knowledge and discussion skills.

The male/female encounter parallels and may overlap the distinction made above between community (mis)understood as a family and community (mis)understood as a professional or business-type operation. Women may tend to interpret the life of the group overly much in terms of relationships while the men may tend to interpret it overly much in terms of professional assumptions. Of course, some men are relationship-oriented and some women professionally oriented and this can lead to bewilderment when the lines are drawn between men and women and not between the more "masculine" and the more "feminine" experience. The latter distinction may be a better one to understand and apply than male/female. Then, when it comes to having special subgroups to deal with these issues, some men might join with women in learning more about "the world" and some women might join with men in learning more about "relationships." In this way, both the positive male and the positive female qualities could free themselves for expression and interaction: within the same woman and the same man, among women, among men, and between men and women. Most Green groups have a long way to go before they reach in practice such levels of consciousness. But they have a shorter way to go than the general society they are seeking to change.

The dearth of other people of color is not a new experience for white-initiated movements. Yet, for the Greens, whose Ten Key Values include a specific call for diversity, it is a continuing anxiety and distress. African American, Native American, Hispanic American, and Asian American activists have, however, made a strong contribution of the development of individual local Green groups. They have also had a marked influence on regional and national Green gatherings through public speeches, small group work, and one-on-one conversation. They have likewise had a continuing impact on the evolution of the Green Program for the '90s which was completed and approved in Estes Park, Colorado, in September 1990. In addition, people of other cultures are active throughout the country within their movements to fight against the pollution and exploitation which disproportionately affect people of color and the poor and working people.

Green locals have a rich opportunity to do at least three things. One is to develop ties with other movements and people of color by joining their struggles. A second is to seek out ways, with them, to build bridges of communication that would emphasize mutually reinforcing multicultural education and multicultural self-help projects. And a third is continually to advertise and practice multicultural values within the local Green group so that many more people of color other than white would feel comfortable and, more important, feel the Green vision and organization is also theirs.

How should decisions be made? Greens throughout the country follow a similar pattern: they resolutely seek consensus. If consensus cannot be reached on a proposal, a motion can be made to go to a vote. The number of votes needed to pass varies with different groups; for some, four-fifths, for others three-fourths or two thirds, and for some simple majority.

Most local groups thus far make decisions by what might be called an informal consensus process: there is discussion of a given proposal led by a facilitator, there is a sorting out of problems with the proposal, it is informally reformulated or redesigned, and it is accepted or rejected without recourse to a formal act of calling for consensus or proceeding to a vote. The smallness of the group makes this informal process workable and natural, much like so much committee work that is done at the present time throughout society. At times, of course, an issue arises that may be sticky or complex and then a more formal consensus seeking process is followed and, if necessary, a vote is taken.

Greater formality characterizes regional meetings and especially the proceedings of the Interregional Committee (the IC). There the trust and face-to-face familiarity is less and the issues are often, by the time they reach that level, more weighty and/or less clearly understood. At that level, effective facilitation becomes a key necessity. Disagreements over decision rules wracked the IC in its first few years and continue to produce tensions. Though local and regional groups achieve much decision making through informal processes, they don't always have a happy time going through those processes. Conflicts embedded in different concepts of community, and in different gender conditioning and different sexual, racial and class experience interface with different perceptions of a given problem and notions of what it takes to solve it. These differences, in addition to ego demands, pile up to produce hard feelings. And long rancorous meetings. Members may begin to stay away, and may gradually drift away altogether.

Periodically, efforts are made to improve the process of group meetings. The best and most promising is the growing commitment on the part of some of the members of local groups, and of certain local groups as a whole within a given region, to call for workshops on how to make meetings work better. These workshops are run by people familiar with group dynamics. In this way, together with asking different members of the group over a period of time to facilitate the meetings, there grows a fund of experience widely shared throughout the group about how to shorten, enhance and enliven meetings and make them productive. In this way, the people in the Green movement, and through them a large number of their fellow citizens, can learn what their society has deprived them of: the ability to interact effectively with other people, the ability to find and have a voice of their own, the ability to cooperate and negotiate with others for common, public ends.

In this way, as well, through the Greens, Americans can discover and learn that they need not leave decision making to the "chosen" leader on the one hand nor to the experts on the other. Greens do have leaders, of course, and inevitably the leaders begin to have disproportionate influence and power; but this does not last all that long because the "nonleaders" demand accountability; and because the leaders of the day are soon joined by others who become leaders. This induces a kind of checks and balances in which the leaders all together themselves constitute a limiting force on leadership as well as a mutually enlivening force for leadership.

Kermit the Frog's plaint has often been quoted by Greens, and by their critics and supporters: "It isn't easy being Green!" This has been especially felt by local groups when it comes to deciding what issues they should get into. Most have been drawn initially to environmental issues and many have stayed with these kinds of issues: anti-incineration and pro-recycling campaigns, save the forests, protect neighborhoods from intense highway construction, stop condominium developments, and so forth.

Several problems have come up in choosing issues. The first is that on the face of it why should the Greens get into a particular issue when other organizations have already made it their special concern? Second, should the action be done in the name of Green or in concert with other groups under some other title? And third, how, in the choosing of issues, can a group most effectively help the neighborhood or region understand that they are not a single issue group or not only an environmental group?

On the first problem, "It's already being done," some groups languished, but others have persisted and come up with various positive responses. One is that "We are not a special interest group. We see, and argue for, the interrelation of all the issues." Action then can take the form of seeking to be a catalyst to get existing single-issue groups into working relations with one another, so that out of this can come a broader understanding of each issue and the development of coalitions with more staying power than before.

Or action can take the form of getting into an issue on one's own, as a separate group, and doing the action in a manner that reveals the full implications of that issue: that is, that solutions cannot simply be piecemeal or for that time and place only, but must seek a more and more comprehensive answer. A favorite example is stopping incineration. Though an action begins with a loud No! of resistance, it continues with a fuller and fuller articulation of, and demand for, a comprehensive solution to the problem of waste: from its source in production policies through the practices of distributors, to the habits of consumers, to the processes of reuse and recycling, and then finally to the careful disposal of the now radically reduced waste components.

One can apply a similar comprehensive logic and attendant strategies of action to energy production, or to transportation, or food production, or health care, and so forth. In each case, a particular local issue (shutting down a nuclear plant, lobbying for renewal of train service, stopping the irradiation of food, demanding better wages for nursing home workers) leads backwards and forwards to the web of problems and concerns in which that particular issue is embedded. Doing actions in terms of this contextual approach clearly differentiates a Green group from the actions of most single issue groups. This does not preclude working with such groups or asking them to help you in doing an action. In any event, if one thinks about action in this way, and follows through, there is no question that Greens can bring something unique and powerful into the swirl and struggle of pressure politics.

Doing actions in the name of Green was, in the early years of Green organizing, something of a question. Groups worried that the name might put people off as being too strange or even faintly unpatriotic. This worry has rapidly faded away, as Green has caught on throughout the United States and the world. On the other hand, since the term Green is even appropriated by Margaret Thatcher, some wonder if it any longer carries a sufficient political meaning to be useful. In response to this fear, it should be pointed out that the use of the word does help, not only to identify a posture of concern toward the environment, but a deeper and more comprehensive political message, a message that weaves together a variety of concerns that the oligarchy's system has systematically sought to keep separate. What the Greens are after is an alternative to the politics of the oligarchy. Their task is to associate the term Green with such a politics.

They can help themselves in this regard by paying close attention to the issues in which they get involved, because these, more than anything, help to project an image and a message. Environmental issues are good for the Greens because they offer an opportunity to focus sharply on the underlying ecological imperatives that now drive society, whether society understands this yet or not. Greens "see" environmental issues that way. Most of the population, and the entrenched oligarchy, do not. They see them as "additions" to all of the other issues; very important, surely, but not at the root of all the problems. So, by concentrating on environmental issues, Greens on the one hand are "doing the right thing" and are helping to associate "Green" with an emerging fundamental politics. However, on the other hand, by concentrating in this way they can also too easily be seen as just another environmental pressure group.

Thus, Greens need to diversify their issues. In what direction? Here choices must be made and are being made by the Green locals. They can move into what are identified respectively as "peace issues" or "social justice" issues or "style of life" issues. But their choices, it would seem, should come "naturally." That is, they should come from the felt inclinations and experience of the members of the group, just as the environmental issues have. A leading natural candidate would seem to be those issues that the wider society identifies as "women's issues": for example, family violence. Choosing such an issue can help the women in a group develop more strength and courage within the group. And it will challenge the greater community, after their initial surprise that Greens are addressing such issues, to acknowledge that Greens are a multi-issue force for change. The Greens in a local group are then in a good position both to show the underlying connections between a seemingly "nonenvironmental" issue,

119

e.g., family violence, and the underlying Green philosophy, and to pro-mote a greater overall attention to the Greens as representing an alterna-tive politics, not just on this or that issue, but on the totality of issues before the body politic.

A stumbling block in the achievement of a more-than-environmental politics by the Greens is a relative absence of a strong political conscious-ness among many members of the Greens themselves. They have not yet sufficiently broken free of the conditioning straitjackets of their society, especially the protest modes of thinking about action and doing it. "Being involved" may still, for many, take the form of showing up at an occasional meeting, participating in a demonstration, making such and such number of phone calls "to help the cause," making contributions now and then, taking turns at the recycling center, and engaging in errands of mercy. These actions are, of course, enormously valuable. But often they are done in a manner and in a spirit akin to the husband who is determined to help out in the household, does the dishes, sweeps the floors, and maybe changes a diaper. He does these separate things, thinking he is involved, even liberated. But he does not take charge mentally, along with his wife, for the whole. He does not comprehend the economics and life of the house-hold as a going concern. He only helps out. So, too, many Greens. They need, perhaps, to be less busy with the minutiae of helping out! They need to help the group develop a greater economy of Green effort and learn to focus it more. That can come only from taking charge mentally, along with others, for the continued capacity of the organization to grow and act on behalf of the Green vision.

Local groups, for this reason, are also slow to develop their line of vision to move beyond only local concerns and to embrace in practical ways the regional and national networks they vaguely assent to but only dimly acknowledge as relevant to their group. Consequently, an inordi-nate burden gets placed on the shoulders of one or two people in the group whose level of commitment is high and who have thought through the implications of the call to an alternative politics. They get burdened with assisting in the building and nurturing of the regional and national net-works as well as with taking leading roles in the affairs and actions of their local groups. However, since the early years, more and more members of active local groups have joined these pioneers, and together they constitute a growing edge of Greenfolk who are in it for the long haul and who un-derstand more and more clearly the implications of the Green demand to act locally and think globally.

The basic lines of development are beginning to reveal themselves. The key is the concept of the community within the community. Greens are on the one hand calling Americans and people everywhere to a restoration of community and on the other hand to a new kind of community, beyond the models of the past, one that creates and sustains a public space and a self-empowering opportunity for everyone. That is the intrinsic value and the ongoing educational power of the Green movement through community. At the same time, as Green communities within the community expand in number and grow in depth, they will be the source and security for the "1,000 organizers" called for by Ralph Nader to spark the formation of a "third party" and create the political muscle necessary to jolt and then finally change the system.

Chapter 10
Green Movement and Green Party

A curious thing happened to the six-year-old Green Committees of Correspondence in the early months of 1990. Organizational and philosophical pressures for a much greater emphasis on electoral politics had been simmering beneath the surface for years at local and state levels and at the Interregional Committee (IC). Yet these pressures were blunted at the Green National Program Gathering at Eugene in June 1989. There, a strong thrust for developing a multiyear strategy leading to active participation in the 1992 and 1996 presidential elections was successfully deflected by Greens skeptical of national politics. Furthermore, or so it seemed, electoral activity itself was given a back seat to other, nonelectoral, forms of action. For example, much fanfare was given at Eugene, and subsequently, to direct action encounters, especially plans for a Wall Street confrontation on or about Earth Day 1990.

But suddenly and quietly, events in several states in the early months of 1990, and then at the IC meeting in March, propelled the Greens into electoral action as never before. As Greens sought to clarify and reconcile apparently independent electoral action with already existing movement bodies at local, regional/state and national levels, there came into being a set of party organizations parallel to and, presumably in a cooperating relationship with, the Green Committees of Correspondence (GCOC).

The implication was strong that a new organizational strategy might be emerging that both separated and reconnected movement work and party work at all levels from local to state to national. But there was a second implication: did it make sense to counterpose party and movement as if they were separate from each other? Wasn't party part of the movement? Wouldn't it make more sense to think of the movement as composed of many different kinds of strategy, of which party work was just one, even though an especially important one?

But this second implication was obscured by the first. Greens pounced on the separation of party and movement, whether in praise or blame, whether in hope or fear. The notion of separation was and is viewed with apprehension by many. Some fear that party work will deflect the energies of Greens away from overall movement building. If, as well, Green parties do not fare all that well in an electoral system that is already biased against third parties, then the Green movement as a whole suffers the stigma of party failure. They point to the marked tendency of the media to be interested in the Greens only to the extent that they engage in elections and party building. Thus, the argument goes, by concentrating on party work, Greens feed a profound misunderstanding of the Green movement: that it is some kind of a "third party," limited to the electoral and governmental realm, and not a fundamental effort to change society from the roots.

Some are also afraid that if party organizations are separate from local, regional, and national Green Committees of Correspondence, they will lose touch with the Green movement as a whole. Party bodies, Green candidates, and Green office holders will not be accountable. They will thus quickly go the way of most such efforts in the past. Even if successful, or perhaps especially so, Green parties will be caught up in the system and quickly domesticated.

These fears are legitimate. The dilemma is complicated by a further perception, however. If Green parties are not given a separate status, or some degree of differentiated autonomy from the other parts of the movement, they may pull the whole movement with them into the electoral orbit, for better or for worse. And isn't it likely that it will be for the worse? Parties are concerned with strategy and power in addition to their concern with vision and goals and policy. Strategy and power considerations are endemic to parties in a manner and to a degree that is either absent from other movement activities or appears there in different form. Furthermore, a Green in office is responsible not only to his or her Green constituency and to the Green Program, but also to all the constituents in their electoral district. This has a tendency to pull the very best politicians of any social movement in two directions at once, and Greens would be no exception.

Direct action, on the other hand, evokes different approaches, a different kind of leadership, and different tactics; similarly for Green educational work or alternative institution building, or alternative journalism, multicultural projects, or even for the mobilization of citizen action on the issues. Mobilizing for action on an issue often leads to taking strong, though narrow, stands and pushing for a kind of encounter with the powers-that-be which the Green Party may find too limiting or too vitriolic.

Seen from this perspective, the immersion of Green parties within the Green Committees of Correspondence, forcing them to accommodate to the pressures and styles of other action strategies, could result in the failure of Green parties to even get off the ground. Or, on the other hand, to the degree Greens are truly serious about party work, it could lead to the gradual displacement and even downgrading of the other parts of the movement in the interest of party success.

The point here is that Green parties need a movement that is generative, vigorous, and nurturing. The same can be said for any other part of the overall movement: direct action, citizen lobbying, alternative institution building. They all need a movement that is alive and well in all its parts. A second point is that Green parties need to be autonomous to some considerable degree: to have their own space and opportunity for growth. And again, the same can be said for the other parts of the movement. And a third point is that all the parts of the movement need to be interrelated, responsive to one another, and to have opportunity to align their strategies with one another.

Alignment of strategies is the creative way forward, not the integration of strategies. In this way, maximum pressure is applied to the prevailing system dominated by the oligarchs. It is maximum because it comes from a variety of sources: the many parts of the movement. And in this way, the sources themselves remain true to themselves and are always able to renew their energies.

This approach, this confederation of the strategies, can be successful. It requires the invention of a new space at the local level and then also at regional and national levels. This space is the Green Community. As explained earlier, the Green Community is a meeting place for people who are different from one another but united around a common vision, common values, and a growing discourse of common interests. It also is and can be, more and more, a meeting place for people who are pursuing different strategies. It can become a place where activists can put their feet up and discuss each other's Green work: electoral action, direct action, citizen action, educational action, and the like. They can plan and take actions together and they can decide to help out one of them at this particular juncture and then another at its time of need. In this way, each one's work is validated, each one's work to some degree becomes the concern of every other one, and each one learns more about the possibilities of aligning their strategy with those of others. This is the promise of the Green Committees of Correspondence, in their further evolution.

It is in this context that the creation and development of Green parties should be viewed. The forward motion of the Greens on the electoral path seems, thus far, to be leaning in this direction, but with many questions and problems encountered along the way. Yet, to the degree that Green activists, in whatever part of the movement they find themselves, understand that the Green Community provides a way for staying united with fellow activists and yet also free to do their thing, to that degree the Green movement will grow into a powerful social force.

In Michigan, a statewide party was born in 1989 and completed its platform and organizational bylaws by January 1990. The Huron Valley Greens, a very active local COC in Michigan, had earlier created, as part of itself, a Working Group on Electoral Action. This working group, however, now also came to be known as a Party chapter. As such, it was considered autonomous from the Huron Valley COC. As a Party chapter, it would have direct official ties with the State Green Party. Its "parent," the Huron Valley COC, however, would continue to have official and direct ties with the Mid-Great Lakes COC. A similar pattern was emerging in California at the local level.

Once Green parties were formed in Michigan and California at the state level, the Greens there had to work out a pattern of connection between the statewide party and the regional COC. In California, the sixty local COCs were grouped in three separate regions, each with its own representation on the national IC. The three regions, therefore, together created a California Green Assembly, whose task it was, among several others, "to monitor the Green Party of California and to hold it true to the Key Green Values."

In Michigan, the regional COC body (the Mid-Great Lakes COC) and the Michigan Green Party decided that they would henceforth meet on the same weekend. The term used by the Greens there to express the connection between the two bodies was that each was a "cooperating organization" vis-a-vis the other.

As spring 1990 moved into summer, these patterns in both states came unstuck. In both, tensions quickly arose between the partyminded and those who now became more and more concerned that movement activities (that is, other parts of movement work) were getting slighted. Some wanted to "bring back" the party bodies into the COCs; others wanted to sharpen even further the separation between the two. Still others wanted to fine-tune the meaning, in practice, of the concept "cooperating relationship." In Michigan, by the Spring of 1991, the Michigan Green Party had ceased to exist. However, a group called the Ann Arbor Greens (an offshoot of the Huron Valley Greens) ran two candidates for that city's Council in April 1991 and came very close to electing one of them.

In California, the statewide Green Assembly proved a nonstarter. However, the party Greens, having formed themselves into the Green Party Organizing Committee of California, created a special liaison committee to promote close contact with the local Green COCs. Yet, this also lapsed. Indeed, in southern California, the Southern California Green Assembly came apart, so that, as of the spring of 1991, there was no regional COC functioning there. Much energy was going into party organizing.

Two related campaigns galvanized Greens in California in a party direction. Mindy Lorenz, active for several years in the Green COC networks at local, state, and national levels, ran for Congress in the Ventura/Santa Barbara area as a write-in candidate. She received 1. 2% of the vote after a spirited campaign, the second highest on record for a write-in candidate. Secondly, the Green Party Organizing Committee decided to push for official status as the Green Party of California. They launched a campaign, aided substantially by Lorenz's campaign for Congress, to register at least 80,000 California citizens by December 1991, the number needed to reach 1% of the voters in the most recent gubernatorial election as required by the election laws. A long-range aim of the California Greens is to develop a steady following for the Green Party of 10% of the voters and on that basis, and in concert with kindred organizations, be able to push the powers-that-be into key structural and policy changes.

Events for the Greens in Maine took a sudden leap towards party formation in early 1990 after several years of "movement building" at the grassroots. The Maine Greens had been founded in January 1984 as a party/movement, perhaps the earliest Green formation in the country. During the next two years, which proved to be very stressful, party-types and movement-types, as they perceived themselves, struggled and slashed at one another. At last, both extremes of these factions left, leaving a small core of people committed to the idea of both a movement and a party, or of a party within the movement. This core then turned to organizing local COCs. The statewide organization remained in place but only as a somewhat passive umbrella for local organizing. A leading member of the Greens, from the western mountain region of the state, ran for the state legislature as a Green in 1986 and collected 18% of the vote in a three-way race with a Democrat and a Republican.

It wasn't until 1990 that the Greens in Maine were ready to return to serious statewide organizing. At a February meeting, attended now by representatives of nine local groups, there was considerable discussion over types of action to be taken in the near and farther term. Some favored issue referendums. Others, not denying the importance of such efforts, argued the importance of developing an electoral strategy. The February meeting set up a "92 Committee" to meet in early April charged with creating an electoral strategy for the '90s. Soon after, a Hancock County Democratic leader and a longtime participant in Maine's Rainbow Coalition, announced her departure from the Democrats to organize a Green Party in Hancock County. This received considerable media coverage, and, together with political ferment in neighboring Washington County, started the Greens rethinking their options and possibilities. The April meeting then took the step of deciding to run a Green candidate for governor in 1990 as part of a long-term strategy. The hope was to get at least 5% of the vote, the amount needed to be formalized by the state as a party, then to field many candidates for state legislative and local offices in 1992, looking to a full field of candidates in 1994 and a serious run for the governorship. The thinking was that if the 1990 campaign yielded less than 5%, the Greens would team up with the Libertarian Party in a referendum campaign to reduce the number of signatures needed on a ballot-access petition from 5% to 2% or even 1%. Campaigns for local and state offices would proceed in '94 and '96 whether or not the referendum was successful.

As it turned out, the chosen candidate for governor decided not to run. Another possible candidate was turned down by the state movement/party steering committee, which then decided to hold off on any governor's race until 1994. Later in the year, the "92 Committee" began working in earnest to prepare for local and state legislative races in 1992. Part of their planning for the '92 elections was to field candidates for county offices. Though county government has long languished in Maine, as in most of the rest of the United States, it was the thinking of the Greens that precisely for this reason Greens should run. This is an opportunity for them to gain experience in office and a chance to rehabilitate and inspire a rebirth of grassroots democracy through the counties.

All of this activity still left the Maine Greens, however, in need of working out the longer-term relationships between bodies devoted to party work on the one hand and the COC structures at local, state, regional, and national levels on the other. New locals were forming in several parts of the state, some in response to the idea of being a party, others more interested in other forms of action. Would new locals—formed in response to "party fever"—adapt to the COC pattern of multidimensional action which, though it includes electoral activity, also engages members in a range of other action strategies? On the other hand, would the already established movement-centered locals readily take on electoral work? Would such work by the local be organized by an autonomous electoral "subcommittee" as in the early Michigan model? Would all the locals together form a Maine Green Assembly, as in the early California model, side by side with the emerging Maine Green Party? Or would some other pattern be found? In the short-term, Maine Greens continued in the manner in which they had been founded, a party/movement.

Similar questions arose throughout the country during 1990-91 as state-wide Green Party organizing took hold in such varied parts of the country as Arizona, Colorado, New Mexico, Florida, Oregon, Minnesota, New Hampshire, and Alaska. But whatever the answers given, there could be no doubt that the Green movement in the United States was now getting serious about party building.

The Alaska effort hit pay dirt. The Greens there decided to run candidates for governor and lieutenant-governor. At first, they were disqualified from the race because, though they submitted a petition of 2,035 signatures, or 1% of the electorate, as required, they did so after the filing date of August 1. They appealed in the courts and won a landmark decision which placed them on the November general election ballot. It became a fourway race: Greens, Republicans, Democrats, and a right-wing Independence Party. The latter came in first. The Greens garnered 3.2% of the vote, enough to crack the electoral nutshell and gain official state recognition as a Green Party, the first in the United States. The Greens spent $6,000. The victor spent $1.5 million; the Democrats $1.3; and the Republicans $.8.[1]

At the national level, pressures to move forward with electoral action resulted in the formation of a national Green Party Organizing Committee at a meeting of the IC in San Diego in March 1990. It happened during a dinner-hour meeting of the Working Group on Electoral Action which had been created by the IC at its previous meeting in Washington, D.C., in October 1989. It was a dramatic moment, and understood as such by the 15 people who participated. They signed their names to the statement which was adopted unanimously. The statement read in part: "The relationship of this new group to the IC and the Green Committees of Correspondence was discussed and the following points were agreed upon. That we consider ourselves a cooperating organization but autonomous from the IC and the GCOC . We consider ourselves morally accountable to not only the Green Committees of Correspondence but the entire Green Movement."[2]

When a report of the meeting, including the above language, was made to the IC delegates in their assembly the next day, the delegates applauded. Whether they fully understood the implications of the action is another matter. It would take months, and perhaps years, for those implications to be absorbed, assessed and understood widely throughout the country, not only among Greens, but also among journalists, scholars, politicians at large, and among the attentive population.

The national Green Party Organizing Committee met at the June 1990 IC meeting in Ann Arbor and met again the following September on the last day of the national Program gathering in Estes Park, Colorado. Mostly, the members shared stories of local and state efforts at party organizing and candidate races. But a fledgling organization was created, membership lists were expanded and clarified, and plans were laid for a national newsletter. The first issue of *Green Paper* came out in February 1991.

The informal session of the GPOC at Estes Park had not set a time for the next meeting. Nor would there be a meeting of the Interregional Committee of the overall Green movement for the indefinite future pending the completion of the work of the Restructuring Committee elected at the Estes Park national gathering. In this vacuum, several GPOC activists decided to call a meeting of the national GPOC in Boston, February 8-9. The purpose was to begin the process of developing an effective organization and formulate some short term goals. Kept deliberately small, the group of 24 came from most regions of the country and 14 states. They established several committees: a Steering Committee, a Fund Raising Committee, an Organizing Committee (to identify and network with state and local Green Party contacts) a Platform/Publicity Committee, and a Committee for Liaison with Potential 1992 Presidential Candidates.

The meeting approved a guiding declaration with respect to the question of support for candidates in either of the two major parties: "We strongly recommend that local and state Green parties concentrate their efforts on mounting their own candidacies and forming their own parties. Endorsements of other candidates and participation in caucuses in other parties should be carefully considered, and undertaken only when they advance the cause of Green ideals and the development of the Green movement."

The meeting also decided to explore supporting the possible bid of Ron Daniels, a leading figure in the Rainbow Coalition, for President of the United States in 1992. With the encouragement of people of color at the meeting, the group suggested that a delegation of Greens ask to be invited to the Atlanta Green Justice Conference for Cultural Diversity and Progressive Movements, in June and sponsored by African American organizations.

The group further decided to call a general meeting of the GPOC to coincide with the fourth National Gathering of Greens to be held in West Virginia in August 1991. It was also decided to plan a GPOC-sponsored conference in March 1992, in Kansas City, to develop skills in party organizing and running campaigns. A critical objective would be to involve activists in kindred movements and explore ways to broaden into a more and more inclusive, independent politics.

Finally, the meeting discussed the GPOC's relation to the Green Committees of Correspondence. It endorsed the proposal of the latter's working group on Restructuring which included in its design a Green Council composed equally of 11 party and 11 nonparty members. This design would be rejected by the Green locals in a close vote in April.

The Steering Committee of the national GPOC, renamed the Steering Council, met in Atlanta at the end of June 1991. It developed proposals for presentation to the general membership meeting scheduled to be held at Elkins, West Virginia, just prior to the fourth national Green gathering there. The proposals included a statement of purpose; the future makeup of the Steering Council (gender balance, equal representation for people of color, specific seats-four out of thirteen-for representatives of kindred organizations); a process to come up with a shift in membership emphasis from general members to state party bodies; an agenda for an intermovement gathering, sponsored by the national GPOC, scheduled for March 1992; a general plan leading to the formation of a Community Presidency (or Run-with-the-Cabinet) ticket in 1996; and an invitation to Ron Daniels, an African American and a longtime Rainbow Coalition organizer, to address the Elkins GPOC general meeting to present his independent candidacy for President in 1992.

The meeting also took note of the defeat of the proposal by the Green COC's Restructuring Committee for inclusion of 11 Green Party representatives in any successor organization to the Green Committees of Correspondence. Calling for unity in diversity, and for the interdependence of bodies such as the GPOC within the scope of the Green movement as a whole, the Steering Council took no action on any specific proposal on the relation between the national GPOC and The Greens. It forwarded several proposals for discussion and debate at the forthcoming general meeting; these ranged from integrating the GPOC wholly within the structures of The Greens to maintaining a separate status for the GPOC but with open lines of communication.

Whatever might come of the specific proposals, it seemed clear that Green Party work was off and running. Experience and a gradually gathering knowledge of how to relate the many parts of the movement will drive the Greens forward, despite tensions, conflicts, and often bitter disputes. It could well be that the Party will go forward on a parallel pathway with other action networks of the movement, organizationally distinct from them, yet related through overlapping membership, common values, and periodic common meetings.

But whatever the exact relationship among particular structures that evolve for party and movement, certain questions will continue to challenge Greens in their effort to keep a balance among various action strategies. For example, what happens if Green parties fail to get significant electoral support? Will the entire Green movement, as well as the Party, suffer from it? Will party fever draw the energy of too many people away from other forms of movement action? On the other hand, will party work, as it gains momentum and therefore draws thousands of people to the Greens, deluge the established locals, and indeed the entire movement structure of the Greens with "party types" who don't understand or don't "give a damn" about the rest of the movement and its commitment to fundamental social and cultural transformation?

Furthermore, if the Green parties are successful in winning elections, will this bring in its train a slew of problems of the sort that electoral success usually brings? Greens will be lionized by the press. Opportunists, who have hitherto hung back, now join in droves. Politicians of the dominant parties will work overtime to create an atmosphere of "responsible leadership" for the newcomers in office. The risk is great that the

Greens will be co-opted and corrupted by the system.

Each of these questions and surmises makes a valid point. Green Party activists who respond point out that the power structure must be confronted at all levels and that party electoral action is one very effective way to do this. It is also an expeditious way to advertise the Green movement and the longer-term Green Program among millions of people who would otherwise never hear of it. Party electoral action can thus also contribute directly to the expansion in the number of local Green groups and thus to the strength of the nonparty side of the movement.

A measure of the critics' concern may be met by establishing a relationship between party bodies and other movement bodies which both differentiates and connects the two in various ways. Each needs a relative autonomy from the rest, and each needs to have some "say" in the councils and decisions of the other. It will take a certain ingenuity and trial-and-error experiments to find a way to balance these needs in actual practice.

Social and political movements have in the past regularly sought unity of organization and have repeatedly tried to make and keep them democratic. They have repeatedly failed on both counts. The unity was broken, and splits occurred. Or the organization became very hierarchic and top-down in its inner and outer operations. Or, third, the organization was deliberately made so loose and low-keyed that the result was diffusion and fragmentation.

The quest by the Greens to find a way beyond these perennial dilemmas may presage a new way of making social change and may be a key in the development of a strong alternative political force.

Organizational differentiation is important. Connection is equally important. The latter is accomplished through such devices as overlapping membership, concurrent meetings, the formation of Green COC liaison committees in the party, and making it a rule that Green candidates must be drawn from those who are, or have been, active in the local Green community (COC). There may need to be exceptions to this rule. In that case, the candidate should be required to go before the relevant Green community for discussion and debate.

In the end, it is the Green community that must play the primary role of guardian as well as nurturer of good Green practice in all parts of the Green movement. The Green community in the first instance is composed of the locals, but also of the various networks (state, regional, and national-and even worldwide) that associate the locals together and form wider and larger communities of Green activists in all aspects of movement work. The Ten Key Values and the Green Program are the documentary basis for that guardianship and that nurturing. But even more important is the mix of people in the community who, because of the community and their participation in it, learn to listen to one another, learn to trust one another's motives and actions, and find ways together to maximize and align their various strategies.

The base, and always the base, is the community at the local level. From 275 Green locals by the spring of 1990, it is not unreasonable to expect a number exceeding 500 by the mid-90s. Some of the Green locals will tend more toward fostering electoral politics and others more towards citizen action, or direct action, or educational projects, and so forth. But most will balance to greater or lesser degree these types of action and all will be successful insofar as they are and continue to be actuated by the spirit of community.

Green electoral politics cannot therefore be judged by the more conventional standards that are applied to Republicans and Democrats. Green electoral politics is closely related to its sources in a movement for fundamental transformation that calls for profound changes in social institutions, in culture, in economy, as well as in the government. Greens need to give each other courage and develop each other's wisdom to accomplish several things at once through party electoral politics: to offer to the public an alternative agenda for dealing with short and long-term problems, to speak to and for the needs of people in the short-term and push for policies in and out of office that can help meet these needs, to protect the work of nonparty Green activists, and to promote through public policies the gradual transformation of society. This is a greater and more difficult task for Green politicians than the tasks taken on by even your best Republican and Democratic candidates and office holders.

Greens need to run for office as Greens, and they are doing so more and more. Large numbers of Green candidates need to take that plunge in the next ten years. As some do it, their experience can be plugged into educational and training sessions for others. Greens should begin with running for local and state legislative offices. After people get experience in campaigning, and get exposure to the public, some should lay careful plans for statewide (gubernatorial) and national office. There are of course exceptions to these generalizations, since particular circumstances may justify a gubernatorial or congressional race in advance of local campaigns in order to spark and generate local Green groups and local campaigns.

As important as running for office, and perhaps even more important, is the need to change the way in which campaigns are conducted. Demanding a level playing field is one part of this: easier ballot access, a fair chance of exposure through the media, and the financing of campaigns that is rigorously limited to public sources. These will not come "at once" or in advance of actually running candidates, but they must be part of a total process of transforming the political terrain of which running for office is one aspect. Running candidates may, initially, be not so much to get into and transform the office but to transform the way in which candidates get there. This, then, also means transforming the way in which campaigns are conducted: less plastic, more reality. It means involving the arts in a creative way, not in the hyper-packaged way of modern advertising. It means down-to-earth exposure of the candidate. It means changing the way TV is used so that it does not manipulate but offers a chance for the candidate and the program to "get across" to the viewers.

Greens should run to educate and run to win. Both. Politics at present is obsessed with winning. There is no reason why this can't be changed and it is up to the Greens more than anyone else to do that. Their emphasis on balance; their emphasis on people as much as on issues; their demand for authenticity; their ability to take risks all combine to make them likely pioneers in rescuing the political terrain both from the manipulators and the issue "heavies."

Not as if the "issues" are not important. Each campaign should carefully develop themes on the issues drawn from the evolving national Green Program and from the local platform; each campaign should monitor how these are received by the public, which ones do better than others and why, and in this way build up a statewide and countrywide knowledge of how best to select, formulate, and promote the issues in Green campaigns.

Local Green groups and their statewide and national bodies need to work out their approach to the Democrats and Republicans. In some instances, it may make a lot of sense to back a candidate of one of the major parties. However, it should be done clearly as a Green sponsorship, and that could mean that the candidate in question may be uninterested. But if the candidate is willing and there is very strong support for doing this in the group, then it could be very effective.

An additional factor in the situation for the local or the state body, however, is whether or not they are running their own candidate(s) in other races, or have a record of having done so. This may be very important in order for it to be clear to the public and to the Greens themselves that the Greens are independent and not a tagalong of a major party. The aim should be to get that political alternative out there, to make it clear.

Greens need to be extremely careful that the language they speak is in the idiom of the people they are trying to reach. The language must be neither ideologically sectarian nor academic. Nor should it be simplistic, which is an opposite mistake. There is here also a serious question of attitude. Green-speaking must be rooted in a sense of common discovery, a sense of reaching towards the truth, not in an assumption of being in possession of "the word," which must then be dispensed to the ignorant. In like manner, Greens need to wrench free of the fateful tendency of 20th-century movements to bury themselves in an ideologically pure system of thought and practice. Instead, they need to liberate their minds by exploring the meaning of ecological wisdom, and they need to apply that wisdom steadily to their internal and external organizing, to their politics, and to the problems of society and the world. This steady effort to understand and evoke ecological wisdom must be undertaken by each local group, by each person in each local, and by each network, and must become the touchstone of the Green political alternative at every level of action and for every kind of action.

A cooperative stance vis-a-vis other politically minded groups with kindred concerns is crucial for the Green parties. Local party chapters and state Green parties, as well as the national Green Party Organizing Committee, should, for example, make contact with the relevant chapters of NOW (National Organization of Women) and work out ways to support each other and each other's candidates. This formula can also be applied to labor unions, to organizations devoted to the needs of people of color, and to environmental organizations such as the National Toxics Campaign, Greenpeace, the National Clearing House on Hazardous Waste, Public Interest Research Groups, and so forth. This is no easy task, but there is need both for great flexibility and for clarity about and unity around the Ten Key Values. It is imperative that the gradual evolution toward a strong alternative party formation effectively and organically includes, from the start, the thinking and planning as well as the needs, interests and values of women, of people of color, of organized workers, and of the "underclass."

An important rule of thumb is that one must try to act in the world from what you know you've got, not from what you imagine you've got. Failing to do this is just about the oldest mistake in the book, padding your numbers, playing PR games, claiming support of members of organizations when all you've got is the paper support of some of the leaders of organizations, and in general fooling yourself (and never fooling your enemies). You've got to know who is of you, who really is with you, and to honor and own and respect that support, however small or merely local it may seem. This builds confidence and clarity and makes you worthy of partnership in the eyes of others. Let the '90s be the decade when people who are leaders in the social change movement drop their overly benevolent and snobbish attitudes.

Running for the presidency must be approached with great caution. 1996 may be too early. Still, there is always the What If? factor. If the Greens develop local groups numbering over 500; if they are able to work out the relation between party and other movement bodies; if they in fact do approach being able to field the 1,000 organizer/activists Ralph Nader was talking about in 1989; and if Greens have been able to mount many effective local, state, and congressional campaigns, then a run for the presidency could be contemplated.

The aim of a presidential campaign would be to return power to local and state and regional levels—and outwards to international bodies. The aim would also be to foster a serious national debate about the major directions of public policy and about the need to come to grips with the stranglehold of the giant corporations on public policy and private initiatives. A campaign of that kind could fire the imagination of tens of millions of people for Green values. The campaign should also feature the Green presidential nominee running-with-the-cabinet, or a "community presidency," as Scott Peck calls it.[3] The Republican and Democratic candidates for president would be challenged to do the same. In the present system, people in the cabinet and other members of the president's team wield enormous power, but are not accountable to the people.

Presidential politics requires a certain astute political consciousness to succeed. Or say that success is to be measured not in terms of winning the presidency but in terms of developing and supporting the power of the grassroots; and in terms of the impact a strong showing for an alternative has on the constellation of powers in society and on the policies pursued by society. In the process of mounting national campaigns, by themselves or in concert with others, the Greens may be able to get people to see things in a new light. Changing the "pictures in our heads," as Walter Lippmann called those fundamental perceptions people have about the world, is a critical element in bringing about the revolution that ends the monopoly of the oligarchy and turns society in a new direction.

An electoral defeat for such a movement/party as sketched in this chapter is not a setback, because the party is firmly rooted in the grassroots and because the local groups each have an economic, cultural and social base in their communities. On the other hand, electoral victories for such a party are not a cause for exaggerated pride but are taken in stride, for elections are only a part of the overall action of the Green movement, not the only thing.

Greens who succeed to office in the next several years are part of the process of shifting the way the people see things. They work on problems, trying to help solve them, but they must show through action and speech what is truly involved in solving them. Any solution to a problem that keeps the power structure intact is really not a solution. Any solution that is a reform that actually precludes being able to take a further step in a creative direction is also not a solution. Any solution that offers just another technical fix is not a solution. Greens in public office can be extremely effective in keeping these questions at the forefront and in putting pressures on their colleagues to deal comprehensively and effectively with problems. Doing this is more important than being successful in office measured by the standards of their colleagues. Doing this, and staying in close touch with their party locals and networks, and in close touch with the Green community, will also help them in remaining accountable to Green values.

The Greens have built carefully for several years. They've been busy laying the foundations of a strong social movement. They have sought to understand the mistakes of the past and not to repeat them. They are now in a position to build rapidly for transformation. They can decisively assist a society in search of answers to overwhelming problems of ecology, community, democracy, and justice.

Chapter 11
Opening a Route to a Multicultural Society

John Vasconcellos made a *bon mot* about Republicans and Democrats during an interview with the author in the spring of 1990. Vansconcellos was then chair of the Ways and Means Committee of the California Assembly and is widely known as the initiator and promoter of the self-esteem movement, at first in California and now also nationwide. He said, "Republicans think of human beings as naturally greedy and selfish. Democrats, on the other hand, have difficulty believing that people can take care of themselves."[1]

Greens believe that people are different. People express themselves in a variety of ways—much like nature itself, for of course as Greens keep telling us, people are part of nature, not separate from it. Nature reveals, for example, almost infinite variations on themes of competition and cooperation. Most often, the same organism reveals complex permutations and weaving together of competitive and cooperative qualities. Human beings are alike in many respects but, just as important, they are also very different, naturally.

The need for unity and the need for diversity are equally true in human beings. The picture is more complex and more interesting than it appears in the received conventional wisdom. Fed by both Right and Left ideologies, the conventional wisdom believes that diversity necessarily leads to competition and that impulses for unity necessarily lead to cooperation. It should be noted parenthetically that the conventional wisdom also believes that competitive inclinations are more natural and the cooperative ones come in as it were afterwards as part of what it then calls our better nature, or our higher ideals. In its moral codes and preachments, therefore, it stresses that "human nature" is naturally greedy and selfish, but that we can mitigate its effects, or even overcome those effects, by high moral living and strenuous self-discipline. The covert message, of course, is that morality is boring, or not terribly useful in the short run, or more blatantly, that "nice guys finish last."

Translated into politics, this boring moral universe finds the Republicans and the Right wing talking realism, as they call it, and the Democrats and the Left wing proclaiming ideals, frequently invoking words like compassion and the welfare of others. The former take the low road and the latter the high road. They prop each other up and belong together. The mutual propping up is furthered by the tendency of the top leadership in each party to restrain those to the right and left respectively. Top Democrats caution their Left enthusiasts to be more pragmatic, to season their idealism with a dash of cynicism; top Republicans call on the Right to be kinder and gentler. In this way, the electorate is invited, brainwashed might be more accurate, to oscillate between two very limited and suffocatingly stereotypical responses to the problems of the day. Our politics needs a strong tug that will pull the rug out from under both.

Contrary to the conventional wisdom, Greens believe that competitive and cooperative inclinations are both natural. Diversity, though it seems on the surface to drive nature towards competition, may also be a powerful force working for unity. And the drive for unity, especially if it levels diversity into uniformity and sameness, may well lead to bitter competition and conflict.

To the Greens, conflict is a natural part of life. They do not anticipate some future glorious time in which there will be some magical "graduation of humanity" to a perfectly harmonious existence. This abstract ideal continues to be prevalent among liberal humanitarian thinkers, in contemporary popular Christian culture, and among proponents of Left ideologies. Conflict stems both from the forces tending towards unity and towards diversity. This happens because, though each organism has its own niche, and the many niches together do tend towards balance, each organism is also a changing, dynamically moving being, both assimilating the old and opening out to the new. In the process of its growth and dying, it naturally interacts with the many and varied beings around it, in competitive and cooperative ways.

In addition to the "imperfect" dynamics of nature, distortions can and do appear in the push and pull of these dynamics. Acting beings engage in the processes of life: things and situations in life are both settled and unsettled and they open to a future that is not totally fixed. Nature is open; it is not a predetermined "whole." Beings therefore experience that things might be otherwise than they are. Choices occur, and are felt as such by the organism, however dimly or unconsciously. Recollections of "good" and "bad" choices linger in the memory, conditioning present action and expectations about the future.

The things experienced by the organism that "might be otherwise than they are" are not only "outside" the organism but are on the "inside" as well. The self, for example, is not a fixed entity, but also part of a developing, evolutionary process, whose boundaries, though real, are also subject to continuing change and redefinition. Thus, it experiences fear and guilt, greed and self-rejection, rage and desire, overweening pride and self-loathing—and it accumulates residues of these experiences from the past. These mix together to produce failures of relationship and loss of communication, including, sadly enough, loss of self-communication. This becomes fertile soil for domination and subjection and for the promulgation of lies and prejudices. Fixed, and institutionalized, barriers appear between people whose only original difference from one another is that they are different. Their natural differences and the accompanying "imperfect" dynamics of their relationships have suffered intense distortion. Under the hammer of the twin forces of domination and subjection, the human species staggers under a heavy load of stress and alienation.

The profoundly typical differences among human beings that have become the occasion for the distortion of relationships and the easy target of the dominator are those of gender, race, homosexuality, language, and religion. And class. Though, as will be shown, class is in a class by itself in the matter of differences.

The quest for community and the need to unite and differentiate activists of many kinds bring into sharp relief the key Green value of diversity. Many Greens consider this value the most important of all. Yet the meaning of diversity and how it may most effectively be applied and realized are not easy to figure out. They are often themselves the cause of angry debate and conflict.

Greens, for the most part, are middle class people. In economic terms, to which one might attach some social signifiers, the middle class is situated between the rich who run things and the underclass who subsist in situations of poverty that separate them spiritually, culturally, and socially from the rest of society. Being in the middle class, Greens reveal many of the same relatively small differences in income and so-called social status that characterize the middle stratum as a whole. They vary from the norm of middle class, however, to some degree. Most Green activists earn less than the college educated members of their age group. Many deliberately change their jobs, or reduce their commitments (and pay) in their jobs, in order to carry on the struggle for Green values and politics. Many adopt a low money-income life-style, do things for themselves (growing more of their own food, for example), or they don't bother with TVs, hair dryers, clothes driers, cosmetics, wonder drugs and the like, or engage in barter arrangements with others in their community.

Very few, if any, Greens are located in the top or the bottom strata of society; that is, top and bottom as defined by degree of wealth, power and socioeconomic status. What distinguishes them from many in the middle stratum is, first, their knowledge that a truly rich and dominant oligarchy does actually exist and that this must be given priority in public awareness; second, their knowledge that therefore to dwell upon the income and status differences among the middle stratum is largely a pointless and politically stupid practice, one that plays into the hands of the oligarchy; and third, their concern about the terrible conditions of the underclass. It is a concern that is not narrowly philanthropic, but is also based on the political knowledge that the continued existence of such conditions for millions of people is deeply injurious to the entire society.

Greens, perhaps, are too sensitive to criticism about their money and class that come from scholars and pundits—whose salaries, one may dryly note, are paid by the oligarchy. Such criticism has much more impact on their psyches than it deserves, partly because Greens are still too accustomed to thinking of life in terms of class distinctions, a heritage of both bourgeois and Marxist traditions. It is a deficiency they need to work at and overcome. It is hard to overcome because the word "middle class" is so often, in liberal intellectual circles, used as an epithet. And when the word white is put in front of middle class, the psyches of even the strongest Euro-American activist for justice, peace, democracy, or the environment shrivels and shrieks in spasms of guilt and self-flagellation.

There is irony in this. It most often is not the middle class who are the primary source or carriers of oppression and prejudice. The source lies higher in the socioeconomic and power structures; and the carriers of oppression and prejudice are the faithful scribes and savants of those "up there." The scribes and savants arrange the furniture of modern political language to suit their masters. But the irony is also tragedy; and it is a profoundly debilitating process whereby activists from different cultural backgrounds, unwittingly taking their cues from the paid scribes and savants, play the master's game with the master's tools.

However, Greens who are white and/or male still do often tend to reveal an outlook towards "the other," be it female, or person of another color, or sexual orientation, or culture, which is characteristic of the oligarchy's ingrained cultural attitudes. The outlook may variously be described as compassion, philanthropy (fine words which have been brutalized by the oligarchy), condescension, or insouciance. It often expresses itself in words that are solicitous or benevolent, that are inherently patronizing, and stunningly unconscious. At best, the intent seems to be to raise up the other to the level occupied by the one being benevolent. It ties in with the moral universe described earlier in the chapter, whereby those (who by their wits and luck and aggressive intelligence have made a buck) should also now be willing to provide charity for the less fortunate, the powerless, the discriminated against, and the persistently lazy.

Welfare programs are immersed in this outlook. The primary assumption of the welfare establishment is that those who are "given" welfare need a chance to rise in society—in society's terms. The unspoken, tacitly understood, governing model is what Audrey Lorde calls "the mythical norm." "In America," she writes, "this norm is usually defined as white, thin, young, heterosexual, Christian, and financially secure."[2] The fact that the norm in question is generally unattainable by these "others" does not deter those Republican and Democratic politicians who indulge in a compassionate politics, nor does it deter the armies of bureaucrats who wax semi-affluent on the backs of the welfarees. The trick is both to keep those others in their place in the face of the intimidating power of the norm and to turn those upward strivers among the "minorities" and the underclass, those who are especially clever and/or gifted, into reasonably close facsimiles of the norm; that is, made over, in terms of life-style and attitudes, into rich, white straight males (whatever their gender or race).

Echoes of this complex set of attitudes, fueled by generations of repressed guilt and sticky sentimentality, are to be found among professional circles in and out of universities, in movements for social change and justice, and among the liberal politicians in the Democratic party. One recalls Vasconcellos' *bon mot*, mentioned at the beginning of this chapter, about Democrats believing that people can't help themselves. They apply this to the poor and the down and out. Leveling people up to some supposed "status quo" norm of achievement and affluence is a widely shared assumption. It is generally an unexamined assumption, which makes it difficult to dislodge.

Greens, by virtue of their critique of consumerism, of GNP-inspired growth, and of the macho/condescending behavior of the oligarchy, should be in the forefront of recognizing and examining that assumption. Many Greens are doing just that. The implication for them ought then also to be that their attitudes toward "others" who are "less fortunate" or "left out" ought also to change. It ought to change, that is, from the posture of benevolence to a more self-critical and inclusive posture of social and ecological transformation. In this new view, a new and examined assumption takes over: that rich people, as well as poor people, middle-class people as well as the rich and the poor, must be challenged, and must have the opportunity, to change their wasteful, prejudicial, self-serving and self-defeating ways and help create a society in which material, social, and spiritual needs are met for everyone.

It is unfortunate, in this regard, that the legislation establishing the self-esteem program in California, an otherwise creative and ambitious pioneering effort at social change, had to be curiously circumscribed in terms of the people to whom it would apply before it could get passed. Originally, it had been intended to apply to all strata in society on the correct assumption that middle-class, and especially upper-class people often have low self-esteem problems that drive them into self-defeating and dominating modes of action and behavior. But the program was limited in its application more or less to the members of the underclass.[3]

Not that the program, as passed and promulgated, is not needed or is not useful. Yet note the implications! Benevolence and condescension again carry the day in public policy. Once again, it's the middle and upper classes coming to the assistance of the underclass to help give them what? Self-esteem? Defined as what and by whom, and applied by whom? There is a tussle here. John Vasconcellos, the author and guru of the project, has a broader and deeper view of the self than that offered by the ego-maximizing models of the oligarchy. He has a view of success rooted in personal growth, not necessarily in upward mobility. But the program is structured to dilute and suffocate that approach. It is aimed at those "down there." The posture of those administering the program can so easily slip into a "welfare" approach, our old friends benevolence and condescension. The tendencies are strong to convert (distort) the meaning of self-esteem into ego maximization. Self-esteem will come to mean getting a leg up into knowing how to "rise" into the ranks of the middle and upper class, who presumably already have such self-esteem. And indeed they have it, in spades—that is, if one means by self-esteem possessing the attitudes and behavior that make for success in the plastic, highly competitive world of the oligarchy and its fellow travelers.

Wouldn't it actually be more sensible, if one had to limit the application of such a program, to limit it to the ranks of the oligarchy? They surely are in need of self-esteem programs that are based on nonmacho models, noninstrumental and nonmanipulative self-education. At present, their sense of their own self worth is seriously in question and it expresses itself in self-defeating behaviors of domination and manipulation.

Wouldn't it actually be more sensible to develop self-help, community-oriented, and ecologically sustainable economic programs for the so-called underclass and leave their psyches alone? Yet the reverse seems to be the net effect of much contemporary public policy.

Greens are steadily moving in the direction of a new and more realistic way of seeing the other. They are beginning to look at their vocabulary, rejecting words and postures that reveal shades of the benevolence/condescension syndrome. They are reevaluating such words as minorities and outreach. They perceive that there are no "majorities" and that society is in fact a vast composition of "minorities." In this picture, the oligarchy are also seen as a minority: a dominant and dominating one. A more accurate word to convey the makeup of our society is "multicultural." Yet even this word is often used to mean "the minorities," those "out there," "the others." Apparently it is very hard for those who prosper from, or are habituated to, cultural hegemony to change that hegemonical posture, and henceforth to include themselves in the circle of "minorities."

Even a new and seemingly more appropriate term such as "people of color" can still mean the same old thing. A genuine feeling for and understanding of diversity would seem to mandate a further step which would employ language such as people of another color, or people of other colors. Such a term could be used freely and interchangeably by every person of color, including white. On the other hand, this might have the effect of depriving the oppressed people of language denoting who the oppressor is (i.e., white). Perhaps whites who feel the problematic nature of the color white in the context of oppressor/oppressed relations, and of the stereotypical perceptions these give rise to, should look around for the another way to describe their color.

An alternative way forward in this thorny thicket of language is offered by the use of such words as African American, Hispanic American, and Native American. Add terms such as Euro-American, Asian American, Jewish American, and Arab American. One could then reduce references to color, or, in problematic circumstances, drop them altogether. One could shift attention away from ambiguous biological differences and focus more clearly on cultural differences; and then on the distortions of those differences and on the oppression that comes with the distortions. This could help the activists in all of the movements for change to communicate more effectively and help move the whole society toward multicultural consciousness and practice.

A multicultural society is one that must confront and dissolve cultural hegemony, or internal oppression as it is also called, no matter how subtly that hegemony is disguised by the postures and language of benevolence. A multicultural consciousness is needed. When such a consciousness breaks through the defense of the psyche and calls into question the institutionalized barriers between people who are "different," the tolerant intolerance of the merely benevolent is washed away.

Greens have still a way to go to overcome in themselves the self-congratulatory and Eurocentric outlook on the world that continues to hold in thrall the dominant oligarchic culture. Yet it may well be the case that Greens are further along in developing a multicultural consciousness than is characteristic of particularistic movements for change. The latter are hobbled by their insistence on "their rights." By concentrating on getting "their rights," they conform to, or get manipulated into, the prevailing concepts of deprivation and upward mobility that are peddled by establishment social science. By concentrating on what is regarded as their particular grievance, they seem to be saying, "We're deprived. We're deprived of what you've got." The "you" that's got it may variously be understood to mean the majority, or the already-established, or the affluent, or those "up there." Action then becomes one of getting access to the imagined joys of the already established.

What is lost to view in this kind of "rights politics" is the need to transform what is valued, and to transform relationships, especially for the affluent and the established. It would make more sense to treat the already established, especially the rich and the powerful, as "deprived." On that basis, imbued with a multicultural consciousness, people can take action together against the patterns of domination of the oligarchy. They can act together for a multicultural society, shoulder to shoulder, across the lines of race, creed, color, gender and sexual preference. This is what the oligarchy shudders to think might happen. Their propaganda engines work tirelessly to keep the semantics of deprivation and minorities and upward mobility alive, to keep the particularistic "rights" pots boiling. Their political brokers work overtime to play one "rights" group off against the others—and to play them off, one at a time, against the "white middle class." The latter, unfortunately, oblige too often.

One reason the word "deprivation" works so well as a semantic, propagandistic tool is that patterns of class prejudice are subtly interwoven with racial and gender prejudice. Often, a person of the middle or upper class (who is a member of what are called the minorities) encounters prejudice because being African American or Hispanic American or Native American or a woman or a union worker conjures up images of lower-class status. Since what are considered lower-class, or underclass, occupations and life-styles are all too frequently held by women, by African Americans or Hispanic Americans or Native Americans, or Arab Americans, or manual workers, and since it is not possible to stop being people of these cultures, even though one is now in the middle class, or even in the very rich class, the consequences are that one is continually subject to being treated as one who is deprived. The interwoven stigmas of class, race, and gender stick with you no matter what, even among those who are supposedly enlightened and liberal, whether oppressor or oppressed! This is so partly because the problem has been put in terms of deprivation.

To some degree it is an understandable reaction. The underclass does suffer overt deprivation of a particularly obnoxious and horrible kind, and their numbers are disproportionately drawn from "the minorities" (including women). By redefining the issues of race, sexual orientation, and gender as not one of deprivation but of the failure to realize a multicultural consciousness and society, one may be launched on the road to greater clarity and by so much, at least, an overcoming of racism, sexism, and homophobia. Greens are moving in that direction.

Emphasis on the building of a multicultural society in which difference is not only tolerated but respected, not only respected but celebrated, would then also encourage the development of a clearer policy on the problems of the underclass. Though racism, sexism, and homophobia are powerful tools in the latter's oppression, treating their racial and/or gender as one of "deprivation" is a truly depressing attitude, a truly disturbing policy. It fosters the notion that to be a woman or a lesbian or gay, or to be an African American or Hispanic American or Native American or Arab American, or to be a worker is to be deprived! This is dumb and cruel, yet this is what is happening everywhere, and all the time.

The focus of the concern about the underclass as underclass must be riveted on the fact that their life needs are not being met. The sense in which they are deprived can be measured, not so much in dollars and cents (though that, too), but in terms of not having or being able to meet basic, fundamental human needs. These needs are the storied ones of physical security, psychic nurturing, food and clothing, shelter, health services, education, recreation, and transportation. Their needs also include a real opportunity to get and keep a job, not just a dead end one and poorly paid, but one they could have if their native talents were given a chance to bloom. Lately, it is also becoming painfully clear that human needs directly include nonpoisoned air, water, land and food-and neighborhoods in which there is at least a semblance of community.

The reader should not imagine that the above paragraph is yet another liberal call for welfare. That is not the intent. All of society is undermined in the degree to which significant segments of the society are desperately lacking basic needs. If the reader cannot grasp this, then he or she may wish to read the vast literature available in the nearest library in which thinker after thinker from the time of Plato onwards, whether considered a conservative, a liberal or a radical, has affirmed the critical importance of a healthy body politic. Such a goal is not a matter of social conscience but a public necessity. For them it is not something that is aimed at indirectly through trickle down and philanthropic policies, but as among the first things that responsible social and political leadership strives for.

This calls for taking a wholly different approach from that pursued by Republicans and Democrats. Society's institutions must aim at energizing and serving the people, and enabling the people to help themselves efficiently, rather than, as our institutions do now, serving first of all themselves. Actually, they are not "our" institutions: they have been taken over by the oligarchy and serve their interests first, and only afterwards the needs of all the people.

Something especially interesting about the above list of needs meets the eye when you take a second look. The last mentioned needs (for nonpoisoned air, water, land and food), though mistakenly thought of by mainstream social scientists as only the special interests of an "upper middle class," are also now more and more perceived to be the imperative needs of the entire population.[4] Nonprofessional working people and poor people are just as much at risk with respect to these "environmental" needs as are people in the "better neighborhoods" and the so-called upper middle class. Incinerators and toxic dumps are "dumped" into the poorer and "minority" neighborhoods. Factories using and producing dangerous chemicals are regularly located in areas where it is assumed people aren't strong or alert enough to mind. Corporate advertisers bombard the underclass with intensive propaganda for their more noxious products. Poor people are realizing this more and more and taking action against the poisoners.

Conversely, the middle class, whom the oligarchy has bought off for decades with the promise and glitter of consumerist affluence, are now becoming almost as much at risk with respect to the first named needs referred to above (physical security, psychic nurturing, food and clothing, shelter, health services, education, and so forth) as the poor have always been. They are at risk from the food they are urged, indeed forced, to eat, the water that is available for them to drink, the air they are called upon to breathe. They are at risk "environmentally" at their job no matter how white or blue collar it is. They are at risk from new diseases such as AIDS (for a decade prevaricatingly described as a disease of homosexuals and the poor). They are at risk at the beaches and from a sun no longer adequately shielded from our bodies by the ozone layer. And, in sum, they are at risk from the inordinate and unnatural stress of industrial life as we have come to know it. As this happens and people begin to perceive and feel it more and more, then the old scholarship and journalism that made careful distinctions between "socioeconomic" and "environmental" problems is revealed to be misguided and, in many cases, "politically" inspired.

Socioeconomic and environmental needs are coming together with a bang: this prepares the way for both to be fought for by both the middle class and the underclass. No more, then, the notion of "special" deprivation. No more, then, either, any justification for treating people in the underclass as a special humanitarian project undertaken by the good souls in the upper class doing good to others "less fortunate." Again, one can see the basis for a turnaround in attitudes. Away from benevolence and condescension and towards a sense of common fate, common need, and common ground. And towards a common action for the social, economic and ecological transformation of society. It's a political consciousness we're talking about here not the same old humanitarian liberalism. The Greens would point all people in this direction!

To sum up: society now requires that diversity henceforth be understood and pursued as a multicultural concept, consciousness, and policy. It also requires the affirmation of a common ground with respect to socioeconomic and/or ecological needs. This is the Green way forward for both the middle class and the underclass together. And for the oligarchy! It's their survival that's at stake, too. But, a hard thing for them to swallow, they need to stop being an oligarchy for that to happen. As a wise person once observed, "It is easier for a camel to pass through the eye of a needle than for a rich man to enter the kingdom of heaven." But as Jesus also understood and taught, nothing of that sort is impossible.

The discussion so far has emphasized how important it is for Greens to develop and nurture a multicultural consciousness among themselves and with others among whom they mingle and with whom they make common cause. What other steps can they take? Three come to mind.

First, Greens can welcome into their local groups and their interlocal networks people of all colors and cultures, not excluding white Euro-Americans. Local groups and networks should monitor themselves on a continuing basis on the composition of their membership and to seek persistently and patiently to become more inclusive. The basis for inclusion are the Ten Key Values of Ecological Wisdom, Grassroots Democracy, Personal and Social Responsibility, Nonviolence, Decentralization, Community-based Economics, Postpatriarchal Values, Respect for Diversity, Global Responsibility, and Future Focus.

Second, Greens can sponsor or join multicultural learning groups. Six or eight activists from each of a variety of organizations and groups, including Green locals, can meet together every one or two weeks for a few hours. Their meetings, beginning over dinner let us say, might go through four stages. They could start by telling their organizing stories to one another. In a second stage, they could spend a bit of time with each other's groups or in one of their projects. On that basis, they could take up mutual and self-criticism. In a final stage, they could sponsor a celebratory event (a picnic, a musical event, a street fair) to which the membership of all the groups they represent would be invited.

In addition to inclusivity of membership and multicultural learning groups, Greens should make short and long-term alliances with other organizations. In this regard, Greens must acknowledge the need for separate organizations and groups who can go to bat for gender, racial, and homosexual justice, for blue- and white-collar workers, for unemployed people, the elderly, young people, and the handicapped. Such organizations are needed both to shake up and wear down the system of domination presided over by the oligarchy and to act as a kind of reality check for movements, like the Greens, who seek to develop a holistic politics.

Examples of this need occur every day. The *Boston Globe* for April 14, 1990, ran a story about a gay Republican, a candidate for the state legislature, who was kicked out of a post with his local GOP ward committee for being openly gay and too liberal to suit his colleagues.[5] Noting that a gay Republican is almost "a contradiction in terms," a top official with the Greater Boston Gay and Lesbian Political Alliance was on the scene to try and give what help could be provided.

Organizations dedicated to dealing with specific instances of bias and hatred against "the other" are in a better position to give immediate help and to fight against the bias than a Green movement or a Green party. However, the particular instance of bias also needs to be related to a broader understanding and a more comprehensive politics. The gay Republican should be supported by the Greens and invited to think about which politics, Republican or Green, will satisfy him in the longer run. But whatever his choice, he will continue to be in need of organizations such as the Greater Boston Gay and Lesbian Political Alliance.

Given the need for alliances between Greens and these separate organizations, on what basis can this be done effectively?

A central goal should be the building of trust and common purpose between the Greens and each separate group and between all the separate groups together, including the Greens. As already affirmed, the idea of community should guide the thinking behind alliance building.

Alliances can take several forms. Green parties at the local, state and national levels can exchange information with the separate groups about likely races and support each other's candidates. This may mean in particular instances that Greens should consider supporting Democratic or even Republican candidates—that they should do it sparingly, and with the understanding of quid pro quo's. That is, if Greens give support to a candidate whose strong suit is women's rights and that candidate is a Democrat, then the Greens may be able to persuade a local NOW chapter to support an acceptable Green (acceptable to NOW, that is) in the next election. Or in the same election!

In addition to electoral cooperation, action together by Greens and separate issue organizations also take the form of citizen-action struggles: campaigns to alleviate a particular problem in the community, or to bring pressure on a particular corporation, government bureau, or legislative body.

Furthermore, direct action of any substantial kind, including civil disobedience, also almost always requires, and is an opportunity for, common action across specific movement lines, and Greens will increasingly be in a position to make common cause.

In all of these alliances or coalitions, both the Greens and the specific movements and groups with whom they join, must aim at more than a scissors-and-paste unity. It is not enough for the top leadership of the various groups to set up a coalition for this event only, and then only with regard to this particular problem or grievance. Something more is needed in the planning, action and follow-up stages of the common project.

"Something more" might well begin with recalling and sharing the memory of previous struggles. Having an opportunity to share each other's stories can lead to acknowledging each other's values, which in turn can lead to greater trust and a coming together on the basis of values. Community must be sought at the gut level, however tentatively at first, but then more and more.

To reiterate, community must be both a goal and a strategy. As a goal for alliance building, community is worthwhile for its own sake, enlivens the participants, and prefigures the kind of society the movement is striving for. As a strategy for alliance building, the emphasis on community building fosters and reinforces a rising consciousness among all the participants in the alliance to unite in struggle for the long haul against the powers and structures of the oligarchy. In this way, a direct action project, for example, relates that day's struggle to the overall revolutionary campaign.

Thus, alliances (whether for electoral projects, citizen lobbying, or direct action) become real insofar as the partners in the alliance view themselves as potential members of a community, seek to share their stories and their values, and through an act of will and trust situate themselves resolutely in the action of the struggle. This makes a gradual growing together possible and fosters the will to do it again, together.

For a last word in this chapter on diversity, one might ask, "Shouldn't the Greens have a majority of women in their membership?" The Greens need to think hard and long about the gender question. Surely, the dearth of women in positions of leadership in direct action struggles and often the relegation of women who participate in direct action to operational roles is just one indication of that need.

For one thing, Green membership, if it is to grow substantially, may have to come from women. An interesting statistic stands out in this regard. Consider male/female attitudes towards President Bush's marshaling of military force against Saddam Hussein. Louis Harris, the pollster, reported in the *New York Times* in early December 1990 that "Though recent polls indicate that Americans oppose military action in the gulf by 61 to 35 percent (with 4 percent undecided), the figures mask an enormous difference between the attitudes of men and women. On attacking Iraqi forces in Kuwait, men split down the middle, with 48 percent favoring such action and 48 percent opposing it. Women opposed an attack by 73 to 22 percent."[6]

It is reasonable to generalize from this and from other indications that the potential pool of women who are likely to embrace Green values and Green politics is greater than the pool of men who are so inclined. Men identify more readily than do women with the macho values and the tendency to formalistic, instrumental, and abstract thinking characteristic of the oligarchy.

Thus, an unsettling but realistic conclusion is that Greens are not likely to attract large numbers of men to their banners; or, if they do, it may even be to the detriment of the movement. Unless, of course, women join in even greater numbers.

Some would argue therefore that for the Greens to succeed in their efforts on behalf of social, economic and political transformation, gender parity in the movement is not enough, that there should be more women than men.

Does this cut into the principle of diversity? Perhaps, in a strict linear sense it does. But on closer examination, a contrary argument can be made. The issue, and the problem, is not gender as such. Rather, it is the degree to which we may realistically expect men or women to have or acquire through self-reflection and social learning the intellectual and political skills necessary to the survival of the planet. It is pretty clear that men in general are still very attached to the old paradigm that fit an earlier age, or which seemed to, but which is now dysfunctional and inappropriate. New approaches are needed. A new discourse. A new way of thinking about life and about relationships. Women are in a better position, having not been as immersed as men in the old paradigm, to have or learn the skills and attitudes that are needed now in this new, ecological epoch. Not that men in numbers cannot or will not join. But the greater numbers that are needed can come only from women.

However, another argument is that women who do wrench themselves out of the "private sphere" and turn in a political direction are often apt to immerse themselves in women's rights issues and organizations, limiting their efforts, and often their consciousness, to a "rights" oriented politics. Partly for this reason, and partly because the terrain of "the political" is new and often unfamiliar territory for them, they do not take the steps that would lead them to a comprehensive, system-change politics. This is a worrisome phenomenon, just as worrisome as the immersion of men disproportionately in the hegemonic thinking of the established powers, or just as worrisome as the tendency of some men to overreact to such hegemonic thinking, opting in favor of anti-politics and a "New Age" pursuit of individual enlightenment.

Thus, on balance, it is problematic if Greens will attract either enough men or enough women to field the force that's needed! What's surely needed is a greater understanding by men and women that these are serious pitfalls, and a greater willingness on the part of men and women to deal with, and work through, these pitfalls. The fate of our country, our civilization, and our planet depends on a deepening and renewal of a political consciousness among those who must make a difference.

Chapter 12
Realigning Economy and Ecology

A visitor from England, old, wise, keen-eyed, and eager for the revolutionary transformation the Greens represent, though not (yet) a Green herself, shrewdly asks, "But what is the Green Policy?" She pauses for an answer, but then goes on: "Well, you know. There is a Labour Policy and a Tory Policy. But what is the Green Policy?"

A fair question. It provokes and deserves both a short answer and a much longer one. The short answer is: stop the equating of profits with growth. Stop the plundering and poisoning of ecosystems on which our lives depend. Liberate people to create new wealth in tune with our ecosystems. Satisfy real needs, not manipulated wants. Build a sustainable life here on this planet. Rethink economy! Restructure it!

A longer answer fills in behind these exclamations. It wasn't very long ago, in the mid-'70s, that bumper stickers appeared on the cars of working people saying, "Eat an Environmentalist." It happened in Maine during the long bitter struggle in the '70s over the proposed Dickey-Lincoln Dam. The dam was supposed to provide peak-hour electricity for wasteful, environmentally unregenerate Boston (a point well hidden from view by those selling the project) at the cost of a good chunk of Maine's ecology. Fortunately, it was finally defeated and attitudes gradually changed, but in the process the people were told that they had to choose between the environment and jobs. Hence the anger of working people and the menace behind the words Eat an Environmentalist. It was and remains a classic instance of an attempt to divide and rule.

The so-called "choice" of jobs versus the environment was propagated all over the country until it achieved the status of conventional wisdom, a bit of settled truth, however unpleasant it might seem to be. Seldom has a greater piece of prevarication been uttered and propagated by corporate executives, by politicians, by scholars, all proclaiming realism; and seldom has such a prevarication had more effect in undermining the foundations of economic life. It continues to work its insidious way throughout society.

Part of the problem was that "the environment" was taken up in a simplistic way, even by the environmentalists. Starting in the '70s it was introduced as if it were just one issue among many others. That is how it came to be dealt with by the platform makers and propagandists of the parties and the candidates seeking office. The environment was not seen or treated as a call for a new way of thinking about creating wealth. It was not seen or treated as

151

the historic opportunity it is to free people to produce truly useful goods and services and to produce abundantly. The rhetoric of abundance was and still is tied to industrial capitalism, a merely pseudo-abundance. What was needed, and still is needed, is a productive environmentalism.

In between elections, environmentalism was made to fit into the already distorted framework of legislative politics as yet another among the hosts of pressure groups vying competitively for favors from the politicians in Washington and the state capitals. The environment became a "special interest," the newest kid on the block, with its special backers, identified as "upper middle-class types."

Yet, the pillage of nature went on, almost unabated. There were particular victories in the '70s for the environment, much of it in response to the panic about steep increases in oil prices early and late in the decade. This helped to create a better climate politically for conservation. But there was little indication of a serious and comprehensive strategy for dealing with the mounting crisis.[1] Even the pressure group tactic, such as it was, also faltered once the Reagan years began. With "growth" policies and military policies more firmly in place than ever, all other demands on government were forced into the pressure cooker of zero sum politics: the environmental lobbies and their "issues," now themselves fragmented and often at cross-purposes, were perceived and treated even more than before as neither better nor worse than any of the other special interests clamoring for a piece of the "fixed pie." Actually, it was a steadily shrinking pie given the explosion of expenditures for the military and the deliberate cutbacks in so-called welfare programs. This meant, for example, that "the environment" was now competing with "welfare" for some trickle-down benefits.

Ironically, the military budget was not an "issue," was not a "special interest" in Washington. It was a *Policy*. Not that there were no skirmishes over the exact height of the mountain represented by the military budget. The different services, the different contractors, and the different committees in Congress fought over how high this peak or that peak should be, but there was no disputation over the massive commitment to the military *Policy*.

The environment requires the status of a *Policy*. By not fighting for the environment as a *Policy*, and by fitting themselves instead into the pressure group framework of the legislative scene, the environmentalists invited the kind of response they got. This judgment applies both to the particular successes of the '70s which they hailed as proof positive that "something was happening," and to the arrogant indifference they encountered in the '80s, which made them justifiably angry as hell at Reagan but insufficiently critical of themselves.

These considerations bring us face to face with the inner connection that must be made between ecology and economy. Growth as hitherto defined (growth as the indiscriminate production and consumption of goods and services) has in fact been the *Policy* of Democratic and Republican administrations for generations. It is this *Policy* the environmentalists should have been identifying as the problem and should have been gathering and honing their forces to combat and defeat. Instead, they have sought through pressure group activity, through rear-guard court actions, and through mediation sessions to stop this bit of pollution here or misuse of resources there or abuse of habitat over there. But they did not seriously address the tilt of the economy, and of public policy itself, towards production and consumption patterns that are inherently polluting and wasteful of resources and human health.

True enough, in the last few years themes of preventing pollution, instead of merely cleaning up the mess afterwards, have surfaced in many quarters.[2] In some businesses and in some areas of government, there is a growing will to find environmentally benign replacements for wasteful and/or polluting products and manufacturing processes. Such efforts to neutralize or internalize environmental costs and to find substitutes that don't pollute or waste, represent the kind of change in policy that the Greens have in mind for the entire economy. But it is just a start, a minuscule start. Or maybe it is just a flash in the pan. Emphasis on prevention is a solid step forward. But a further step is needed, the relative absence of which has crippled environmental politics in the past two decades quite as much as its willingness to get sucked into the pressure politics game in Washington. That step is to push for positive, productive environmentalism.

Beyond the prevention of the production of things that are bad for the environment and human life lies the positive need to create the wealth on which our livelihoods depend. If industrial corporate capitalism can't do it, and it can't, new businesses are needed, as well as the liberation of many old small businesses, which can and will produce goods and services that meet human and ecosystem needs.

The environmental movement has stressed conservation in the past several decades. This does get at the problem of production to a degree. Perhaps what is needed is a creative conservation, promoted by state and local governments, one that stimulates people to form individual and co-operative businesses that get more out of less energy and create quality goods and services primarily for community markets.

What are the major features of a Green Policy? Eight may be identified.

First is the theme of sustainability as a central and guiding philosophy for action by private and public persons.

Second, a different way of measuring economic performance is desperately needed.

Third, regional, local, and community contexts must more and more become the thrust of economic design; at the same time, supranational (world, regional, and global) contexts must be expanded.

Fourth, environmental costs must henceforth be put up front in investment decisions by private and public decision makers.

Fifth, ownership of the means of production must move from oligopolistic and monopolistic gargantuan corporations, whether private or public, to decentralized and mixed patterns of ownership.

Sixth, social justice must henceforth be seen and treated as part of the principle of sustainability.

Seventh, population problems must be seen and treated as both a challenge to overcome poverty and to give social and psychological support to women around the world.

Eighth, runaway consumerism in both rich and poor countries must be carefully addressed by enabling people to reach a new life-in-community and by providing people in communities with control over technologies.

Sustainablility

Sustainability is a way of saying that henceforth economy must be placed within the framework of ecology in our thinking and in our practice. Ecology is the wider and deeper concept because it represents the fundamental imperatives of our livelihood. Water, air, land, and resources-in-the-land are all primary. What is implicit in the specifics of water, air, land, and so forth is the fact that they exist within an intricate web of relationships. They are not just separate elements and they have their being in contexts of place and habitat from small and local to large and planetary. The earth as a whole and in its parts is alive. An intervention in one of these elements, or in a given habitat, has reverberatory effects backwards and forwards throughout space and time.

Through human technologies and by the application of human labor, both physical and intellectual, the elements and properties of nature are worked up into capital and culture. Thus, land, or rather nature, is the primary category, and such other important categories as labor and capital and culture are dependent on the category of nature.[3] These are facts that in olden times were "instinctively" understood and were taught, sanctioned and mandated by magic and religion. This tended to prevent, or at least slow down, the unsanctioned, unsacred, unholy exploitation of nature.

When the lore of the ancients wore away, when new and more interventionist religions emerged,[4] when, indeed, religion itself was either secularized or put on the shelf as a dinosaur of past superstition, then nature was opened up for massive assault and exploitation. Then, what was primary, land and nature, was subordinated to the categories of labor and capital and culture. A profound reversal took place: economy got away from ecology and set up shop on its own: labor, and then those who came to dominate labor, the owners of capital (true of comrades as well as of capitalists) thought of themselves as independent and lords of the earth. The spirit of the human lost its moorings in the realities of earth and cosmos and began to roam homeless through the creations and recreations of its own brain.[5]

What Greens press for is a reversal of that reversal. They want it to be accomplished via a new sense of the interrelationship of the human and the natural. Greens are persistent in affirming that the human in the natural and the natural in the human are part of the intricate web of "all things." The web is neither fixed nor determined. It is itself evolving and the interventions by the human are part of that evolution. The intervention can be thoughtless and destructive or it can be thoughtful and enhancing. For it now to become thoughtful and enhancing, the human intervention must cease its "domination over nature" obsession. Part of that change involves bringing economy into a relationship to ecology whereby economy is a subset of ecology instead of ecology being a subset of economy. Considerations of the intricate web, considerations of how that web is itself composed of smaller webs (bio-regions), and considerations of the specifics of water, air, land, and resources must now become the fundamental considerations of economy.

The webs and their specifics are the basis for sustaining a human population. Below, the discussion will linger for a moment on the population-question. But here the point is, very simply, that the fundamental guide to decisionmakers in the economy, be they private or public, must be the sustainability of the webs and their specifics. If that is sustainable, then human life is sustainable and can prosper. But if prosperity is purchased by undermining the real capital of life (those webs with their specifics) then no amount of success in the present is worth a penny. It is this kind of thinking that must come about if we are to survive. And it is beginning to happen: the people are beginning to understand this. But their present leaders, the entrenched powers of the oligarchy, remain confused, or intellectually lazy, or deliberately obtuse. Or all three. In the meantime, they hang on to their privilege, power and profits at all costs.

Sustainability must be thought of primarily in positive and creative terms, not first of all in terms of prevention. As mentioned earlier, the generation of wealth must now be seen as getting a powerful stimulus precisely from that quarter which seemed adverse to production, the environment. Ecological principles for production, based on a creative conservation, offer efficiencies never dreamed of by the founders and votaries of industrial capitalism and industrial communism. These principles also encourage diversification of goods and services, encourage the production for community-centered markets, and stimulate a closer and more responsible relationship between the maker of the good and its consumer. This enlivens sustainability, true enough, but it also ensures the quality production of needed, and wanted, goods and services.

Redefining Progress

Given the need to think sustainability makes it obvious that a much better way to measure state, regional and national growth is crucial. GNP, The Gross National Product, is not only inaccurate and misleading, but it actively distorts public policy by giving a false picture of how and where and how much growth is taking place. The work of the household, for example, is not included. Nor is there any distinction between healthy, useful, and truly productive activity on the one hand and, on the other, the increasing amount of activity that is required to make up for the deficiencies caused by the production and distribution of harmful and wasteful goods and services.

By the terms of its stupefying irrationality, GNP measures those latter goods and services as positive additions to the national product. Cigarette sales are part of GNP when as a matter of fact they cause the death of 300,000 people per year and all the financial, physical, and emotional expense these deaths entail. Similarly, all the "economic" activity that must be devoted to dealing with the more than 50,000 deaths yearly on our highways is treated as if it "added" to our growth. Or consider the number of new prisons being built. These, it is said, are desperately needed to combat crime. But the number of prisoners is partly a function of an irrational drug policy. It is more deeply a function of the wretched economic and social conditions in which a growing and helpless underclass is forced to exist. These prisons are, from the distorting point of the view of the GNP, a contribution to our growth. Destroying vanishing farm land for a shopping mall is growth! Stimulating people to use yet more energy in order to show more profits for the utility is growth!

A measurement of growth must be a measurement of genuine livelihood and wellness, and though the attempt to do this is not easy, especially in the face of GNP as holy totem, that attempt must be made, and soon. This is a critical feature of Green Policy.[6]

Sustainability includes, of course, the point made earlier about the need for producers to internalize environmental costs. Responsibility for assessing these costs and striving for ways to eliminate them must be woven into the investment decision at the start of the production process. Producers of goods and services must henceforth find and apply benign and nonwasteful substitutes for polluting and/or wasteful products and processes. They must find substitutes for, or eliminate the need for, working conditions that are harmful. They must seek ways to capture and recycle chemicals and gases that presently escape into the air or are irresponsibly taken to a dump. In general, they must create products and services that are recyclable, repairable, durable, and enjoyable. This must apply to all businesses and the way to begin would be the drawing up of Charters of Social and Environmental Responsibility to which all companies, public and private, would have to adhere. It could not be accomplished overnight, but the critical thing is to put the Policy in place so that it would be clear to the entire economy that henceforth these are the rules of the game.

Such measures would already constitute something of a revolution in the nature of the economy. It would, for example, eliminate nuclear power as presently designed. It is doubtful if utilities and/or the consumers of electricity would care to pay for the thousands of years of disposal costs of nuclear waste. Similarly, how many executives in high places would continue to love fossil fuels if in the price of oil and gas and coal there would be included the staggering costs of environmental degradation their products unleash on the planet and on its inhabitants, including people?

As the hidden costs of nuclear and fossil fuels come into the light, the perceived costs of conservation and of solar power will come down dramatically. Their costs would also come down absolutely because of the much greater research and development that would then be put into solar energy and conservation. But even more than that, it becomes clear that not just one major energy source will be the "silver bullet" on which the economy must run. A variety of renewable energy sources, adapted to different regions, with a different mix in each region, would then come into focus and sharply influence the way economists, businessmen, labor leaders, and politicians would think about the priorities and the efficiencies of successful production.

Here, one should also reflect that tried and true rules of the old economics such as economy of scale and comparative advantage are not necessarily the best or most efficient way to produce and distribute goods and services.[7] These old so-called laws have pushed business toward bigness, bureaucracy, overspecialization, and monoculture. Again, the message for the future is toward greater regionalization and decentralization and toward variety and quality. Agriculture, for example, will have to move toward more organic methodologies in which the interfacing of crops and integrated pest management are accepted as a far better way to produce food than the use of insecticides. Similarly, in transportation, greater regionalization and decentralization calls for much more variety in the way in which we get around: less dependence on cars and trucks, more on trains, bicycling and walking. The latter, of course, becomes more possible, and attractive, as industry and business are sited closer to home.

The picture that emerges is one of greater focus by the economy on regional and community life and greater responsibility of business to the region and the community in which they locate.

Mixed Forms of Ownership

What will this mean for the form of ownership? Greens are not yet fully clarified on this critical question: views extend from rejection of markets and private ownership by some to an eager embracing of free enterprise by others. Most Greens, applying the principle of balance to this question as well as to others, believe in a variety of ownership patterns that would, and should, vary from region to region and even from community to community.

Virtually all Greens, however, do agree that the giant corporation as a central unit of the economy is both undemocratic and ecologically unsound. They call for rigorous accountability to social and environmental priorities in the first phase of an application of Green Policy; and then, gradually, a breaking up of the large corporations and a shift to other forms of ownership, both public and private. As for public ownership, they strongly favor community-run enterprises. Nationalization does not appeal, and even state ownership is regarded with skepticism.

One may readily see that the argument for democracy is a cogent one. The giant corporations are too dominating in their external relations: the market, the halls of government, and the culture. As for their internal relations, they tend to be and remain, in spite of continued efforts at reform, highly hierarchic, centralized, and bureaucratic institutions that dominate and exploit the working and personal lives of the great majority of American citizens!

Besides the democratic argument, other important arguments must also be made against the giant oligopolistic corporation. Economy, as noted, needs to be brought more into keeping with habitat, community, and regional ecology. The size of the firm therefore needs to be congruent with such decentralization, and though cases may be made in some limited instances for national and even global corporations, under strict guidance from the public, the great majority of giant corporations today should be broken up in the interest of successful adaptation to ecological imperatives and patterns.

Furthermore, giant corporations, because of their size, are bureaucratic behemoths that are relatively unaware of how they affect their human and natural environment. The management is dangerously insulated from the true extent of their corporation's degradations on nature and society. Their personal decency in many cases runs shockingly parallel with corporate policies that dominate, exploit, and even terrorize the bio-regions and neighborhoods of the people. The corporation's ledgers show growth even while the ecosystems the growth ultimately depends on are under brutal corporate assault. Breaking up such corporations is a necessary condition for developing a better fit between the firm and the bio-region.

Finally, the giant corporation is disproportionately staffed at the top by men (though some women have reached these heights) whose mind-set is steeped in the old paradigm that believes in "man over nature," linear progress, amoral technology, and limitless growth. Breaking up the giant corporation is a necessity if society is ever to get out from under their domination.

Unlimited Growth a Chimera

Ecology tells us in so many unmistakable ways that, whether in the short or the long run, whether relatively or absolutely, there are limits. There are limits to the amount you can poison the water, air, and land before irreversible effects take over, locally, regionally, worldwide. There are limits to the extraction of materials before they give out or become too expensive to recover. There are limits to the amount of energy that can be produced at given times and places relative to the amount of energy used in producing it. There are limits to the degree of human intervention into a bio-region relative to the ecological balances that bio-region must maintain if it is to sustain human habitation. And so forth.

The notion of limitless, linear growth is therefore a chimera, a myth. Yet it has been this myth that has been used by the powers-that-be, thoughtlessly and irresponsibly, to cloak their drive for domination of nature and by implication, of all other people.

Limits, relative or absolute, demand that an economy becomes a supporter, not an enemy, of sustainability. Growth, if understood in a context of sustainability, is possible. Not only possible, but to be expected. But it is a temperate growth that weaves into the fabric of nature and human life new patterns of getting more out of less and new technologies and discoveries that add to the sum of available energy. The crucial question is not growth as such, but finding and maintaining the careful balances on the basis of which true growth becomes possible.

Social Justice

This sharply brings to the fore the relation of social justice to sustainability. The failure of both capitalist and socialist industrial societies to solve the problem of poverty in spite of rising levels of social wealth and capacity for producing more than any previous form of productive forces is obvious. Caring people have long pressed for succor for the poor, the underclass, on humanitarian grounds. Yet the embarrassing (and widely repressed) truth of the matter is that in spite of all programs the problem not only does not go away, it gets worse.

The humanitarian argument is valid in itself. But it is easily co-opted. It is made to camouflage the inherent structural distortions of these societies. Humanitarian appeals and protestations become "flags of decency" behind which rich capitalists and powerful commissars despoil the world and con the people into buying needless things when critical life-needs have not been met, nor even produced.

An ecologically derived argument must be added to the humanitarian one. To put it bluntly, capitalism (and socialism as well) have been socially blind in their pursuit of production. They've used up vast amounts of the planet's true capital, its resources and energies, and they've poisoned vast sections of the planet's bio-regions in producing and overproducing the wrong kind of goods for the wrong kind of people. First priority, whether through the market or through administrative decisions, has gone into the production of goods and services for those that could buy them and/or had the power to obtain them. This has meant that the nonpostponable needs of life—food, shelter, water, and so forth—have regularly taken a back seat to (a) "luxury" goods for the rich and the powerful, and for those who ape them, and (b) to military armament.

In capitalist countries, this has been accomplished partly through government decisions, but largely through the reduction of goods and services to the status of commodities. By means of the latter, an ever enlarging number of consumers has been lured into buying indiscriminately goods that are needed and goods that are not needed: presumably, it doesn't matter if nature's substance is used up and poisoned on behalf of fully postponable wants and luxuries so long as the GNP goes up. But of course it does matter. A consumer and militarist society has no standard by which to judge what is socially valuable and what is ecologically necessary to survival and sustainability. The so-called standard it does rally behind is supposed to be the market, but that is a circular argument, since the market is composed of the sale for money of all the objects of production whether needed or not needed.

In countries of "real existing socialism" as the Communists (until very recently) have sought to call themselves, nature's substance has been disproportionately used up and poisoned on behalf of (a) militarism and (b) the nomenklatura class of Communist Party and its appointees in government, industry, and culture.

Both societies have failed to assess what is socially necessary, given the limits of nature. If they had, and if industrialism had commenced under the aegis of a philosophy of natural limits, the story of humankind in the past century would have been very different. It may not yet be too late to change decisively toward a concept and *Policy* of sustainability.

Sustainability, socially understood, demands a society in which, whatever the form of ownership or degree of market activity, there exists a socially approved provision, a settled *Policy*, that nature's substance, and the investment decisions that transform it into goods and services, be used (and, through recycling, reused) for the nonpostponable needs of all citizens. Housing, clothing, food, water, air, physical security, transportation, education, energy—all these and the like are the sorts of goods and services that must be provided for first, given the limited substance of nature. They can be provided through capitalism or through socialism, or, better still, through a combination of both. But the type of capitalism and socialism that is needed rules out huge centralized corporations and huge centralized government-owned industries. On the assumption that the true basics of life are given priority in public policy and in investment decisions, other goods and services that may be categorized as luxuries, or as being available through disposable income, should also be produced. Produced, that is, consistent with sustainability.

The Pressures of Population and Consumerism

Population. A critical part of sustainability is the question of demand. Two important determinants of demand are the number of people in the world (population) and the pace and character of their consumption patterns.

Greens have argued, often vehemently, over the population question, some siding with zero and minus-zero population advocates who would put population control at the top of society's concerns, and others insisting that population is a problem (and a function) of poverty first of all. Most Greens argue for a balance between these either/or approaches.

There can be no doubt, that if there are limits prescribed by nature, then there is also a limit to the number of people a bio-region, or a planet, can or should support.

The education of the world's poor women must be placed in the center of efforts to stabilize and reduce population to sustainable levels. This education must of course include knowledge and availability of contraceptives. But even more importantly, it must include general knowledge and specific technical skills. Women must have the opportunity to develop support systems for themselves, in terms both of their livelihood and protection against male violence.[9]

At the same time, consumer habits worldwide, but especially in the "rich" countries and among their middle and upper classes, must be given a chance to moderate themselves. How can this be done? It is a question quite as important as the problem of overpopulation. It is so, because one may imagine a decline in the increase of population and yet at the same time imagine a steady, even enormous, leap in the consumption of resources. Now, some of that jump need not be ecologically depleting or damaging if recycling becomes an integral part of industrial and consumer behavior. Aluminum cans containing soft drinks can reappear as aluminum cans. In other words, we should be able to graduate from throwaway behavior and a throwaway society. We must if we are to survive.

However, the passion for buying things and yet more things, now at the level of an obsession for hundreds of millions of people, constitutes a grave threat to sustainability, even supposing all the features of a Green Policy described here were to have been put into effect. If buying and consuming goods and services at the pace and at the level now "normal" for the "rich" societies, were to continue unabated, and to become the goal of "poor" societies, nature's limits and tolerance would be overwhelmed.

Greens argue that people get addicted and obsessed if they cannot find satisfaction through balance. The antidote to the supposed "materialism" of people is not the "spiritualism" of a new morality or the inculcation of "higher" norms and ideals. Greens feel that what people lack, and a big reason for accumulating things, is an absence of authentic, satisfying, trusting and loving relationships. In a word, what modern peoples of the world are increasingly longing for, because they have been wrenched out of it by industrialism, is the reality and experience of community.

That is why Greens make much of the need for community, for themselves and for everyone. Their expectation is that if people are able to find, and are given an opportunity to find, a life in community, the psychic hungers that now manifest themselves in possession and accumulation will be tempered. Their energies will go into active and creative work, art, and play rather than into passive and consumption-oriented behavior. If, in addition, the power of the giant corporations is curtailed, or eliminated altogether, then the social landscape will also be liberated from the grip of their ubiquitous, often deceitful, and falsely alluring advertising.

This is a Green faith about human beings, rooted in a realistic reading of "what people really want." It has much power and pertinence. The Green Policy of uniting the concepts of ecology and economy and of applying the principle of sustainability to society as a whole also, then, adds community as an integral feature of the good life.

The good life of the future is the sustainable life of temperate, balanced growth. In such a society, personal and social development and freedom, and the quality of life, will be as important, perhaps even more important, than the increase in the number of goods and services. The latter will be judged in accordance with human and natural needs, not in accordance with abstract notions of growth-to-no-end or the accumulation of so called profits.

A Better, Deeper Public Life

Such reflections underscore the fact that the Greens, more than any other political or social movement, argue for, look for, and understand what is meant by, a flowering of public life. By public, they do not mean in the first instance the government. They mean something broader within which government is an important agent of action, but by no means the only one. The word public is closely associated with the word community: the public "happens" wherever people take mutual responsibility for things in common. Some of these things eventually may need the say and sanction of government action. Yet in many, if not in most, cases, those things can be handled short of government intrusion.

What things? Such controversial ones, for example, as abortion, or pornography, or divorce, or drugs. These issues are tearing contemporary society apart. The debate in each is deeply flawed. It is polarized between those who insist that government "do something" and those who, when all other argument fails, fall back on the rights of what they call privacy.

Both have an important point to make. The one insists on the responsibility of society to each member of that society. The other insists on the right of each member not to be intimidated and invaded by the government.

A Green kind of argument is that of course we are our sisters' and brothers' keepers and that of course governments are poor instruments at best to "enforce" such keeping, that governments are ill-suited to such determinations. Greens can make an argument for taking these issues out of the sterile debate between Individual and the State, and for reframing them as issues to be resolved by a reconstituted concept, and practice, of the public. The public is where people interact with one another to find solutions to situations in which "the right" is not wholly one side or the other, but is mixed in the complexities of human relationships. Relationships must be the focus of problem-solving.

Problems involving drug abuse, or abortion, or divorce, or pornography are very relationship oriented. They occur in contexts of interpersonal conflict. Government is much too blunt an instrument for this. So is recourse to private rights. Society has evolved methods of interpersonal communication to deal with complex and tortuous issues. Such methods as peer-counseling, mediation, and arbitration are outside the sphere of "law and government" as such, even though in many instances government officials may steer people in conflict toward these noncoercive and nongovernmental attempts at resolution.

We must restore the creative social powers of people working together to deal with contexts of interpersonal conflict. Government is needed to deal with physical violence, but much conflict and self-abuse needs the healing process that comes when "the sides" can mutually acknowledge each other and a social force is established which, without taking sides, helps generate new perspectives and a will to seek mutually acceptable solutions. This places responsibility on the voluntary will of human beings, guided by advice and wisdom of people and processes they can trust.

But the sides in any crisis must be fairly equal in their economic, social and psychological strength. Otherwise, the social process that is being used, say mediation, will become a camouflage for continued, or even intensified, domination of one side by the other. Mediation in the field of environmental conflict, for example, has scored some significant success in balancing—or, rather, in rebalancing—the multiple concerns of corporation, government agency, people immediately affected, the ecosystem, and the general public interest. But mediation has also often played into the hands of those who went into the mediation with most of the power, and most of the cards, stacked in their favor. They have usually been the corporation or the government agency."[10]

The government does have a legitimate role to play in helping society develop those basic equalities of strength and of helping individuals gain access to finding such strength. No less an agent in this regard is the economy itself. A healthy economy, ecologically grounded, would provide the kind of life-support systems for people so that they could, regardless of gender or sexual preference or race or class be able to enter into public encounters of mediation and arbitration relating to drugs, divorce, abortion, or pornography with the confidence and assurance necessary to their dignity and survival.

Part IV

Green Party

Chapter 13
Groundwork

The spirit of movement building rather than party building fired up most Greens in the United States when they began organizing in 1984. Locals, pursuing a variety of strategies for change, sprang up in most parts of the country. They banded together in loosely formed regional networks. The regions associated together in a national Interregional Committee (IC). We adopted the name Committees of Correspondence, later changing it to Green Committees of Correspondence, commemorating thereby the network of the founders of the American republic in the decade before the Revolutionary War.

The beginning, at the national level, took place at what is now remembered as a historic meeting in St. Paul in August 1984. It was initiated by Charlene Spretnak, who, together with Fritjof Capra, had just written *Green Politics*, a book about the emergence of the Green Party in what was then West Germany. The book was an instant hit among the considerable number of people in the United States who combine an ecological awareness with an equally strong awareness that it's the antidemocratic politics of the republic that must change. The St. Paul meeting undertook to create a set of guiding principles, commissioning Charlene, Mark Satin, and Eleanor McCain to come up with the wording. Their efforts were approved and the principles have come to be known as the Ten Key Values: ecological wisdom, personal and social responsibility, grass roots democracy, nonviolence, respect for diversity, post-patriarchal values, decentralization, community economics, global responsibility, and future focus. They are a creative and potent force in helping to promote and develop Green ideas and principles; and in helping Greens to stay united in spite of the stresses and strains that have threatened to pull them apart.

The Interregional Committee (IC) met three times a year and was the primary decision-making body in the early years. Later, starting with the second national gathering in Eugene, Oregon in June 1989, the ultimate decision making power came to be lodged with the Assembly of the national gathering, made up of delegates from dues paying locals and regions. The gathering was also open to individuals who paid dues both to their locals and to the national clearing house in Kansas City. The national gathering met first in Amherst in 1987; then in Eugene, Oregon in 1989; in Estes Park, Colorado in 1990; and in Elkins, West Virginia in 1991.

By the time of Elkins, Greens in many states were beginning to create statewide Green parties. A national Green Party Organizing Committee

(GPOC) had been formed the year before and was drawing fire from various Greens. Some critics were opposed to electoral politics altogether. Others were fearful that party-minded Greens, and their state parties, would get out from under the control of movement forces; or would separate altogether; or, on the other hand, would come to dominate and overwhelm the movement.

The Elkins gathering in 1991 presaged a split in the Greens nationally. An essentially new organization was created at Elkins to replace the Green Committees of Correspondence. Called the Greens/Green Party USA (G/GPUSA), it claimed sovereignty of both movement and party activity. Dues-paying activists, representing movement locals, commanded its structure. State parties were not represented in the annual national Congress, the policy and rule making body. This frustrated those who had been active in the national Green Party Organizing Committee (GPOC) and they created the Green Politics Network (GPN) in the spring of 1992. One of its major goals was to help form an association of autonomous state Green parties.

There ensued a drama of different, and often competing, organizations at the national level but then also involving some locals and some state parties. Most Greens, though in different ways, strove to find a concept and a workable structure that would accommodate the rising tide of Green state party building and would also preserve the prestige and vitality of other movement activities. This striving found a focus when Greens from 31 states came together just ten days after the 1996 elections in Middleburg, Virginia to launch an Association of State Green Parties (ASGP). The ASGP fulfilled the hopes and early organizing efforts of the Green Politics Network. Ralph Nader's candidacy for President under the banner of the Green Party was the vital factor in bringing many more Greens together to form a national party based on autonomous state Green Parties.

The Middleburg event has led to three successful follow up meetings of ASGP by the time of this writing, December 1998. The three were held respectively in Portland, Oregon in April 1997; Topsham, Maine in October 1997; and Santa Fe, New Mexico in April 1998. Twenty four state Green Parties affiliated with ASGP during this period, comprising almost all of the states with viable Green party organizations. In the face of this, the old organization created at Elkins in 1991, G/GPUSA, was under heavy pressure — from moderates within its ranks and others — to adapt its structure and soften its skeptical attitude towards party building. Moderates formed a Unity Group, hoping to persuade G/GPUSA to shift from its primary foundation in movement-oriented locals to a broader structure that would effectively include state Green Parties. But at G/GPUSA's national gathering in Lawrence, Massachusetts in August, 1997, the moderates were defeated in their effort at reform. Feeling that they had gone about as far as they could go with G/GPUSA, most of the moderates turned to ASGP as the vehicle of choice for bringing forth a full scale federation of state Green Parties.

There is, consequently, strong evidence that the struggles of almost a decade and a half will now propel the Greens into a national party, via ASGP. It will be rooted structurally in state parties and conceptually in the idea of a "party of a different kind." By this phrase or rallying cry is widely meant a party that is grounded in the Ten Key Values and a party that draws energy and discipline from grassroots organizations, both party and nonparty, that are devoted to community building, civic engagement, and popular issues.

In my account of our beginnings in Part Three, most of which I wrote in 1991, I emphasized the importance of community to the Greens. I introduced the phrase "community in the community." I wanted to convey the idea of a social movement, lodged securely in the local habitat, whether urban or rural. I wanted to feature the social movement as a catalyst for basic change within the larger community on issues of self-reliance, justice, environment, and democracy. This involved creating a multifaceted Green organization in as many locales as possible throughout the country. I saw the local organization as a group of people engaged in a variety of strategies: educational and cultural projects, struggles over social and economic issues, study circles, life-style modelling, counter-institution building, and, yes, electoral work as well. Not all Green locals would necessarily do all of these things; some would focus on two or three, others on only one, and some would strive for as many as possible.

This was the incubation period of the Green movement in the United States. Greens were pretty solidly agreed that the basis of the movement was in the community-centered local groups. Yet from the start there was conflict over the fundamental ideological orientation or soul of the Green movement. It was a fight over structure and over philosophy, and embroiled us in two related conflicts.

The first was a central debate between, on the one hand, an anarchist-inspired municipalist social ecology articulated by Murray Bookchin, of the Social Ecology Institute in Burlington, Vermont, and his followers in several parts of the country, including such Green leaders as Brian Tokar and Howie Hawkins; and on the other a strong emphasis on ecological wisdom that was advanced by Charlene Spretnak, David Haenke, Lorna Salzman and others. There was some seeming affinity between this latter group and various schools of deep ecology, among them Earth First! Murray Bookchin and his colleagues were sharply critical of deep ecology and Earth First! Murray's battle cry, often repeated, was that the domination of human over human led to the domination of human over nature, not the other way around. He and his followers attributed "the other way around" doctrine to deep ecology—hence Murray et al.'s choice of the prefix "social" in front of ecology. They were worried that the Green movement would turn away from social justice and would begin to devalue human beings in the presumed interest of "the animal kingdom"; or would ignore social justice and issues of economic structure in favor of personal life-style changes. Deep ecologists (among them Arnae Ness, George Sessions, Kirkpatrick Sale, Dave Foreman) emphasized the rights and status of nonhuman nature. They condemned the anthropocentric and superiority attitudes inculcated in human beings by a posture of domination over nature. They noted the threat such attitudes pose in human relations with other humans. The implication of their thinking was that the human/nature relationship had to be dealt with first and foremost and only then could or would the "social" relationship (human-to-human) be capable of being ameliorated.

The arguments and counter-arguments tended to become polarized and were often conducted in a combative and sneering manner.

Murray Bookchin aimed his criticisms and his often vitriolic wit at James Foreman and other leading members of Earth First!, but then also visited his polemical style on Charlene Spretnak and other California Greens, often coupling them in an indiscriminate way with Earth First! This created a furor among many Greens, especially women in the movement who affirmed feminist values and who felt that adversarial polemics always got personal, inevitably produced polarization, and were totally inappropriate to Green discourse. It left a residue of hurt, anger, and frustration that built up over several years and fostered later organizational ruptures.

The second conflict grew out of the first. A Left Green Network began forming in late 1987, after the first Green Gathering in Amherst that summer. Howie Hawkins, as principal founder of the new organization, travelled widely about the country. He was concerned, drawing on Murray Bookchin's arguments, that the emerging Green movement would become nothing but a narrowly environmentalist movement that lacked a fundamental socioeconomic, anticapitalist critique in both its program and its practice. He was also concerned that the new national organization, the Green Committees of Correspondence with its Interregional Committee (IC) structure, was too loosely organized. It was also too fixated on the consensus mode of decision making, he argued. Though anarchistic in his general outlook, Howie insisted that the national organization must have highly structured bylaws. During the years leading to the Elkins gathering in 1991, he brought forward many draft bylaws to the IC that were very detailed. He sought to unite anarchism and strong national organization, "unified" being his battle cry. He wanted to create an organization based on majority rule and minority rights and based on a process of decision-making whereby the delegates of local bodies would vote strictly on the basis of binding mandates from their locals. Unless we did this, he argued, we Greens, in our development, would veer from grassroots accountability, and we would easily be co-opted in our practice if not in our values by the established order. As he told me at the Austin meeting of the IC in January 1988, he formed the Left Green Network both to "Green" the left and to "left" the Greens. That may have been his intention, but, as the years went by it became evident that he and the people he attracted to the Left Green Network, put far more emphasis on trying to remake the Greens into a Left fringe sect than on any greening of the Left.

Howie and I had worked side by side up to that point, not always agreeing, but generally cooperating both in the New England Committees of Correspondence (NECOC) and in the national Interregional Committee (IC). When he launched the Left Green Network, I saw the value of educating Greens on social and economic issues and thus to balance the tendency of some Greens to push only for environmental issues, narrowly construed. Howie and I continued to communicate for a time; but, caught up in the struggles, we drifted farther and farther apart. It would not be until our debate at Boxford, Massachusetts in May 1997, sponsored by the Massachusetts Green Party, that we would have a chance to compare notes face to face and probe each other's positions in a spirit of non-adversarial encounter.

I did not join the Left Green Network, and found myself associating more and more closely with those Greens who, though sympathetic to both deep ecology and social ecology, felt that the devotees of each tended to the extreme. One such person was Dee Berry who founded and directed the Kansas City Clearing House from 1984 to 1989. Under her dynamic leadership the Green Committees of Correspondence flourished and grew from a smattering of locals scattered across the country to over 300 participating local organizations.

Dee was an ecologically oriented systems-thinker before she joined the Greens and tried to bring a systems approach to the Greens through her work at the Clearing House. She was particularly impressed with the writings of W.I. Thompson, especially his critique of either/or logic. This critique was reinforced in her mind by her study of many feminist authors who were pointing out how patriarchy is rooted in either/or thinking and how this feeds into the polarization of opposites, myths of inferiority and superiority, patterns of "invisible" domination, and an adversarial, exclusivistic attitude towards the world.

Since my own thinking was moving along similar lines, strongly influenced by such authors as Audre Lorde and Paulo Freirie and by a rising tide of eco-philosophic and post-modern criticism of industrial society, Dee and I began to see eye to eye on many fundamental issues, both of theory and practice, facing the Green movement. We spoke up, and spoke out, in favor of a logic and a practice that featured a both/and approach to life and politics. Instead of dividing things up into dichotomous opposites and becoming adversarial, we argued, we Greens need to find and acknowledge difference, respect diversity, and take the kind of action that promotes balance, looks for common ground, and finds solutions that respect difference and diversity. This is the way we were reading nature as well: that nature is diverse, dynamic, interactive, replete with difference, and always open to evolutionary change. We began to use the word transformation to convey this idea.

Dee's fellow activist in the Kansas City Greens, Ben Kjelshus, also strongly advocated respect for diversity and balance, as did other activists like Mindy Lorenz of Southern California, Danny Moses, Charlene Spretnak, and Kent Smith of Northern California, Blair Bobier of Oregon, Betty Zisk near Boston, Margeurite McMillan in Western Massachusetts, Sue Conti in Virginia, Greg Gerritt and Matt Tilley in Maine, and Eugene Bronson in New Jersey. In the early nineties, we were joined by Tony Affigne in Rhode Island, Christa Slaton in Alabama, Karen Mayo in Maine, and Barbara Rodgers-Hendricks in Florida. Still later, we would be joined by Linda Martin of Hawaii and Virginia; Sam Smith of Washington D.C.(1993); Hank Chapot of Northern California; Nancy Allen, Jane Livingston, and Tom Fusco of Maine (1994); Thomas Linzey and Annie and John Goeke of Pennsylvania (1994/5); Linda and Richard Heffern of Missouri (1994); Steve Welzer of New Jersey (1995); Ronnie Dugger, organizer of the Alliance for Democracy; Bert Garskof of Connecticut , and David Draper of Maine(1996); and then, with the coming of the Nader campaign in 1996 and the formation of the Association of State Green Parties at Middleburg, Virginia in November of that year, with a whole flood of "old" and "new" Greens.

I was beginning to formulate in my mind, and to talk with my new found Green peers about, transformation as a central, if not the central, concept in an emerging Green philosophy and practice that could draw from both social and deep ecology. At the first Green Gathering in Amherst in 1987, I spoke of the need to walk on two legs, a spiritual one and a political one, a phrase picked up by Jay Walljasper of the *Utne Reader* for his article on the Amherst gathering. In the same article, he also quoted me as calling for a politics in which we Greens would be "wise as serpents and innocent as doves."

The political, as I thought of it then, involved a cluster of strategies of which the electoral, though important, was only one among many. In my mind's eye, I had not yet seen what I now believe to be true, that electoral politics and Green party building have special importance if we are "to change the world." I think most of my Green peers, at that time, in the late eighties surely, and into the nineties, felt about it much the way I had. However, a theme was emerging among us that was later to push us decisively towards electoral politics and party building as *primus inter pares* (first among equals). We began to realize, and to argue, that in any case, no matter what our favorite strategy or approach, we had to become a movement/party speaking to and with ordinary people. We were determined not to get into sectarian or "in-group" ruts of past movements, we would not be content with any kind of sandbox within which we would talk only to ourselves.

Thinking such thoughts in the late eighties, we became alarmed at the increasingly strident and sectarian tone of commentary, criticisms and manifestos coming from the Left Green Network (LGN). They were holding conferences separate from the meetings of the IC in various parts of the country. They wrote often in the monthly IC Bulletin that Dee Berry and office volunteers produced as part of the Kansas City Clearinghouse's activities. At IC meetings and in annual Green Gatherings they became more and more confrontational.

The Left Green Network aimed much criticism at the IC. They claimed the structure was too loose, there was not enough accountability, and the method of consensus seeking teetered between "the tyranny of structurelessness" (in which those who took initiative on a project were often sickeningly micro-managed) on the one hand and way too much leeway for separate projects on the other, and thus undemocratic.

They had a point. Nevertheless, they were so obsessed with these faults of the IC structure that when they got their own chance to create a new structure, as happened at Elkins in 1991, they sought to "unify" it to a point that smothered diversity and initiative.

The Left Green Network's structural critique of the IC went hand in hand with an insistence on a militant anticapitalist posture. This became, for them, a kind of litmus test by which to judge whether Greens were truly Green. Often this went hand in hand with an insistence on what Murray Bookchin described as anarchistic municipalism as the one true alternative for Green activists and for the world.

The leadership of the Green Committees of Correspondence were not anticapitalists. We were not pro-capitalists either. We thought of ourselves as neither left nor right; we wanted to be out in front of these entrenched ideological polarizations of the twentieth century. We were also alarmed at what seemed to us the ideological rigidity and intolerance of the Left Greens. They often seemed to us to exude all the trappings of a left activist culture, a kind of ideo-fundamentalism more concerned about the letter than the spirit, and about being pure of dogma rather than actually bringing about change. We got angry at what seemed the mistreatment and bullying of people who didn't go 100 percent with a supposed correct line.

We argued for diversity of ideological viewpoints, of cultural identities, and of social groupings within the context of the Ten Key Values. We also applied the concept of diversity to organizational forms. We wanted a popular politics and mode of organizing. We saw the limitations of particular-issue campaigns, demonstrations at Wall Street, yet more marches on Washington, and lobbying for this or that specific reform. We began to look more and more to the electoral terrain as a public space in which to meet and talk with our fellow citizens and tell the Green story. This understanding grew steadily as we turned more of our energies into building Green parties in our own states.

The Left Green Network misinterpreted our growing push for electoral politics as the first step towards accommodation with the establishment, capitalism, business-as-usual politics, and opportunism. Some even felt that we must be headed for elitism and right-wing reaction. They apparently had no conceptual tools to understand us differently, being immersed in a traditional "left versus right" picture of political ideologies. If we were not left, in the terms in which they understood it, then we had to be on the right. In addition, because we favored a politics of engagement with the electoral system and representative government (which is steeped in hierarchy to their anarchist way of thinking), we could not be truly democratic. They distrusted us, felt we were pulling the Green movement in the wrong direction, and some were jealous of our leadership.

At the August '87 IC meeting in Kansas City, right after the first Green Gathering in Amherst, I became the principal coordinator of a project to develop a national Green program. It came to be called Strategy and Policy Approaches in Key Areas, or SPAKA for short. Almost all of the active local Green groups in the country got involved in this multi-year endeavor. At the second Green gathering in Eugene, Oregon in June 1989, we pulled together the hundreds of papers, resolutions, and attempted syntheses into a working document featuring our philosophy and practical recommendations in each of 21 major program areas. We adopted these provisionally, the idea being to give the local groups and a new program committee an additional year in which to make changes, get even more input, and give the document a more consistent style.

The principal coordinator during the additional year was Christa Slaton, a founder of the Hawaii Green Party and a member of the Alabama Greens to which state she had recently moved. I remained as an advisor to the new program committee. Under Christa's leadership, the SPAKA process deepened the grassroots generation of ideas and perspectives with which we had begun. The document was eventually adopted at the third Green Gathering in Estes Park, Colorado in September 1990. But this occurred only after a tumultuous and tragic confrontation, which began with a widely distributed letter in August from members of the Left Green Network, spearheaded by Howie Hawkins and Brian Tokar. In this letter, they scathingly denounced the SPAKA process as "undemocratic." The criticism was unmerited and was delivered in a manner that seemed like a personal assault on Christa Slaton. It poisoned the deliberations in Estes Park, and, the criticism continuing, Christa resigned as program coordinator. She left the Gathering and the Green movement. The movement lost a brilliant and strong spirit, a superb organizer, a person deeply committed to Green values and to feminism.

The attack on Christa shocked me deeply, as I had been earlier by the assault on Charlene Spretnak by Murray Bookchin's followers at the first Green Gathering in Amherst in 1987 (including epithets of "fascist" flung at her). During that gathering, Dee Berry and I were among those asked by Charlene and Murray to participate in a mediation session led by Margot Adair. After three difficult hours, we all thought we had come to a solution of sorts, and an agreement to respect each other's politics. But in the aftermath of the Amherst "detente," the attacks from Murray and his followers continued, particularly a harsh article by Phil Hill of the Washington D.C. Greens. This left a bitter residue and led to Charlene's withdrawal from an active role in the national Green movement and party building.

We of the transformational politics persuasion had also been troubled by the acerbic and we thought often gratuitous criticisms heaped upon Sue Conti (our first fund raiser) by members of the Left Green Network and others sympathetic with their politics. She found it difficult to continue, and after great emotional turmoil, finally decided to resign. She, too, left the Greens.

It seemed we were faced with an opposition that especially singled out women for criticism. It was also a type of criticism that traded on adversarial, antagonistic language and polarizing personal put-down. A third element in this pattern was an attack on our rising commitment to electoral politics.

We were puzzled as much as hurt by this mode of argument and struggle. We felt we were being treated by the Left Green Network, not as fellow Greens, but as people no better than capitalists, Republicans, reactionaries, if not indeed worse. It was as if we had become, in their eyes, betrayers of the true faith. We continued to affirm the importance of diversity, including the diversity of philosophical points of view within the overall umbrella of The Key Values. We sought to place the Left Green Network (LGN) within the Green movement and as an important voice within the Green Committees of Correspondence. But what puzzled us was the message that LGN's was the true voice, that their politics had to prevail, and ours must be overcome.

We asked ourselves again and again: how does one fight an opposition which assumes an antagonistic stance without yourself becoming, or appearing to be, antagonistic? This was an especially difficult and agonizing question since, given the remoteness of things national to most Greens, the great majority of Greens in the various states and locals saw any appearance of struggle as prima facie evidence that both sides must be equally guilty of egoizing, creating conflict, etc. They thus resisted or dismissed the need to deal with the substantive political and philosophical differences. Many would have come to our aid if they had been willing to listen, to abide with the problem, instead of tuning it out. In this way, those who foment antagonistic strife often tend to come out ahead. This seemed to be happening for a time, but eventually the tide turned.

As we moved into Green party building, we encountered heavy going in many states where the Left Green Network and non-left, anti-electoral Greens were active. This occurred in Oregon, California, Missouri, Pennsylvania, Massachusetts, Wisconsin, Ohio, Virginia, New Hampshire, New York, and New Jersey. It did not happen either in Maine or Rhode Island or New Mexico where the party and movement had early found a way to move in step with one another.

In Oregon, Blair Bobier led the effort to create a Green political party but was rebuffed by some Green locals. He and other electorally minded Greens had worked closely with kindred groups such as Greenpeace during the Gulf War in early 1991. Out of that came ferment to create a party. Instead of fighting with fellow Greens who were holding back from politics, they decided to sidestep confrontation by forming a Pacific Party. It has since developed robustly as a Green party based on the Ten Key Values.

In California, opposition to forming an authentic Green Party was fierce. Mindy Lorenz, active at the national level in the leadership of the Green Committees of Correspondence, was also leading the way in California to get locals aroused about electoral organizing and electoral campaigns, with a view towards building a strong Green Party in California. She drew intense fire from LGN Greens in her area of Los Angeles. At one of the meetings, Mindy was physically assaulted, another attack on a strong woman and for the sin of building a party. We also viewed it as a further instance of adversarial, antagonistic politics.

We had our work cut out for us! Not only were we bucking an anti-electoral and left-sectarian bias within the Left Green Network. We were discovering that many Greens shared the prevailing American culture's distaste for "politics," period! They pursued life style transformation, alternative institution building, educational and cultural development, and/or specific issue campaigns. Not all were hostile to electoral politics by any means, but many were, especially the more vocal ones. We kept arguing for a variety of strategies in which electoral politics was given its fair share and recognized for its importance. The Left Green Network and those favoring alternative life-style/institution building were not hearing this. They feared full-scale electoral politics. They argued that it took energy and focus away from their favorite strategies. In any case, they said, we needed to build up these other strategies first, including a strong effort at multicultural organizing, before going electoral. Otherwise, the party might slip away from control by "the movement" and become "politics-as-usual."

A critical and challenging answer to these fears and concerns, then as now, was to build a party of a different kind. But the argument was not made strongly enough by us, I now feel. Nor were we clear enough in our efforts to affirm a "neither Left nor Right" philosophy and politics; and to score the Left Green Network for bogging us down in outworn 19th century ideologies. We centered on arguing for a variety of strategies. In an article I wrote for the Green Bulletin in 1991, I called it the House of Green. The House of Green has many rooms with different strategies located in different rooms, all of them connected to a "Commons," the Green Community.

But if we had been able to make an argument for a "party of a different kind," would that have helped?

Chapter 14
First Steps

Could we who worked to build an authentic and credible Green Party have prevented the confused and checkered journey of the Greens after the Elkins gathering of 1991? Could we have done it by putting forward more clearly, more stoutly, our belief in the importance of the electoral terrain, the importance of building a strong and durable national Green political party, and the transformational potential such action has for society and government? Could we have insisted that this terrain must be reclaimed for freedom, justice, and truth telling; and that if Greens are ever to make direct and close contact with our fellow citizens on the fundamental issues, that this can only fully occur in the electoral sphere? Could we, in sum, have aroused most Greens to the task of building a party of a different kind?

One answer is "maybe." Another answer is "probably not." We ourselves were groping for a full understanding of what we should be striving for. The concept of a party of a different kind was on our lips but we didn't really know what that might mean. We needed more actual political experience. But even in the states where Greens were active electorally and in office, the steps being taken were still tentative. Furthermore, we had our hands full trying to cope with the resolute resistance from both the Left Greens and the New Age Greens to even small steps in that direction. And we faced the many barriers put in our path by the dominant two-party monopoly. To our deepening chagrin, we came to know just how hard our chosen path was going to be.

A third answer, however, is that we did make a start! A small but noticeable one came already at the second Green gathering in Eugene, Oregon in June, 1989. Brian Tokar in a *Z Magazine* article for March 1997, entitled "The Nader For President Fiasco," identifies me as the one who, "at the very first decision making national gathering of representatives of Green locals in 1989 in Eugene, Oregon . . . proposed a long range strategy of Green involvement in the presidential campaigns of 1992 and 1996." Brian presents this as something unfortunate, being committed as he is to only tolerating electoral activity if it is subordinate to protest-oriented activists in non-electoral local groups. Building a real political party, one that engages fully in the electoral sphere, including campaigns for the presidency of the United States, is not something the anarchist-prone activists Brian idealizes feel they can control. Nevertheless, his accusation indicates that "already" back in 1989, we party-builders were pushing and promoting a long term electoral strategy.

Brian might have added that I also proposed to the fifty Greens crowded into the workshop on strategy in Eugene, that we should think of running a community-presidency campaign, and think of doing it by 1996 (not 1992). A community-presidency would feature, in addition to the presidential and vice presidential nominees, several other persons with specific qualifications corresponding to cabinet posts. All would run together as a team. This was partially realized in 1996, when Ralph Nader ran with seven different Vice Presidential nominees, though only one, Winona LaDuke, was listed on the ballot in most of the states. The idea I wanted to get across to the strategy group was for us to think in new ways about a national political party and presidential campaigns.

A further step was taken in the fall of 1989, at the October meeting of the Interregional Committee (IC) in Washington, D.C. Matt Tilley, my co-representative to the IC from Maine, and I presented a proposal for the creation of an Electoral Action Working Group. Left Greens were very critical of this idea, the debate was intense and for a while I thought it would go down to defeat, but in the actual vote it was approved by a vote of 90% in favor.

At the next IC meeting in March 1990 in San Diego, the Electoral Action Working Group, having grown rapidly in the intervening four months, transformed itself into the Green Party Organizing Committee (GPOC). The GPOC declared itself to be an autonomous and cooperating body within the overall structure of the Green Committees of Correspondence. The IC delegates, when presented with this as a proposal the next day, approved the move.

At the IC meeting in Ann Arbor in June, members of the Left Green Network, clearly alarmed at the notion of autonomy for a budding political party, insisted that the GPOC go back to being a Working Group. Later that year, at the third national Green Gathering in Estes Park in September, there were also expressions of dissatisfaction from Left Greens with GPOC's push for electoral politics and for autonomy. But the argument was upstaged by discussion of the new Green Program, and by plans for wholesale restructuring of the Green Committees of Correspondence.

But this resistance to GPOC's activities was more than matched by a rising interest in the nitty gritty of forming state Green Parties. A workshop on electoral politics at that Estes Park gathering drew over fifty people from across the country. This signalled that a growing number of people from the several states were getting active in politics in their states, and were looking for ways to connect with one another for mutual assistance. California Greens, for example, kicked off a registration drive that fall which by the end of 1991 would yield them 96,000 signatures and party status. Also, that fall, the Alaska Green Party would become the first to achieve ballot status, as Jim Sykes garnered more than the 3% necessary in his run for governor on their behalf.

The GPOC met briefly at the end of the Estes Park conference and decided to meet within six months, not waiting for the next annual Green gathering in order to do so. Time and place for such a meeting were not specified however.

After the Estes Park gathering, three things happened that together prepared the way for a big argument at the next national Green gathering scheduled for Elkins, West Virginia in the summer of 1991. The first was a four-day meeting near Kansas City in November of a nine-member Restructuring Working Group which had been elected at the Estes Park gathering. Their task was to come up with a proposal for a new structure to replace the IC. The Group was co-chaired by Dee Berry and Charles Betz, a Left Green and a recent newcomer to the leadership. The proposal would be voted on by the Green locals the following April.

The second was a call that came from Mindy Lorenz of the California Greens and me for a meeting of the GPOC in Boston in February 1991. The third was a campaign launched by Howie Hawkins to oppose the proposal of the Structural Committee and to promote his own alternative.

The Restructuring Committee unanimously agreed on what they justifiably felt was a creative bicameral approach. They proposed a Green Council of eleven members for movement-oriented locals and a parallel body of eleven members for state parties. These two bodies would meet both separately and together. If this plan had been actualized, it probably would have prevented, and surely would have moderated, the splits and the confusion of the next several years.

The plan was sent out for several rounds of input from all of the participating locals and was finally presented for ratification in April. But, at the instance of Charlie Betz and other Left Greens, a "unified structure" plan which Howie Hawkins had come up with the previous summer and submitted to the Estes Park gathering, was also presented and given equal weight on the ballot along with the Working Group's "bicameral" plan. Then, for reasons that remain shrouded in mystery, still a third plan, an apparent "hybrid" of the other two, was also placed on the ballot.

The Restructuring Working Group had been elected at the Estes Park gathering from diverse geographical regions and wings of the Green movement. They had been elected specifically to create a better design for a national organization. They were confident that their "bicameral" plan would appeal to both the GPOC and the Left Green Network (LGN). The idea did appeal to the GPOC at their meeting in Boston in February but was rejected by Howie and the Left Green Network. He attacked it as a threat to Green unity and he called for "a unified national structure."

By playing on the theme of "a unified structure," Howie attracted both Left Greens and New Age Greens. The two groups had little in common, but both were skeptical if not hostile to electoral politics and they did not want the party people to escape the control of local Green groups in which "social movement" and/or "life style" activists were prominent. There was also the mystique of "being unified" that attracted both groups, for different reasons — the Left Greens because that is what their tradition teaches them to think about organization; and the New Age Greens because they wanted harmony and togetherness above all. Neither group seemed very hospitable to, or very knowledgeable about, newer concepts of organization that feature diversity of forms, solidarity of side-by-side organizations, and the cooperation of people through their difference.

The April vote by the locals narrowly defeated the Structural Committee's bicameral proposal. Down to defeat as well went the hope that at last the Greens had found a way to unite the social movement and the political party. What ensued thereafter, at the Elkins gathering that summer and beyond, was a confused and bitter conflict, lasting for years. But there was also learning taking place and that too is still being felt.

The GPOC meeting in Boston in February 1991 was a galvanizing experience for the two dozen participants. The leading message of the meeting was for people to go home and start a state Green party — and encourage friends and contacts in adjoining states to do likewise. Plans were also laid to assist in the development of already existing Green parties, and to create an effective network of these parties and of new ones as they emerged. In addition, the group anticipated holding meetings that would build bridges among the many third parties that were sprouting up in the country. Since the participants had a record of doing things and getting them done, word quickly got round the country that the GPOC was strong and effective. The group announced that the next meeting of GPOC would take place at Elkins, West Virginia in a two-day session just prior to the annual gathering.

Word also got round very quickly that we had excluded from the meeting Howie Hawkins and a fellow member of the Left Green Network, Guy Chichester of the New Hampshire Greens. It was an action that was risky given Green sensitivities on issues of inclusion and exclusion. We felt it was necessary given the long record of opposition to party building, much of it hostile, from Howie, Guy and other leading members of the Left Green Network. If we let them come in, we reasoned, they would be disruptive of our fundamental purpose, and possibly derail what we were now determined to accomplish. But, of course, if we refused them attendance, we would stand accused as exclusivistic, elitist, separatists and the like. This happened.

A Steering Committee of GPOC met in Atlanta in late June. We firmed up ideas for a democratic structure for GPOC based on the state Green parties. We envisioned developing support systems for these parties, and for hosting a meeting for a variety of third parties in the spring of 1992. We also tried to prepare for what loomed now as a difficult meeting in Elkins.

We didn't know the half of it. Scores of Greens, including many members of the Left Green Network, came early for the Gathering in order to attend our GPOC meetings if they could. They were "let in" by our secretary, Phil Rose, who had come under the strong influence of Charlie Betz. Charlie, in a July letter, had primed Greens throughout the country to the "dangers" represented by the GPOC. He was a member of the Left Green Network, had been at the Boston meeting of GPOC, had been a leading participant in the Restructuring Committee that had called for a "bicameral" Green Council, and had been an invited participant in the Atlanta meeting of GPOC's Steering Committee. But now he was changing his mind. In his letter he accused GPOC of intending to separate from the Greens. He excoriated us in harsh language and warned the Green locals to resist our plans. Charles apologized for this letter six months later, but the damage had been done.

New Age Greens, Left Greens, Greens unattached to any caucus or particular faction came to Elkins determined to "do something" about the GPOC, since we presumably were "out of control" and out to do our own thing. They stormed their way into our meetings, very much on edge, frightened that we would leave (as one shrewd observer put it), yet angry at us for forging ahead with party building plans. Some clearly were itching for a fight, others wanted information, others wanted to be reassured. Our every move was subject to intense scrutiny. Even our ad hoc sessions of an early morning in which we sought to develop some ways to deal with the fact that our meeting had been "taken over" and that we would not be able to work on Green party building, even these small group meetings were denounced as clear evidence of "back room" politics, elitism, and other unimaginable horrors.

In the sessions on Wednesday and Thursday, and on Friday morning of that Elkins gathering, we sought to calm people's fears. We argued the importance of party building, we argued the importance of giving authentic structural room for that activity within the overall national organization. We did not argue for the special importance of party building. Maybe we should have. But we were interested only in being given a chance to work at party building as an autonomous activity within the Green structure as a whole, one that fit into a concept of "The House of Green." The House of Green has many rooms, there is free access from room to room, there is a common room, but there is also the reality of distinct spaces (autonomous rooms) for different kinds of activities (of which party building is one). This approach was either not believed or was not understood by enough folks there. Nor did we argue the need to create a party of a different kind. We might have done that had we focussed more clearly among ourselves on the question: just how important IS party building in comparison to direct action, issue politics, alternative institution building, and the like? Why didn't we apply the idea of alternative institution building to political parties? That might have gotten some people's attention. We had pieces of this kind of approach but they hadn't come together, and we tended to give primary focus to the argument for diversity of structure. On that issue, quite a few heard us, but many people who might otherwise have been with us, shied away because they had been led to believe that this was a code word for going our separate ways.

We also tried to focus attention on the substantive struggle between the GPOC and the LGN. We pointed to the ideological chasm between the latter's philosophy of eco-anarchism and our transformational philosophy. I remember that at one point Lorna Salzman tried hard to point us in that direction, but we didn't fully engage. We didn't because we believed in unity, in solidarity, in the possibility of discourse across difference. We didn't want to "split" the Greens, even though that was part of the charge against us.

It would have helped our cause hugely, of course, if more Greens had given more thought to what "unity" means. It could, for example, mean unanimity, uniformity, and nitpicking control, which is what we felt Howie and others really meant by it. Or it could mean solidarity, cooperation, side-by-side coexistence, and so forth, which is what we meant by it. Many Greens seemed unable to imagine a non-unitary unity. It would also have helped hugely if more Greens had understood that we were trying to get beyond an either/or logic in favor of a both/and logic. We saw this as a battle of the old paradigm still rooted in Cartesian, mechanistic thinking, versus a new transformational paradigm; and we placed the Left Greens squarely in the camp of the old, for that is what their insistence on a "unified structure" meant to us. It meant control, bureaucracy, long and complex bylaws, and the drying up of initiative and innovation. Our forebodings were not unjustified.

By late Thursday afternoon, with the promising GPOC plans for party building a complete wreck, and the turmoil of argument having reached an apparent stalemate, the by-now large group of over 70 people took up somebody's suggestion for "the key players" to meet that night to try to come up with a proposal that could then be taken up Friday morning for decision. This was suddenly agreed to.

183

The Thursday night session is one of those meetings where everything seems to hang by a thread. I cannot remember everyone who was there, but as I now visualize the table around which we sat I can see Valerie Ackerman, a fair minded Green from Ann Arbor who was on neither "side," though she favored a social movement approach to Green organizing; Brian Chambers, also from Michigan, similarly inclined; Mindy Lorenz; Dee Berry; Danny Moses (meeting facilitator); Barbara Rodgers-Hendricks; Charlie Betz; Howie Hawkins; Kwazi Nkrumah, an African American social movement activist from California; and Suleiman Mahdi, an African American from Atlanta who had been with us in Boston, had hosted our GPOC Steering Committee meeting in Atlanta, and who seemed to have an immediate grasp of what a "side-by-side" concept of politics and organizing should mean. But I believe now, in retrospect, that he limited that concept to race relations and did not think of it as something to apply as well to organization theory and practice.

Initially, the discussion bogged down over the same arguments we'd been hearing since Tuesday evening. During a break, Mindy Lorenz tried out a possible compromise with Dee, Suleiman, Barbara, and me. We liked it, even though it did not provide all that we felt the party-side of the movement needed by way of structural identity and support. We felt, however, that it was a plausible and promising step forward.

When the meeting reassembled, Mindy presented the proposal. After a long and difficult debate, everyone agreed to it except Howie and Charlie. Charlie was on the verge of agreeing. At one point, Valerie, who had Howie's confidence, made an eloquent and touching appeal. She pleaded with him to "rise above principle." A powerful and loving person, trained in pyschological theory and practice, she was trying to convey the importance of looking beyond the words we use to give form to our principles, and instead to delve into the real relationships of persons to one another that often go beyond words. Principles, she suggested, are often confused with verbal statements. The room was very quiet as she talked. It seemed for a moment that Howie might be moved, but then he squared his shoulders and said that he could not. Charlie then stayed firm as well. Our Green history for the next several years, if not much longer, would have been much different had they responded to Valerie's appeal.

Kwazi Nkrumah and Suleiman Mahdi spoke. They recalled an instance in the black movement when two factions "almost" overcame their fierce opposition to each other, but the moment passed, and the way forward was deeply damaged thereafter. It was a prophetic remark.

We looked at one another with blank faces. Howie and Charlie were unrelenting. Then someone, recalling Quaker practice in achieving consensus, a practice which many Green groups also used, suggested a way out and forward. We could declare consensus provided Howie and Charlie would agree "to stand aside." They were amenable to this, or so it seemed to us. Was it a farcical naivete that overcame us at that moment? The meeting was over, we were all in various stages of euphoric shock. Only Suleiman was worried and kept shaking his head. We reassured him, and decided that we would all come early the next morning just before the meeting started and sit together to symbolize the consensus reached.

We all assumed that our "consensus" proposal would be the only one to be presented to the general meeting next morning. I now put quotes around "consensus," because it really wasn't, given the way Howie and Charlie interpreted how "to stand aside." That night they crafted their own proposal for presentation the next day, calling once again for a "unified structure." Some of us, in retrospect, recalling the intensity of those days, are willing to give a charitable interpretation of Howie and Charlie's mis-interpretation of "to stand aside." Others, more skeptical, believe that "they played us for suckers."

Next morning, Howie and Charlie got their proposal in first with lots of copies. The "consensus proposal" got in a little late. The meeting never understood that there was such a thing as a "consensus proposal." Most "saw" two proposals, signifying a continued split. Even our sitting together ("our" being all of us except Howie and Charlie) was misinterpreted by more than a few as typically GPOC "elitism." This, too, was strange since half of us "sitting together" were not members of, nor identified with GPOC; in fact several were members of or close to the Left Greens.

Both proposals were debated with renewed ferocity. Finally a vote was taken and the "consensus proposal" (seen as the GPOC proposal versus the Left Green proposal) was favored over that of Howie and Charlie's by a 60% to 40% vote. But since by GPOC rules, passage required two-thirds, the proposal was defeated. The halcyon GPOC meeting was over. The regular meetings of the Green Gathering were about to begin.

They proved an anticlimax to us in the GPOC. We gave it a good shot. Mindy Lorenz, and Barbara Rodgers-Hendricks of the Florida Greens, volunteered for the Structural Working Group and I attended all of the inter-minable sessions as an observer, Friday through Sunday. The arguments were repetitious of what had gone on for days during the GPOC sessions. The day-long, night-long sessions reached a point of stalemate on the fun-damental issue of state party participation in the overall structure. The best that the working group could do was patch over the continuing breach by calling for an ad hoc Working Group to meet during the coming year on the issue. This was duly accepted by the convention on Monday, Greg Gerritt of the GPOC would be a member, and on Tuesday a seeming spirit of unanimity was proclaimed in the conference as a whole. Mindy Lorenz was the only member of the GPOC/transformational politics group to be elected to a new Steering Committee. My name had been put in as a nominee for the Steering Committee and I did not have the heart, or the wit, to withdraw the nomination, though I knew there was no chance for me to be elected by the Left Green dominated gathering. I was right.

In addition to a Steering Committee, the new structure also created a Green Council, replacing the old IC. Its members comprised representatives of several identity caucuses (Environmental Justice, People of Color, Women, Gays and Lesbians, and Youth), as well as representatives of the regional groupings of locals, plus several people elected directly from the annual Congress, the policy making body composed of delegates from local groups.

State parties were not part of the structure. We in the GPOC had lost and lost decisively. The Left Green Network was riding high. Their pundits, Phil Hill in the lead, proclaimed Elkins as the victory of the Left in the pages of the Guardian, an article quickly xeroxed and prominently distributed across the country to all the Green locals by the Kansas City clearinghouse, which was now securely in the control of the Left Greens. Presumably it was a victory over the right, meaning us. They had their leading people in all the leading places in the new organization, which they somewhat pretentiously (and prematurely) called The Greens/Green Party USA. Indeed, the GPOC would no longer be called the Green Party Organizing Committee but the Green Party Organizing Caucus, signifying that now a firm control has been placed on party building.

We did a lot of soul-searching. It was a set back yes. But with the defeat came also a growing and deepening realization that the struggle, though far tougher than we had ever thought it could be, was truly worth it. We had begun on a course, when we created and developed the GPOC, that could lead to a genuine national Green Party resting securely on the participation of autonomous state Green Parties. We had actually won a plurality of Green votes, 60% to 40%, from among 80 people participating in the GPOC conclave on Friday morning, most of whom were not members of the GPOC. That fairly decisive plurality was for a structural proposal that did give a substantial degree of room, call it autonomy, for the state party side of Green politics. Though it lost because it failed to get the two-thirds our GPOC decision-rules called for, nevertheless getting 60% under the adverse conditions of the Elkins meetings clearly showed we had considerable support among the Greens generally.

Yet, perhaps we had gone too far too fast. We'd frightened people both because we were talking party language when they were not ready to hear it; and because we projected an image of organization (unity through diversity) that they did not understand; or they felt that it threatened the unity they seemed to want above all. We were dealing with the fact, as we came gradually to realize, that many people came to the Greens not because they wanted to change the world, but because they wanted a secure home away from home. We were up against a strong sand box mentality.

We were also up against a hard knot of Left Greens resolutely opposed to serious party building and who were prepared to co-opt any party building going on, the better to subject the party-side of things to the control of the "social movement." We didn't think that the structure they had created at Elkins could work all that well, replete as it was with lengthy and stupefyingly complicated bylaws, and we would be justified in that estimate. We also knew that the New Age Greens, many of whom had allied with the LGN in their struggle against us, would not continue to support them.

From our growing contacts with our brother and sister Greens in Europe, we realized that we were not alone in this struggle between a movement oriented around the activities of nongovernmental organizations (NGOs) and a political party; between a militantly left ideological persuasion and a set of principles rooted in ecological wisdom. Since, in Europe, these struggles saw the emergence of viable political parties rooted in the practical issues of ecology, democracy, and justice, we took comfort and hope from their experience. But we also felt it would be harder for us in the United States, because the U.S. electoral system lacked proportional representation. This meant that it would take longer to create and develop viable political parties and that this in turn would slow down the experience and consciousness of doing real down to earth politics.

Yet we were convinced that the logic of political development of the Greens was in our favor. Greens were increasing their engagement in electoral politics all the time. In more and more states, fledgling statewide parties were forming. As this happened, we figured, the idea of a national Green Party based on statewide parties would catch hold. We also figured that we could and should wait upon developments in the states. We turned more of our attention to building statewide parties in our own states. At the same time, we wanted to keep alive and to nurture the idea of a Green party at the national level. In addition, we wanted to initiate and foster cooperation among the various third party efforts in the country.

Consonant with these thoughts, we also looked more closely at what we meant by a new politics. We raised questions among ourselves on this order: what did a new politics mean for the kind of electoral campaigns we and other Greens should/would conduct? What would be a Green approach to money in politics and campaign finance reform? Suppose a Green could ever become President, would he or she be able to function effectively? If he or she had the power, could it be used to decentralize bureaucracies, institutions and corporations sufficiently so that the fundamental Green values of community economics and political decentralization could be realized? What could it mean, our belief that spirituality must have a bearing on the political world?

We were talking the language of "a party of a different kind" but we hadn't yet formulated it well enough, either in concept or in its application to party organization, to focus clearly in that direction.

Chapter 15
Breaking Free

The banner headline read "Confederation of State Green Parties Takes Shape." It was the summer of 1993, and this was the lead story in the first issue of *Green Horizon*, a journal of news and commentary published by the Green Politics Network (GPN). The headline heralded optimism, although only four state Green parties — Hawaii, Maine, Missouri, and Rhode Island — had given their formal blessing to the idea of a confederation. No delegates were named by any of these state parties and there was no meeting, but the idea was now fully out there. It would be more than three years, however, before it actually materialized in an Association.

Before that took place, before it *could* take place, we had to take our leave of the newly formed Greens/Green Party USA (G/GPUSA). We had to strike out on a distinctly party pathway. To enable us to head in that direction we created the Green Politics Network. We sought a kind of organization that would not itself become a national Green Party, but would be a catalyst to help bring it into being.

To take this difficult step, we first did some serious reflection. We had to focus our spirits and our energies on the long term goal of bringing into being a national Green Party, a party of a different kind. To accomplish this, we had to dispense with distractions. We came to realize the degree and depth to which we had become co-dependent on our adversaries in the Left Green Network, now astride the national Green organization that had given itself the name Greens/Green Party USA. We were in a "bad marriage" with them and we had to stop trying to make the relationship work. We had been trying this for several years. It had been a crash course in futility. If we were ever to re-enter into relation with them that was sensible and productive, we would first have to get out of the marriage.

However, after Elkins, we of the now shipwrecked Green Party Organizing Committee continued at first to temporize. That is how we see it now, but at that time we felt we should give the new organization, G/GPUSA, the benefit of the doubt. Mindy Lorenz participated eagerly in the conference calls of the Steering Committee. Barbara Rodgers-Hendricks took seriously her role as elected delegate from the Florida region to the new Green Council. Greg Gerritt tried to get things going as secretary of the ad hoc Structural Working Group created at Elkins that was supposed to come up with a new proposal for state party representation in G/GPUSA. Dee Berry and Ben Kjelshus in Kansas City continued their efforts to create a viable and inclusive Missouri Green Party. Dee launched a campaign for Lieutenant Governor. I had just finished my book *The Greens and the Politics of Transformation*; and, as I read it now, there is no indication in it of any plans to create a new national organization.

But the door was slammed shut in our face. Mindy was often a minority of one on issues before the Steering Committee. She came more and more under attack, personal as well as political, from the Left Greens on the Steering Committee. She was also targeted by Left Greens in her home district in southern California, where she had been a candidate for Congress as early as 1990 and where she continued to take a lead in building local party bodies and a statewide Green Party. She was a leading force in the successful effort, completed in December 1991, to enroll almost 100,000 citizens of California in the California Green Party, enough to give the party official ballot status. Smarting under many attacks and feeling desperate, she would eventually decide to leave the Greens, a grievous loss to the Green movement and party.

Barbara went to the first meeting of the new Green Council in Dallas that fall and ran into severe weather. In one encounter, she found herself, the only woman, under heavy verbal abuse from eight men. The pasting she got centered mostly on the sins, imagined and otherwise, of the Green Party Organizing Committee, even though that organization no longer existed. It was, as she later recalled, one of the most bitter and hurtful experiences she had ever endured. She would never to go back.

Greg Gerritt accepted responsibility as secretary of the Structural Working Group to facilitate the drafting of a report for the next annual gathering of G/GPUSA. He found it difficult to get steady participation, but he did eventually cobble a report together by including what had been sent to him by others on the committee. In his report, he identified who had contributed what, and then also included his own views. In his comments, he added the argument that it was both illegal and immoral for state parties that are based on broad citizen participation to be subject to the control of a national body composed of representatives of dues paying activists in nonparty locals. The leadership of G/GPUSA did not receive this kindly. He was sent a letter of censure from Charlie Betz, Coordinator of the Clearing House in Kansas City. The letter was said to have been signed by six of the seven members of the Steering Committee of G/GPUSA. Greg was later told by two members of the Steering Committee, Katherine Adam and Howie Hawkins, that they did not sign nor had they known anything about the letter. In any event, most of the Structural Working Group members, other than Greg, treaded water and it was not long before the Green Council abolished the working group.

In Missouri, Dee Berry ran into Left Green opposition, both in her campaign for Lieutenant Governor and in efforts to nudge into being a

Missouri Green Party. Opposition came from two leading members of the Gateway Green Alliance of St. Louis, Don Fitz and Jeff Sutter, both prominent members of the Left Green Network. In an article in the Gateway Alliance's newsletter, published just after Dee had announced her intention to run, Jeff Sutter accused her of "misappropriating" funds of the Prairie Greens, a regional organization of which she was co-chair. He xeroxed the article and sent it to all members of the budding Missouri Green Party, including all members of the Kansas City Greens, Dee's own local. He was immediately called upon to withdraw the allegation. This he eventually did and apologized. But Dee's campaign came to a halt and the damage done to the Missouri Green Party's organizing efforts still plagues it.

Meanwhile, in the pages of the *Guardian* that fall of 1991, I was described by Phil Hill, not only as an inveterate right-winger but a McCarthyite. My indignant rejoinder was not published.

We had said to ourselves in previous years that we were being picked off one by one: first Charlene Spretnak, then Sue Conti, then Christa Slaton. Now, as it seemed to us, we were in danger of being picked off all together and at once.

There came a time in late 1991 that we made a decision. To me it was the hardest political decision I ever made. Now I look back and realize it shouldn't have been that hard, I should have had more sophistication and, to be very blunt, I should have "cared" less. "Teach us to care, and not to care," writes T.S. Eliot in a line I had often lingered over. I might have applied it then and saved myself a lot of anxiety and sleepless nights. I proposed in a letter to those associated with the now defunct GPOC that we create a new national organization. It was greeted with instant relief and acclaim by most of us. Relief because we needed protection and mutual support. Acclaim because we knew we had much work to do to help a national Green party to come into being, one capable both of being an effective network for emerging state Green parties and a catalyst for cooperation among many third parties. And acclaim as well because we knew we had to explore and deepen the meaning of spirituality in political life.

We wanted to create a different kind of organization, in structure and in process, and we wanted it to make a difference in the wide world of people's lives. Not the sandbox for us.

We met at the Hartland Conference Center in Kansas City in late March 1992. During the first three days, Wednesday to Friday, we founded the Green Politics Network and for the last three we hosted the first of our Third Party conferences.

We were joined for the first time by Tony Affigne, a prominent activist and leading member of the Puerto Rican community in Providence, Rhode Island. He had been involved in environmental and community activism since the 1970's, and had run for governor in 1986, the nation's final campaign under the banner of the Citizen's Party. He had participated in the deliberations of the Green Party Organizing Committee in Boston in February, 1991. He was strongly committed to a transformational philosophy of life and politics rooted in ecological wisdom.

As a person of color, Tony is fluent in his articulation of the Green value of respect for diversity. He taught us much about what that means conceptually, how it plays out in everyday life, and how it applies not only to personal relationships but also to organizational theory and practice. Firmly rooted in the social movement, he was equally at home with party building.

Tony was a bracing influence from the start. He helped give discipline and definition to our thinking and our practice. He helped us to see what had been happening to us and what had been done to us, and he located all that historically, so that we had a clearer sense of our direction. He also helped us not to take ourselves too seriously.

In the Mission statement we produced in Hartland, we said that "The Green Politics Network will develop a nationwide, democratically structured home of Green activists, foster the development of state and local political parties and organizations that share our values, provide a forum for the development of new ideas and strategies, offer resources for education and skill development, build communication with Green parties around the world, nurture coalitions of kindred organizations, and create a space for people to connect with the spiritual universe."

"Our holistic politics," we said, "will be based on the principles of Ecology, Social Justice, Nonviolence, and Participatory Democracy. We are committed," the document continued, "to a new political process which recognizes our responsibility to the Earth and to future generations; embodies respect for diversity; promotes nurturing, cooperative behavior; facilitates responsible and accountable participation; encourages initiative, and demands integrity. We insist that how we treat each other is as important as achieving our goals. . . .

"Our intention," we concluded, "is to act together and singly as facilitators, catalysts, and enablers of organizations and projects, already existing, or yet to be created, that advance the transformation of power and policy in our communities, states, nation, and globe."

The themes are interesting as one looks back on this after seven years. Party building is there; pursuing politics of a different kind is there explicitly; and applying this to political parties is there implicitly; treating people with respect was a very big part of our deliberations, understandably so, given our experiences in the struggle with Left Greens; connecting with the spiritual universe was and is near the heart of our enterprise; and just as important to us was the creation of autonomous projects.

We tried to be careful not to present ourselves as competing with the new national organization created at Elkins: G/GPUSA. We did not want to be a G/GPUSA-type of organization. We were creating a structure in and through which we could develop separate projects, each of which would be autonomous. We envisioned that a number of our projects would become self-sustaining and eventually move on and off into the big wide world by themselves, and we would gladly let them go. This in fact has happened to four of GPN's most important projects: first, the idea and early development of what is now the Association of State Green Parties (when originated by members of GPN, it had the name Confederation of Independent State Green Parties); second, the Third Party Coalition Project, also called Third Force; third, *Green Horizon*, at first a newsletter and now an independent quarterly published by Leopold Press; and fourth, a Food Circle of Greater Kansas City, a pioneering effort to link farmers, processors, retailers and consumers in the production and consumption of organic food.

The Third Force project began already at the Hartland Center that March of 1992. On the weekend, we hosted representatives of more than a dozen parties and organizations. We explored what we might have in common. The conference agreed to a general statement signifying our commitment to an alternative politics and laid plans for communication in the future.

The GPN also made plans to promote, both nationally and in the various states, the networking of Greens who were engaged in party building. Greg Gerritt and Tony Affigne took a lead here and soon developed a proposal for a confederation of independent state Green parties. The proposal was approved by the Missouri Green Party in January 1993, by the Maine Green Party in March, and by the Rhode Island Green Party in April of that year. Tony brought the proposal to the California Green Party plenary in June, where it was discussed informally, though no action was taken. Later in the fall, Greg sent a letter asking Green parties in Wisconsin, West Virginia, Pennsylvania, New Mexico, Colorado, Arkansas, and Arizona to sign on to the Confederation. Though the proposal provoked discussion, no action was taken by these states at that time. It was an idea that needed time to percolate, especially since it was perceived as being in competition with the G/GPUSA.

However, we were drawing a line that would become more and more clear and definitive as the years went by: that we were for a national Green Party based solidly in autonomous statewide Green Parties. We were already contrasting this to the inability or unwillingness of the Left Green Network, and of the G/GPUSA organization they had created, to provide a

193

home for state Green parties.

What we did that weekend was of course a challenge to G/GPUSA. They did not take it kindly. On the other hand, they also misconceived the challenge. They thought we were out to replace them, that GPN was itself presenting itself as the national party. There is much irony here. G/GPUSA was trumpeting itself as the national Green party when in fact no state parties participated in its founding and none at the moment were affiliated. Later one or two did, but feebly. The other part of the irony was that GPN, though reminding and reassuring everyone that we were not a national party and had no intention of becoming one, nevertheless began to be looked at by many, in praise or blame, as a national party, at least in embryo.

True enough, we sought to be a catalyst for a national party, but the national party we wanted would only come about when and if the various and individual state parties would associate together of their own volition. It was self-empowerment we were after. We were offering the table and chairs (the space), but — as Tony Affigne sought tirelessly to tell all and everyone — it was up to grassroots forces, the Greens in each of the states, to take up the offer and fill that space.

The Left Green leadership in G/GPUSA were furious. Instead of putting a good face on it, as they might have, and welcoming the initiative, they chose to take severe umbrage at what we were doing. Their restrictive left ideology apparently constrained their minds and robbed them of flexibility. They sought to paint us as renegades (a word often used) and as splitters of the movement. We were apostates, worse than heretics even, certainly worse than Democrats and Republicans. They phoned and wrote warning letters to the invited participants in our Third Force weekend in March of 1992, urging them not to attend, saying we were falsely pretending to be the national Green movement/party. They never tired of flailing us as "rightists," "elitists" and "politicians." They had at last discovered an "enemy": us. On the other hand we were said to be just a small band of discontented political hacks, of no account, and not to be paid any attention to. For years, they have had regular access to the pages of *Z Magazine* for their articles depicting us in these terms. Our efforts to respond in the same forum were as regularly turned down.

It is true that we were only a band of individuals, but as individuals we were each of us parts of local, state, and national networks of activists. GPN was a network of networks: not formally organized that way but each of our members was informally involved in multiple milieus of political and cultural work. Thus our influence and our power (relatively speaking) was considerable, both in our respective states and nationally. Small wonder the Left Greens and their G/GPUSA adherents were worried, given their misconception of our intention. It seemed to us a willful misconception. They wanted an enemy. They wanted, perhaps needed, someone to blame.

We were glad to be free. Though we heard Left Green fulminations against us, it was as if from a far distance. We were not held hostage in our projects and initiatives to their controlling harassment, as we had been for years. We could move ahead with what we called in a statement struck off at Hartland, "Urgent Tasks of the Green Movement." These included sparking Green parties in as many states as possible, developing a network of such parties, finding people to run for office, running for office ourselves, developing new organs of communication, fostering talk and action across third party lines, and, as the election of 1996 approached, seeking a presidential candidate.

As we expected, we were in no small measure aided in these endeavors by the growing activity of Greens running for office in many parts of the country. In the fall elections of 1992, Blair Bobier ran for Congress in Oregon, Linda Martin for U.S. Senate in Hawaii, Jonathan Carter for Congress in Maine, Abraham Guttman for state legislature in New Mexico, Mindy Lorenz for Congress in Southern California, Barbara Rodgers-Hendricks for Congress in Florida, Mark Dunlea for state legislature in New York, Jeff Barrow for Congress in Missouri, Carolyn Campbell for Congress in Arizona, and Dee Berry , in a petition drive, sought to get on the ballot to run for Lieutenant Governor in Missouri. And many Greens ran for local, nonpartisan offices. Jim Sykes had already gained party status for the Alaska Green Party in 1990 with a run for Governor and Kelly Weaverling had become the much acclaimed mayor of Cordova in that state.

Some of the candidates who ran in '92 were members of the Green Politics Network (Barbara, Blair, Carolyn, Mindy, and Dee) but most were not. As Greens made their foray into the political/electoral terrain, as they dealt with the nitty gritty of doing a campaign, reaching out beyond the "sandbox," they soon saw the limitations of an overly ideological purity. They saw the importance of reaching out to the mainstream and meeting them as fellow citizens and not, in the first instance, as militant activists.

During the next four years, 1993-96, we gradually added politically minded, ecologically grounded, organizers and activists to our membership. Each of us was active in our own local Green group and in our emerging statewide parties. We developed wide ranging contacts with like-minded Greens and with those in third party and political reform organizations. We did this primarily through three projects: we held a series of national conferences, beginning with the Third Force conference in March 1992; we promoted the idea of a confederation of independent state Green parties; and we published a newsletter/journal, *Green Horizon.*

In February, 1993, Becky Koulouros, the office coordinator of the Environmental Studies Program at Bowdoin College in Maine, and I organized a four day "alternative politics" conference at Bowdoin on the theme of "Doing It the Grass Roots Way." We did this in concert with many student organizations. All of the candidates mentioned above were invited and most came. They were joined by Sam Smith of the *Progressive Review* in Washington D.C.; by Mike Feinstein of the California Green Party who had just helped organize a very successful "Green Parties of the West" conference; by representatives of the Reform Party; by Ron Daniels' Campaign for a New Tomorrow; and by the Center for Voting and Democracy, a national organization dedicated to promoting proportional representation.

The Bowdoin conference sought to describe what an alternative politics could be and ought to be like. It was a breakthrough for all of us in the sense that we were now no longer arguing whether or not to engage in electoral politics and no longer embroiling ourselves in endless and vituperative rhetoric about its precise relationship to the rest of the movement. For the first time we could start with the assumption that we must be engaged in electoral politics and party building. And this enabled us to ask a fundamental question: what kind of politics, what kind of party, should we be thinking about and putting into practice? One of the sub-titles of the conference was "Fostering Public Conversation." It was an intimation of our growing consciousness that far more than "winning office" was at stake (though we took that seriously, too) and that we must henceforth view running for office as itself a way to change the dynamics and the structure of political parties and campaigning in the United States. We were reminding ourselves that in addition to just learning the ropes of campaigning, we needed to question the quality of politics itself.

These were substantial gains. But an equally significant gain for our continued political development was the entry into our GPN circles of Linda Martin and Sam Smith. Linda came to the Bowdoin conference fresh from her impressive run for the United States Senate in Hawaii in which she garnered 14% of the vote, the most any Green would receive for a national office until Carol Miller's 17% for Congress in New Mexico's Third Congressional District in April, 1997. Linda, who later moved to Virginia with her husband Michael Cornforth, brought to our organizing a powerful, focussed energy, and infectious enthusiasm, that would help spark several more national conferences, each more ambitious than the last, and would catapult us into Ralph Nader's campaign for president. Linda would become the director of the national Clearinghouse for that campaign.

Sam Smith brought a different style to our organizing and party build-

ing. His perspicacious wit, common sense understanding of political realities, and compelling insight into the political squalor of Washington D.C.
kept us balanced. He kept us aware that our major concern was to challenge Democrats and Republicans, not get embroiled in disputes with Left
Greens. He pushed us gently but persistently to search for a politics that
could communicate with ordinary people and build towards a new mainstream. His monthly *The Progressive Review* provided a continuing tonic
and outreach, his work with the D.C. Statehood Party and on many talk
shows spread the word for an alternative politics, and, though a self-styled
non-organizer, he nevertheless joined our team of conference organizers
for an alternative politics.

The team consisted of Tony Affigne, Linda Martin, Sam Smith, me,
and — beginning in 1994 — Hank Chapot of Oakland, California. Hank
joined us as a major figure in the Green Party of California, a candidate for
the state legislature, a gardener by profession, and a man of shrewd wit,
decisive action, and strong commitments. He took the lead in organizing a
conference in Oakland in June 1994. Its theme was "New Politics '94:
Nuts and Bolts for State and Local Victory." In addition to familiar themes,
we added a panel featuring representatives of several third parties, and
another panel featuring Greens-in-office at the local level. The third parties represented there were the New Party, Labor Party Advocates, Patriot
Party, Green Party, and California's Peace and Freedom Party.

During the remainder of 1994, most of us were caught up in political
campaigns in our respective states and in building our state parties. In
Maine, Greg Gerritt ran for the state legislature for the second time. In his
previous run, in 1986, he got 16% of the vote in a three-way race. This
time, again facing a Republican and a Democrat, he got 20.2%. These
totals indicate the substantial strength the Green Party does command. It
exceeds the numbers obtained by Green Parties in Europe, for example.
But, whereas in Europe, their vote totals of between 5% and 15% secure
many seats in Parliament and considerable political leverage, here in the
United States, even 20% in a three-way race yields no representation for
one fifth of the voters, and gets barely a mention in the media. The difference is that in Europe, as in almost all democracies, the voting system is by
proportional representation, not the first-past-the-post system still in operation in the United States.

In the 1994 campaign, I threw myself into Jonathan Carter's gubernatorial bid, a campaign that attracted wide public attention. Jonathan's run
for Congress in the 2nd District two years before had netted him and the
Greens over 10% of the vote, a total that infuriated the Democrats who
blamed the Green Party for enabling Republican Olympia Snowe to defeat
their candidate Pat McGowan. Since Olympia, having survived a possible

defeat in 1992, would later run successfully for the U.S. Senate, the Democrats started blaming the Greens for Olympia's rise. Whether this was truly the case or not (exit polls by Maine Public Radio in 1992 showed Jonathan getting a substantial Republican vote as well as votes from Independents who otherwise would not have bothered to vote), in the eyes of many politicians and the press, the political landscape in Maine was beginning to shift because of the Greens. On election day in November of 1994, Jonathan received 6.5% of the vote in the gubernatorial race, enough to qualify the Green Party as an official political party along with the Ds and the Rs. It was the first officially recognized Green Party east of the Mississippi.

In New Mexico, the Greens came alive in 1994. Abraham Guttman had run for a state legislative seat in 1992, preparing the way by getting over 40% of the vote. Now, in 1994, the Greens recruited Roberto Mondragon, former Democratic Lieutenant Governor and a much respected member of the Hispanic community, to run for Governor. His running mate was Steven Schmidt, a talented strategist and political savant, who had worked closely with Jerry Brown and his campaign for president in 1992. The Mondragon/Schmidt campaign put the Green Party on the political map in their state with over 10% of the vote.

Both Abraham and Steve, though not members of GPN, were kindred spirits and as the years went by we drew closer and would become strong allies in 1996/97 in the formation of the Association of State Green Parties. In the '94 campaign, Steve put a great deal of effort into a comprehensive Green Platform for New Mexico, one that would later inform the Nader presidential campaign. It would also become a foundation stone thereafter for the Association of State Green Parties.

Steve and Abraham both worked closely with Cris Moore in building the New Mexico Green Party. Cris had won a nonpartisan seat on the Santa Fe City Council and soon became a leading figure there, as well as a strong voice in New Mexico and nationally for electoral politics and party building of a kind that was broadly rooted in fighting for people's issues and community strengthening at the grassroots. We in GPN were impressed and gratified by his politics and his alliance with Abraham and Steve. Cris was a Left Green with a difference. His experience with the nitty gritty of campaigning and as an elected official spurred him towards practical and yet principled action. The working relationship that Cris developed with other leading figures in the New Mexico Green Party has proved extremely beneficial. It was also important nationally. Cris would take a big initiative in 1995 by calling a national gathering, independently of G/GPUSA, of Greens of all persuasions and organizations. It was held in Albuquerque in early August of that year.

In Hawaii there were several kindred spirits deeply engaged in Green political work: Barbara Bell and Ira Rohter, often in the leadership of the Hawaii Green Party as co-chairs, and Keiko Bonk and Toni Worst, leading candidates for office. Though not members of GPN, they talked and walked a kind of politics that we supported and sought to learn from. Keiko was the only Green to win a partisan election in the United States up to that time, having been elected to the County Council on Big Island, a powerful position in a body that was split evenly between Democrats and Republicans. Toni Worst ran a strong campaign in 1994 for state legislature in the Manoa district and got over 40% of the vote.

In California, Kent Smith ran for the U.S. Senate in the Green primary, Hank Chapot ran for the state legislature, and Danny Moses campaigned for Lieutenant Governor. Danny had taken a leading role in the Green Committees of Correspondence and was a consistent ally in our struggles with the Left Green Network. After the Elkins gathering in 1991, he dropped national politics and concentrated his Green work in California.

In Rhode Island, Tony Affigne, though not himself running for office, provided major support for Jeff Johnson in his Green Party campaign for Lieutenant Governor and Anna Cardillo Martin's run for State Senate for Providence's North End.

In Missouri, Terri Williams, member of GPN, won an astounding upset victory for mayor of Webster Grove. Matt Harline, a kindred spirit, won re-election to the Columbia City Council. And in Pennsylvania, Thomas Linzey, about to join our Third Parties '96 Team, was a Green write-in candidate for governor of Pennsylvania.

These were budding times. Those of us in GPN found ourselves in touch with most Greens who ran for office and/or with those who won office. There was an instant "sympatico" relationship. We were all talking a similar talk and walking that talk. GPN was a strong voice in the country for taking electoral politics and party building seriously. At the same time we were learning, through our practice and our reflections on that practice, to take seriously the need to build a party of a different kind.

Chapter 16
Crossing the Threshold

1995 was a watershed year for national Green political development. The Green Politics Network team of Tony Affigne, Hank Chapot, Linda Martin, Sam Smith, and I organized two national third party get-togethers that led to a turning point conference in January 1996 under the rubric of Third Parties '96. Cris Moore, together with the New Mexico Green Party, successfully brought together Greens of all persuasions for a national Green gathering in Albuquerque in late July. Steve Schmidt, of the New Mexico Green Party, working closely with Mike Feinstein and Greg Jan of the California Green Party, initiated a "40-State Green Party Organizing Effort" that aimed to coalesce with a hoped for campaign of a Green presidential candidate in 1996. These efforts converged in stimulating Ralph Nader to agree in late November 1995 to run for president in California's Green Party primary in 1996. By early '96 he had decided to run in many states under the Green banner. This move from consumer advocate to political partisan by a respected and famous national and world figure spurred Green Party building in dozens of states.

Immediately following the November election, representatives of 31 state Green parties met together with Ralph Nader in Middleburg, Virginia to launch the Association of State Green Parties. With this action, Greens in the United States finally crossed the threshold into the realm of national politics with a clear intention to build a party of a different kind based on autonomous state Green parties.

Finding a Presidential Candidate

For a time, however, it seemed that the various Green projects of 1995 might diverge and splinter. The major theme of Third Parties '96 was "Transcending Left, Right, and Center: Building the New Mainstream." We had two goals in mind: first, to bring together a loose network of as many third party and kindred political organizations as possible; and, second, to look for, find, nominate, and run a candidate for president.

On the other hand, the trio of Steve Schmidt, Michael Feinstein and Greg Jan — though supportive of our coalition strategy—promoted a distinctly Green Party approach. They figured that a Green presidential candidate would spark the building of Green Parties in many states. They also, Steve especially, wanted to begin working on a national Green platform—based on the one developed in New Mexico for the gubernatorial campaign in 1994. In conversations at the Green Gathering in Albuquerque, and thereafter, the Third Parties '96 team and the trio maintained close communication. We were positioning ourselves to go either way, depending on the candidate and how he or she wanted to run: on a coalition ticket under an appropriate name, or on a Green ticket.

In June, 1995, the Third Parties '96 team brought together a broad spectrum of over two dozen parties and kindred political organizations in Washington D.C. We looked for things we had in common rather than lingering over things that would keep us apart. The more than one hundred participants included representatives of the Libertarian Party, Reform Party, New Party, Natural Law Party, Labor Party, Socialist Party and Green Party.

We produced a document called "Common Ground Declaration." It contained 17 items on which there was complete agreement and over a dozen others that got "near consensus" (at least 60%). The statements on which we reached complete agreement included the following.

We support proportional representation.

We support campaign finance reform to provide a level playing field in elections.

We believe that all economic activities should improve and protect the health of the earth, while promoting the happiness and prosperity of its inhabitants.

We must end corporate welfare.

We would encourage, through economic measures and education, the practices of source reduction, reuse, and recycling, and we advocate the elimination of toxic, nuclear, and other environmentally harmful substances.

We oppose race and class distinctions in exposure to environmental hazards, in communities and workplaces, including the siting of toxic waste facilities, employment in hazardous industries, and the location of energy and mining facilities.

We support people's right to control their own sexual and reproductive lives.

We would cut military expenditures dramatically, AND provide for displaced workers.

We believe that economic decisions should be made democratically, with participation by all affected workers, communities and consumers.

We support the maximum empowerment of people in their communities, consistent with fairness, social responsibility and human rights, to meet local needs, and to defend those communities against exploitative forces.

Rob Hager, an investigative lawyer and friend of Ralph Nader, contacted

Linda as a result of our June Third Parties '96 conference and its Common Ground Declaration. He had written a paper giving an analysis of corporate domination and the possibilities inherent in the American political situation for mounting a strong counter-force that drew on a large number of political tendencies and constituencies.. He liked our "neither left nor right, new mainstream" approach and considered it a refreshing change from both sectarian left politics and from the corporate-bound liberalism of progressives still hanging in with the Democratic Party. He began to think that Ralph Nader might be persuaded to run for president. During that summer and fall he bent his efforts in that direction.

He and we were hoping to persuade a number of progressive leaders in the country to think of themselves as a presidential team, one of whom would be the official candidate, the others supporting him or her as part of an unofficial cabinet. We and Steve Schmidt sought to persuade Jim Hightower of Texas to join such a team and indeed to think of himself being the candidate. And through Steve Cobble, a leading organizer in the Rainbow Coalition and member of the New Party, we were seeking contact with Jesse Jackson to propose a similar possibility to him. During this time, I also tried to involve the New Party in our national conferences. Both Joel Rogers and Danny Cantor, founders of the New Party, had responded to a degree. Danny and Sue Wall, a New Party organizer in Portland, Oregon, helped to plan the Oakland '94 conference, and Danny participated in some of the Washington D.C. Third Parties '96 discussions. I now sought to persuade them to join us in fielding a presidential team and finding a candidate.

But the New Party hung back. Jim Hightower decided to stick with the Democrats, in spite of his towering rhetoric condemning the corporate policies of the both major parties. Jesse Jackson did not respond.

Yet the pressure was building for a progressive to run for president in 1996. Ronnie Dugger wrote a thrilling and instantly famous article in the *Nation Magazine* in August, 1995 calling for a breakthrough in national politics, one that would take a clear stand against corporate domination of both major parties. He received over 1000 letters. On that basis, he and others went forward with plans to develop a national alliance, one that eventually bore fruit in the formation, in November 1996, of the Alliance for Democracy. But at the time, the fall of 1995, it was but one more current in the progressive political winds.

In a different key, IPPN (Independent Progressive Politics Network), a movement that grew out of Ron Daniels' bid for president in 1992, held a national conference in Pittsburgh in August. They were particular about who was and was not "a progressive," and thus critical of our Third Parties '96 new mainstream approach. They also put less emphasis on electoral politics and party building than we did. Nevertheless, they now declared their support for action by progressives in the electoral sphere. Linda Martin was invited to give a talk at their conference.

By early fall, Rob Hager was having conversations with Mike Feinstein and other Greens in California and there was more and more talk of a possible presidential run by Ralph Nader. A group of leading Greens and progressives in California made a strong plea to Nader to consider this.

In November, the Third Parties '96 campaign went to Boulder, Colorado for a follow up conference to the one in June in Washington, and as preparation for a possibly decisive conference to be held in Washington in early January 1996. In the morning of the last day of this conference, we got the news that Ralph Nader had given his okay to run in California's Green Party primary for president. Spirits soared, and we headed for the Washington conference with proposals for an expanded Common Ground Declaration and, we hoped, a kind of kickoff for a national campaign for the presidency headed by Ralph Nader. However, at this point Ralph had only committed himself to run in the California Green primary

At the December Council meeting of the Maine Green Party, I proposed that we call on Ralph to be our state party candidate for president in 1996. The call, which passed unanimously and with great enthusiasm, was immediately sent to Ralph. Linda and I, on behalf of Third Parties '96, wrote Ralph urging him to attend the conference. Through the good offices of Lance Tapley, a Maine friend of Ralph's, I spoke by phone with Ralph two days before the conference. He invited me to lunch at Andy Shallal's restaurant just up the street from his Center for the Study of Responsive Law on P Street in Washington.

At this lunch, the day before the conference, Ralph announced that he planned to run in Maine, all the way, and to do the same in California. His reasons for running in Maine, he told me, were to help the Maine Green Party to grow; to help get the American people to think seriously about an alternative to the two major corporate-dominated parties; and to "send a message" to President Clinton. It was assumed that he meant he was open to running in many other states as well, but Ralph was reluctant to affirm this. He would instead get into the presidential campaign on a state by state basis during the coming spring and summer. Some felt the process took much too long, that we missed opportunities to get him on the ballot in many states, that instead of the 21 states where this did happen it might well have been 40. In any case, I urged him again to join us at the Third Parties '96 conference and it was arranged for him to address the group the next day.

That night, Ralph came down with a bad cold, and could not attend. The conference on Friday and Saturday continued to expand on the Common Ground Declaration. But plans for follow up on the Nader campaign and continued coalition building, intended for discussion Sunday, were interrupted and cancelled by an immense blizzard. Still, in the next few days, by phone and email, we laid the groundwork for a national Nader for President Clearinghouse to be located in Washington. Linda Martin would take the lead. Local Greens across the country were contacted and got involved. These, plus the contacts we had made in the preceding years, helped her and the many people she attracted, to develop a national network and to assist state groups to get Nader on the ballot. Communication, though not always smooth, did develop between the Clearinghouse and the 40 State Parties project of Greg Jan, Mike Feinstein, and Steve Schmidt.

Thomas Linzey was among the people who joined Linda's ambitious endeavor. Thomas, a young lawyer in Pennsylvania, had run for governor in that state in 1994. He had also founded the Community Environmental Legal Defense Fund and was becoming an expert in election rules and law. He was later to become the legal counsellor for the Association of State Green Parties when it was launched in Middleburg, Virginia, immediately following the '96 election. In working with Linda's Clearinghouse, he proved to be a catalyst for organizers and provider of critically important legal and administrative information for the groups that formed in dozens of states around the Nader for president campaign.

As we moved into the Nader campaign, the "coalition building" side of our political endeavors took a back seat, though we did make a serious, but unsuccessful, effort to get someone to continue the Third Parties '96 effort. We would later come back to coalition building, but now building the Green party was closer to our hearts. Not only was it the chosen vehicle of Ralph Nader, but the Greens seemed more and more the one third party that could embrace the hopes, longings, and convictions of millions of Americans.

We saw the need to reach out in a respectful and genuine way to other third parties and kindred political organizations, but primarily we wanted to promote, cajole into being, and work like hell to fulfill our dream of a national Green Party.

Close Encounters Once Again

This, however, meant having to deal once more with the Left Greens and with the organization they dominated, the Greens/Green Party USA (G/GPUSA), though now from a position of strength. For several years we in GPN had paid only minimal attention to the goings-on of G/GPUSA. We had been greatly relieved to wrench free, organizationally and emotionally, from the infighting that had begun to demoralize the internal politics of the Green Committees of Correspondence in its last two years. We heard tales of the same thing happening to the successor organization created at the Elkins Green Gathering in 1991, G/GPUSA.

Following Elkins, G/GPUSA worked hard to make its next gathering in Minneapolis in August 1992 a success. They attracted a large number of Greens. They added to and revised certain portions of their national program. I was pleased that they improved the section dealing with the economy, which formerly had a knee-jerk anticapitalist and pro-socialist cast to it. They also appeared to acknowledge the rising statewide Green parties (perhaps to head off a confederation of state Green parties) by opening their Green Council to representatives from state parties. The state parties, however, would continue to have no representation at the annual Congress, which remained the policy making and directive force in G/GPUSA.

Few states responded. The Alaska Green Party joined, but only provisionally since they were dissatisfied with the Green Program. Much later, a New York Green party, led by Howie Hawkins, would also join. But most states temporized or refused to join. They decided to put the idea of a national organization on the back burner. It was clear to a growing number of Greens that Greens, once they got serious about creating a political party, were not overly enthused by an organization that made little room for them.

After Minneapolis, the fortunes of G/GPUSA declined precipitously. Poor management pushed them ever deeper into a debt that reached nearly $45,000 in a few years time. Infighting over the location and control of their Clearinghouse consumed most of their energy for two years. Betty Wood won that battle and established the G/GPUSA headquarters, near Howie Hawkins, in Syracuse, New York.

The organization perhaps hit its nadir in 1994, when less than a score of Greens showed up for its annual gathering in Boise, Idaho. Via the lavish use of proxies, just a few persons from a few locals now controlled the organization. These locals were in St. Louis, Syracuse, and Southern California, in each case led by deeply committed Left Greens, skeptical of, if not strongly opposed to, electoral politics, unless it was clearly accountable to social movement activists in local groups.

The crisis of G/GPUSA, widely perceived as such, pushed Cris Moore to take his own initiative. Cris had always been favorable to the Left Green approach and philosophy. But he also believed sincerely in electoral politics and had won a seat on the Santa Fe City Council. His experiences and his native political smarts made him less and less enamored of the more intense Left Greens who had come to have much influence, if not outright control of, the G/GPUSA. He and the New Mexico Green Party agreed to call a national gathering for late July/early August of 1995 in Albuquerque. They did this without the approval of G/GPUSA. The latter, however, had no choice but to go along with Cris's very popular initiative.

In the spring of 1995, partly in preparation for the Albuquerque conference, there emerged a proposal to convene a national "Green Coordination." It came about this way. Mike Feinstein and I had been having phone conversations off and on since the Bowdoin conference in 1993. We discussed the gamut of Green affairs in our respective states, in the nation, and especially in Europe where Mike had attended many Green conferences and about which he had written a book (*Sixteen Weeks with European Greens*, 1992). We kept coming back to the perilous condition of the Green movement nationally and how frustratingly slow was our evolution towards an authentic, credible national party. I argued for building a network of independent state Green parties, both for its own sake and to push the G/GPUSA into either going along or going off in their own direction. Mike, though agreeing that we must build the national party as soon as possible, thought it could best be done through a transforming process within G/GPUSA. I kept pointing out that we had tried that. "Been there, done that," was my riposte. He kept saying, "Well, let's try again."

Shortly before the scheduled Third Parties '96 conference June 1-4, Mike and I talked about the recently created European Federation of Green Parties. The founding of that federation in Helsinki in June, 1993 (attended by both Mike Feinstein and Linda Martin) was greatly facilitated by the previous formation of a loosely organized network called "The Green Coordination." Each of the participating Green parties in Europe had equal representation. It was for talks only, not for making decisions. Out of those talks however came the basis for the founding of a Federation.

We saw the possibility of adapting this idea to our national situation. We would call for a free and open convening of a Green Coordination in which all the national organizations (meaning especially, both G/GPUSA and GPN) would participate equally. Indeed, state parties would also be invited, and the implication was that any interested local would also be welcome. No decisions would be made at such a meeting or follow up meetings. But here would be a safe space to sort out differences and conflicts. Hopefully, this would lead to a way forward acceptable to all.

After the close of the Third Parties '96 conference, on a Sunday evening at Sam Smith's house in Washington, a large number of Greens got together to talk and "hang out." There I presented the idea Mike and I had come up with. It was well received by the wide variety of Greens, including Cris Moore, who would shortly be hosting the Albuquerque conference. Tom Cadorette of the Virginia Green Party, a member of both G/GPUSA and GPN, volunteered to get it on the agenda at the former's Congress that was scheduled to take place following Cris's Albuquerque conference.

Several state parties signed on to the proposal in the next few weeks. At Albuquerque, over a dozen of us connected with GPN approved it on behalf of GPN. G/GPUSA's Congress had difficulty accepting it, but in the end approved, after making some changes in the language.

We now thought that maybe some modification had occurred in the steadfast claim of G/GPUSA to be the only legitimate national Green organization. We were to be disappointed. That fall, an effort to convene a meeting of the Green Coordination by two "unaligned" Greens in Colorado, Dean Myerson and Allison Burshell, was squelched by members of the Green Council of G/GPUSA. This was followed, in December, by an announcement from the St. Louis Gateway Greens, a strong bulwark of G/GPUSA, led by Don Fitz and Jeff Suter, that they would host a Green Coordination meeting in St. Louis the following spring. There had been no prior consultation with the original signatories, nor with any state Green party, nor with GPN. The meeting would be held simultaneously with, and presumably be part of, the regular meeting of G/GPUSA's Council. GPN, in a strong letter to all the state parties and to G/GPUSA, declined to attend. The Green Coordination was dead.

Meanwhile, Mike Feinstein went forward with his plan to host a national/international Green Gathering in Los Angeles in August '96, which he hoped would also be a nominating convention for a Green presidential candidate. His dream was coming true. By the spring of that year, Linda Martin's national clearinghouse for the Nader campaign was in full swing, as were the endeavors of Mike, Greg Jan, and Steve Schmidt in their "40-State Green Parties in '96" project.

The Los Angeles conference was done in the style of the Albuquerque gathering of the year before. G/GPUSA was part of it, but only in the same way as other Green organizations. This is the way Mike wanted it. He got a great deal of grief as a result. He had trekked to St. Louis in late March to consult with their Green Council and was roundly, even bitterly, attacked, but he and his cohorts persevered. There would be a place for G/GPUSA but they would not have the guiding, deciding role.

The conference ran from Thursday through Monday the third weekend in August. By Sunday evening, after many workshops and plenary sessions on a variety of topics, the gathering began to shift gears. On Monday morning there was a session of the Congress of G/GPUSA, but a press conference by Ralph Nader also took place late morning, leading to the nominating convention in the afternoon and evening.

Late Sunday evening something happened which, at this eleventh hour, might still have resulted in unity among the different Green organizations. During the preceding three days, I had been approached by various Greens, sounding me out on my current feelings towards interaction of some kind with G/GPUSA. Jana Cutlip, the President of its Green Council, was one. She had participated in the first Third Parties '96 conference. A number of people wanted to take advantage of the presence of so many Greens of a variety of persuasions at the gathering. There was a fairly chaotic informal session early Sunday evening that expended itself in much talk.

But there was an interesting proposal that was going to be brought forward by Cris Moore at the G/GPUSA meeting the next day, Monday. He was calling for the abolition of their Congress and the transformation of their Green Council into a body representative of the state Green parties. Chris was taking this action with the backing of the New Mexico Green Party. The latter had just passed a bold resolution calling for the "establishment of an Association of State Green Parties for the purposes of being a National Committee to take care of the electoral needs of the Green Party."

Cris's proposal was a harbinger of the actual Association of State Green Parties that would form after the November election, and it borrowed much from the idea of a Confederation of State Green Parties which GPN had been fostering for several years. Cris had strong Left Green credentials, he had been the guiding force in the national gathering of Greens in 1995, and he represented a state that was widely regarded among the Greens in all parts of the country as a leading exponent of a party of a different kind. Here he was advocating a national association of State Green parties! Many of us were impressed. . . and delighted. We felt that this could lead to something creative at the national level of Green Party organizing.

As I mulled this over, thinking that his proposal would nevertheless run into heavy weather the next morning in G/GPUSA's Congress, it occurred to me to suggest amending the plan. Don't abolish the Congress, was my thought, but call upon it to continue to meet as an advisory body to the newly minted Green Council composed of representatives of the state Green parties. I ran across Cris Moore in the halls that Sunday evening and he said he would not object to such an amendment.

Somewhat later in the evening, Jana and I happened to cross paths. We began talking and it was soon apparent that we both had come up with the same idea! Our enthusiasm built and we worked out a proposal that Jana would make the next morning in conjunction with Cris's proposal. I checked out my idea and our plans the next morning early with other members of GPN. They were skeptical but supportive.

The Congress meeting turned out to be a great debacle. An inordinate amount of time was spent by the delegates in getting started. Some of them challenged the way the meeting was being run and who was running it. In retrospect, this was probably intended, since a number of delegates apparently did not want Cris's proposal and the amendment to come to the floor. The fracas ate up the time. Eventually the proposal was brought up, with very limited time available. Nader's press conference was due to start. Most people in the hall felt quite positive about the proposal and about our amendment. There was some criticism but also strong support. Then, Kwazi Nkrumah, a leading force in the G/GPUSA for years, rose and spoke in favor, but on condition that the new state-based Green Council as proposed would retain representation for the various identity caucuses (people of color, environmental justice, women, youth, and gays and lesbians). He asked me if I would support him in this. Though I had, over the years, enthusiastically promoted such special representation, I had also begun to question its usefulness. But I thought hard and told him I would support that. He then gave a strong endorsement to our proposal. It seemed clear that the tide was turning in the hall towards approval. But in the vote on a procedural motion whether or not to bring it to the floor, the motion lost. The locals from St. Louis and Syracuse, deeply opposed to the proposal, and led respectively by Don Fitz and Betty Wood, had the proxy votes to defeat it.

The meeting disbanded amidst great turmoil, anger, confusion and general distress. Don Fitz, nevertheless, proclaimed the vote as another victory for democracy. From his perspective and convictions, and those of the Left Greens generally, it was not as outlandish a claim as it appeared to many there. Had he not defended the integrity of the G/GPUSA Congress? Was not the Congress the chamber of representatives of local groups of activists, and were not these activists dedicated to a social-movement kind of politics that far outshone in real value mere electoral activity and party building? That's how it must have seemed to him and his supporters.

Yet, the fact that proxy votes, wielded by two or three people, gave Don Fitz et al the victory, was viewed by many as the antithesis of democracy. In addition it came to be known more widely that, in cases of uncertainty as to who was entitled to how many proxies, the decision was made by Betty Wood as Clearing House Coordinator. But Betty was also casting votes, her own and that of several proxies. These anomalies, adding to the other problems of G/GPUSA, eroded their credibility as an organization.

As I left Los Angeles and returned to my campaign for the U.S. Senate in Maine, I realized more sharply than ever that Don Fitz, Betty Wood, Kwame Nkrumah and others of the Left Green persuasion were interested in a different kind of organization from the one that we favored. Yet, what was frustrating to us was their determination to keep party building under the control of people who were not interested in, nor even very good at, doing electoral politics and party building. Why would they not let us proceed to do our thing?

On the other hand, why were so many Greens who wanted to go forward with party building continuing to stay in G/GPUSA? Why stay and try to squelch, in the name of transforming the organization, those Greens who were deeply committed to a social-movement type of organization? Why not just leave the organization, as so many were doing and let it be what it apparently wanted to be? Were they being fair to Don Fitz and others of a like persuasion? Why not acknowledge that here was a clear case of apples and oranges?

After that bruising event, the Nader press conference and nominating convention went forward with elan the remainder of the day. It was a stirring occasion. 600 delegates and friends jammed the auditorium. A representative of each state in which Nader was on the ballot or in which he would be a write-in candidate had the opportunity to affirm that Nader was indeed their candidate and to declare why he was. This was followed by speeches from Winona LaDuke, the eventual Vice Presidential candidate; Keiko Bonk of the Hawaiian Green Party and twice-elected County Council member on the island of Hawaii; Ronnie Dugger, founder of the *Texas Observer* and of the Alliance for Democracy; and Dan Hamburg, former Democratic Congressman who changed to the Green Party and would later be the Green Party's 1998 candidate for Governor of California. Nader entered the hall to great acclaim and gave a powerful and persuasive acceptance speech. It probably set a US record for length of a presidential candidate's acceptance speech, running 2 hours and 15 minutes.

The Green Politics Network had a successful retreat on Tuesday and Wednesday following the conference, after which we all returned to our states, most of us to electoral campaigns.

I had hardly gotten back to Maine, when I received a phone call from Mike Feinstein. He had just learned that, unbeknownst to any of us at the Los Angeles meeting, the G/GPUSA leadership had two weeks earlier submitted an application to the Federal Elections Commission for official status as the Green Party of the United States. In it they claimed for their own organization all the Green candidates for national political office of the past several years. Most of these candidacies (like Abraham Gutmann's for U.S. Senate in New Mexico, or like mine for U.S. Senate in Maine, and scores of others) were conducted wholly separate from the auspices of G/GPUSA. We had run as candidates of our state Green parties. Indeed few if any of us ever even thought of G/GPUSA as having any electoral connection or electoral interest. In addition, G/GPUSA had contacted almost no one from among those whom they claimed as "their" candidates to see if they would agree to be so listed., even though this is required by law. A motive that probably figured strongly in this desperate move was the possibility, however slight it might be, that Ralph Nader would get 5% of the vote, in which case, a national Green Party would be eligible for several million dollars in matching funds in the next election.

Mike was extremely upset at what he regarded, quite rightly, as deception, even fraud. As was Steven Schmidt, whose race for Lieutenant Governor in New Mexico in 1994 had been claimed for G/GPUSA, without his knowledge. It was a turning point in Mike's political evolution. Thereafter, he was ready to consider seriously the creation of a national political party separate from G/GPUSA.

Hank Chapot was another whose candidacy was claimed by G/GPUSA. Hank immediately filed a brief with the FEC, contesting G/GPUSA's application as misleading and invalid. It was an opportune and effective intervention. In the week following the election, the FEC turned down G/GPUSA's application.

Full Court Press for an Association

We decided to press again, and more forcefully now, the case for an association of independent state Green parties. We found a vigorous ally in Bert Garskof in Connecticut. Bert was taking a lead in the Nader campaign in Ralph's home state and, along with Tom Sevigny and others, was building the foundation of a Connecticut Green Party. He pushed for an Association via email during the six weeks before the November election, stimulating considerable debate and various other proposals, some stemming from people still attached to G/GPUSA.

The campaign for the U.S. Senate in Maine was moving at a dizzying pace by late September. Almost every day there was a debate somewhere in Maine with my three opponents. Linda Martin and Thomas Linzey were also fully absorbed in the work of the Nader Clearing House in Washington. We felt, however, that we had to think beyond the election and have a strategy in hand. I remember urging Linda, Thomas, and Bert that we must call a meeting of all the statewide groups involved in the Nader campaign as soon as possible after the election. The national Nader for President Clearing House, which had the respect of Green organizers across the country, would be pivotal in drawing people to the meeting. But it would disband soon after the election. The level of enthusiasm and commitment to a new politics, inspired by the Nader campaign, was bound to taper off if we waited until spring, as some were advocating. They agreed.

Linda, ever resourceful, had located a spacious home in Middleburg, Virginia for the meeting. Elaine Broadhead would make her elegant and homey Glenora Farm available. We drafted a call and received the unanimous approval of the Connecticut and Maine Green parties to issue it in their name. We worked out a date with Ralph Nader so that he could be there. This proved difficult because of his full schedule and because many weekends were already taken up by other meetings important to at least some of us, including the founding convention of Ronnie Dugger's Alliance for Democracy. But we finally focussed on the weekend of November 15-16, only ten days after the election.

I remember well the feeling of urgency. It was partly fueled by the futility of dealing any longer with G/GPUSA. We had tried the Green Coordination, only to have it hijacked and made of no account. Similarly, the "great compromise" as Jana Cutlip of G/GPUSA and I considered our friendly amendment to Cris Moore's proposal in Los Angeles, had been spurned by G/GPUSA's Congress. These debacles were followed by the disclosure of a possibly fraudulent and certainly misleading and unilateral application to the FEC by G/GPUSA. We had gone down the road of seeking a *modus vivendi* more than was necessary or sensible. It was time to move to a genuine association of state Green parties.

In the wording of the letter that went out to all the states that had fielded Nader campaigns, we were concerned that we not leave anything unclear on the central issue. The letter therefore read as follows: "The meeting is not about whether to form such a union of state Green parties, but is intended to proceed to its formation effectively, building on the momentum and enthusiasm generated by the Draft Nader effort in more than 40 states."

The Middleburg gathering fulfilled our hopes and exceeded our expectations. Representatives from 31 state Green parties/groups came together for two days. Eleven state Green parties had empowered their representatives to enter into an Association, which they did. Ralph Nader was joyously received by the conferees. Rudimentary bylaws were adopted, beginning with this statement of purpose: "1. Assist in the development of state Green parties. 2. Create a legally structured national Green Party." The word "federation" would be added at the next meeting in Oregon, so that number 2 would read: "Create a legally structured national Green Party Federation."

The Gathering Strength of ASGP

This was a new beginning for Greens in their long quest for a national Green political party. The eleven state Green parties that launched the Association of State Green Parties (ASGP) were Arizona, Arkansas, Connecticut, Washington D.C. (the Association acknowledges the host of our nation's capitol as a free state) Maine, Nevada, Oregon, Rhode Island, Tennessee, Utah, and Wyoming.

The Association attracted five more state Green parties by the time of its formal establishment in Portland, Oregon the weekend of April 4-6, 1997: New Mexico, Virginia, Ohio, Colorado, and Michigan, in that order. Four more— Hawaii, Massachusetts, New Jersey, and Pennsylvania— joined in the interval between the Oregon meeting and the next meeting in Maine, October 3-5, 1997. A thorny and competitive situation in New York did not deter either claimant to the Green banner in that state from joining, one gaining provisional status at the Maine meeting, and the other coming on board six weeks later. By the time of the spring '98 meeting in Santa Fe, New Mexico, April 24-26, 21 state Green parties had come together and the ASGP was zooming towards the formation of a national Green Party rooted in autonomous state Green parties. In early summer, 1998, the Minnesota Green Party and the Georgia Green Party applied to join the Association and, following a positive report from the Association's Accreditation Committee, were accepted unanimously.

The California Green Party voted to apply for ASGP membership on November 21, 1998. It was a close vote. The party Bylaws required an 80% majority to pass. The final tally showed 80.5% in favor! A small group loyal to G/GPUSA lobbied strongly against joining; they had been successful two years earlier by a very narrow margin. But by '98 the momentum for joining was too strong for a holdout group to succeed in preventing what the overwhelming majority favored. The addition of California is a milestone and moves the Greens nationally more closely than ever to a credible and politically serious national party.

The new Association, at the Middleburg meeting that launched ASGP, formed a Coordinating Committee composed of two delegates from each of the member state Green parties. This across-the-board numerical equality of representation was preferred by the member states as a way to get started. At the Maine meeting, a year later, a seven-person Transition Committee was elected to explore options for a proportional allocation of delegates, both to the ASGP Coordinating Committee and to a presidential nominating convention in 2000. The attempt would be to establish a proportionality that is fair to both small and large states (which may be at various stages of development and success) and to fairly represent the diversity within and among state Green parties.

In their report to the Santa Fe ASGP meeting in the spring of '98, the Transition Committee recommended, and the meeting agreed to, a continuation of the two representatives per state arrangement for the Coordinating Committee. They presented a time line for a gradual shift to some degree of proportionality as between big and small states, however, so that by the year 2000, the parties in the bigger states would have more representation than the smaller ones on the Coordinating Committee (some were suggesting a cap of no more than five for the bigger states). The Transition Committee would also be recommending a proportional arrangement for the presidential nominating convention in 2000. Their findings and recommendations would be presented at the next meeting of the ASGP, scheduled for the spring of 1999.

The Coordinating Committee, at their face to face national meetings, elect three Co-Chairs, a Secretary and a Treasurer to serve until the next national meeting. Thomas Linzey of Shippensburg, Pennsylvania, who had been providing legal and administrative services for member state parties, was confirmed in the Portland, Oregon meeting in April '97 as the ASGP legal advisor and counsellor. He was also given the go-ahead to develop a Clearing House for the Association. Several committees were established and plans went forward to develop a decision making methodology for email. Almost all of the delegates are on line.

One of the most significant features of the new Association was that many of the people forming it were Greens new to the national scene and/ or people new to the Green party and movement. For the most part they had been drawn into the Green parties in their states by the Nader campaigns; or, they had been active in their state Green parties or locals but had not gotten involved in the national Green scene. Those of us who had taken the lead for several years were suddenly joined by a host of new or returning Greens ready to take leadership roles.

From the start of the Association, therefore, its leadership was a blend of "old" and "new" people. Gradually, still newer people would be coming in and this distinction would also be swiftly transcended. The fortunes and destiny of the new organization, feeling its way to a fully fledged national Green Party, was now securely in the hands of the member state Green Parties and their own elected and responsible leaders.

Sorting Out the Backlash

Though it seemed that everything was coming up roses at Middelburg and subsequently, there were still plenty of thorns. At first, after Middleburg, it was mostly thorns. Mike Feinstein had predicted, during our meeting at Middleburg, that there would be an outcry from G/GPUSA. He also predicted that thereafter things would settle down and ASGP would be able to move forward. This turned out to be the case. But it was more than an outcry, it was a cascade of anger and excoriation. The vehicle for the outburst was the internet's Green Forum which had somewhat over 100 Green email subscribers.

The objections were primarily based on the fact that a conference like Middleburg was called at all. G/GPUSA had for years claimed to be the national Green party and movement all in one. Now an apparent upstart had dared to stake a claim.

The critics missed two important facts. One was that ASGP did not claim to be "the movement." More importantly, ASGP did not claim to be, as yet, the national Green Party. It was establishing a new principle for a national Green Party: such a party must be based on autonomous state-wide parties. This sharply distinguished it from G/GPUSA which contin-ued to be controlled by bodies of activists in a few scattered locals across the country. These bodies, in turn, were controlled by people whose pri-mary concern was social activism and not electoral politics. Thus, a com-pelling argument could be made that ASGP and G/GPUSA were two very different kinds of organizations.

But these points were lost on the critics in and about G/GPUSA. They saw a competitor; they saw a competitor already up and running and claim-ing the whole enchilada. They loudly condemned this "unauthorized" or-ganization. The triggering factor in the explosion of criticism was the hue and cry raised by Peter Robinson, a member of the Virginia Green Party and of the G/GPUSA. He accused the leadership of the Middleburg confer-ence of excluding Jana Cutlip, at that time still President of the Green Council of the G/GPUSA. Whether this was actually the case or not, or whether she had acted in a manner to provoke what then seemed exclu-sionary action on the part of our host at whose home we were meeting, was not considered either by him or by those who, upon hearing of this from him in a one-sided way on email, took up the hue and cry. The intent was to discredit the conference, and discredit the new organization.

After Middleburg, and on into 1997, a number of Greens around the country who were critical of G/GPUSA but were also not ready to advocate affiliation with ASGP, formed a Unity group. Leaders were Holle Brian, Lowell Nelson, and Joel Sipress of the Minnesota Green Party, Greg Jan and Dan Solnit of the California Green Party, Dan Coleman of the Chapel Hill Greens in North Carolina; and then also Peter Robinson. Ron Stanchfield of the New York Greens and Cris Moore in New Mexico were also leading voices for a time, but they fairly soon shifted towards ASGP.

Though the Unity group's initial motivation seemed to be one of a "pox on both your houses," they eventually settled down to an effort to get both organizations to come together and work towards a common organi-zation. They sent around a unity statement that over 450 Greens around the country signed.

We in ASGP were unsure that the Unity folks were not just another stalking horse for G/GPUSA. In our minds the problem between the two organizations was not one of personal dislikes and misunderstandings, which is what many Unity folks seemed (quite naively) to think, but real political and philosophical differences.

On the other hand, we were somewhat mollified by the fact that sev-eral in the Unity group and others active in G/GPUSA were starting to

criticize G/GPUSA articulately. It's centralism, its questionable use of proxies, the continued refusal of Betty Wood, its Clearing House Coordinator,
to share information about who was in the organization, the fact that its
national membership had declined to about 450, and that only about 4 or 5
locals constituted its base, all came under scrutiny. David Ellison of the
Ohio Greens, an effective activist both in Ohio and in the councils of G/
GPUSA for several years, assembled a stinging critique of G/GPUSA which
he put on line.

Nor was the point lost on us that the Unity Group, by posing the issue
as a need for negotiation between two perceived adversaries, affirmed the
legitimacy of ASGP.

In addition, we noticed that the Unity Group was not all that unified,
and that while some like Holle Brian and Peter Robinson continued to lean
toward the G/GPUSA model of a national organization, more and more of
the others were advocating a model similar, even identical, to that of ASGP.

Linda Martin and I worked with Unity Group members Greg Jan and
Morgan Vierheller of the California Green Party, and with Holle Brian, to
produce a statement for ASGP's Portland meeting in the spring of 1997
supporting unity talks; but we were careful to emphasize that the unity we
were talking about was that of a national Green party based on autonomous state Green parties. The statement passed unanimously in Portland
with two abstentions.

Later in the spring of 1997, Howie Hawkins and I were invited by the
Massachusetts Green Party to debate our respective views at their annual
picnic in Boxford. Howie agreed with my vigorous promotion of a state-
based national Green party. He did so, however, on behalf of a hybrid form
of organization in which groups of dues-paying local activists dedicated to
the social activism would have direct representation along with state parties. It was a hybrid which he hoped would still make the national organization in general, and the electoral wing in particular, accountable to the
non-electoral social-activist leaders. Those of us who were familiar with
Howie's decade-long efforts to push the US Green movement towards this
old-left model, were not overly impressed with his approach. It seemed a
plausible tactic on behalf of the same old strategy.

The Unity Group sponsored a small meeting in Minneapolis in early
June, 1997, attended by some G/GPUSA leaders in addition to some members of the Unity Group. Pressure was put on Howie, Kwazi Nkrumah and
others of G/GPUSA who attended the meeting to push for structural reform at their upcoming Lawrence gathering in August. This concern was
relegated to the background, however, by a proposal generated at the meeting for immediate negotiations between G/GPUSA, ASGP, and "unaligned"
state parties. After a few weeks of mulling this over via email, the Coordi-

nating Committee of ASGP decided that though negotiations should take place, they could only be meaningful after G/GPUSA had their national gathering. Would G/GPUSA agree to a national Green Party based on state parties?

This turned the focus back to what could or would happen at the meeting of the Congress of G/GPUSA in August 1997 in Lawrence. During late summer, several leaders of the Unity group and others wanting reform in G/GPUSA, pressed for reform on email. They then also attended the Lawrence gathering as delegates. But they were unable to budge the core leadership of G/GPUSA. Nor was Howie Hawkins able to get his proposal passed that would have provided for a bicameral body composed of both local movement activists and representatives of state parties, something he had so assiduously and successfully fought against in 1990/91. A three person committee for talks with ASGP was approved at the Lawrence gathering, but there was very little give on the decisive question of changing the basic structure of the G/GPUSA. Keenly disappointed, the reformers in the following weeks turned away from G/GPUSA and towards ASGP as a more likely vehicle through which to achieve a national Green Party.

This accorded very much with what many of us in ASGP had been saying with increasing confidence. G/GPUSA and ASGP were not antithetical organizations was our argument. They were two different kinds of organization, a case of apples and oranges. While we sympathized with the reformers, we had also cautioned them to have a care for the political and philosophic sensibilities of the inner core of G/GPUSA's leadership. Why lure or force them into a kind of politics that they found uninteresting and ideologically unacceptable?

It seemed to us that we who were committed to a popular Green politics and to a national party that is based on statewide parties could now see light at the end of the tunnel. Or, to vary the image, we were crossing the threshold. What lay before us now was the daunting and exciting task of deepening and expanding the national party that we had founded.

Zooming Forward to Green Party, American Style

The Santa Fe meeting of ASGP in April, 1998 confirmed and deepened the momentum begun at Middleburg just 18 months earlier. As a delegate from Maine, sitting in a large circle with delegates from twenty other state Green parties, I sensed a surge of spirit and confidence. Delegates were becoming more familiar with one another. Their interaction was animated, timely, and responsible. The New Mexico Green Party provided experienced and effective facilitators. A set of "Interim Position Statements" were developed and adopted, preparing the way for a full-scale

Platform in the year 2000. This was accomplished in a brisk and lively manner and in a cooperative and trusting spirit. It seemed that the Greens had arrived at a degree of maturity that had often escaped them in the past.. A new Steering Committee was elected by proportional representation composed of Nancy Allen of Maine, Anne Goeke of Pennsylvania, and Tom Sevigny of Connecticut as co-chairs, Tony Affigne of Rhode Island as Treasurer and Dean Myerson of Colorado as Secretary. They would be in office until the next meeting of the Coordinating Committee, set for the spring of 1999. The ASGP was beginning to act and sound like a national party. By January, 1999, the European Federation of Green Parties, on the eve of their biggest ever Congress to be held in Paris in late February, declared their decision to recognize the Association of Green Parties as their partner in the United States. Delegates of the ASGP would be received in accordance with the spirit of this declaration. There would be meetings at the Congress to develop and adopt a Common Ground statement.

These are the Interim Position Statements, with a preamble, adopted in Santa Fe in April 1998:

"The Association of State Green Parties is dedicated to the values of the international Green movement. Our goal is to create a just and sustainable society based on the Ten Key Values of Ecological Wisdom, Social Justice, Grass Roots Democracy, Nonviolence, Decentralization, Community-based Economics, Feminism, Respect for Diversity, Personal and Global Responsibility, and Future Focus. To work toward this goal the Coordinating Committee of the Association of State Green Parties has adopted the following positions reflecting the sense of the Association in anticipation of the adoption of a national platform.

**We support human rights nationally and internationally.

**We will work to end racism, sexism, discrimination based on gender status and sexual orientation and discrimination against people based on age, disability, religion or nationality.

**We advocate the use of true-cost pricing in energy and resource management to protect our natural resource heritage for future generations.

**We call for a new definition of wealth that includes clean air and water, biodiversity, health, education, and peace as measures of economic security.

**We support legislative, institutional, and economic policies that will accelerate the development of decentralized, nonpolluting renewable energy technologies.

**We call for immediate decommissioning of all nuclear power plants without passing the cost on to ratepayers.

**We support permanent, above-ground, locally-based storage sites for nuclear waste to minimize the hazards of waste transport.

**We support immediate decommissioning of all nuclear weapons production facilities, date-specific destruction of all nuclear weapons, and the signing of oversight treaties calling for drawing down of nuclear stockpiles.

**We call for a declaration that the U.S. will not use a first strike and an end to funding for any new nuclear weapons research.

**We advocate proportional representation for state and local elections, fair ballot access and campaign finance reform.

**We will work to increase public participation at every level of government through strategies such as initiative, referendum, and recall, and to ensure that our public representatives are fully accountable to the people who elect them.

**We advocate the creation of community-supported alternatives to corporate-owned media.

**We oppose bioengineering, irradiation, and other unsustainable agricultural practices and processes.

**We reject the USDA's current proposed organic foods standard.

**We support decentralized local agriculture.

**We support legislative and land use policies that preserve and restore biodiversity (genetic, population, species, ecosystems) at the local, national, and global levels.

**We oppose economic globalization and international trade agreements that threaten workers rights, the environment, and local self-determination.

**We advocate building community-based fair and sustainable economic systems.

**We acknowledge the importance of small business and cooperatives for the preservation of local communities, for keeping money circulating within local regions, for providing meaningful jobs, and in providing counterpoint to multinational globalization.

**We will actively work for universal health care and we believe that everyone has a right to decent, affordable housing, education, and medical care.

**We support a woman's right to choose safe, legal abortion and believe that reproductive and health issues must remain a medical matter between individuals and their health care providers.

**We will work to build alliances with environmental groups, labor, social justice groups, and alternative political parties that share our vision of a just and sustainable society.

**We support economic systems, resource use, and foreign policies that promote world peace.

**We need to explore, promote, and institute nonviolent solutions to break the cycle of violent crime, and eradicate the inequities inherent in our criminal justice system.

**We support community-based crime prevention programs that address the roots of crime by creating educational and recreational opportunities for all, as well as protecting the safety and peace of the community.

**As a matter of conscience, we oppose the death penalty.

These affirmations reveal a politics in a new direction. It is neither Democratic Party, Republican Party, Socialist, Fascist, or Communist. It is a politics for the 21st century. It takes a giant step beyond the ideologies of the 19th and 20th centuries, whether of left or right. Indeed, it is a politics beyond ideology. It is a politics that is rooted in vision, dialog, and practical need, not in fixed doctrines that operate like ideological straitjackets and blinders. It is also a politics that goes beyond mere compromise. What is first is the seeking of new common ground, not the compromise between entrenched positions and seemingly incommensurable goals. This politics recognizes that compromise at times is necessary and effective, but only if it is done on behalf of finding new common ground.

Action for a Green Century

If the next century is to be an ecological century, and a new era for the open society and the free citizen, then it will happen because Green Parties and the Green Movement around the globe helped to make it happen; were, in fact, the inspiration and catalyst for enabling it to happen.

There are many voices, some of them commanding great respect, who say that humanity has only 30 years left in which to temper and turn the forces that are hurtling the human race and the planet to destruction. One hopes that such dire predictions are overdrawn; and there are voices who condemn such predictions and try to supply us with reassurances. But soothing reassurance is not the response we need.

A Green response is timely action, dedicated organizing, thoughtful reflection on what works and doesn't work, and then more action, organizing, and reflection. Ecology, like democracy, is a program and it is a method. Both. It is a vision and a way to the vision. We human beings are part of nature, and nature, ecologically understood and practiced, opens always towards a richer and more abundant life.

Nearing the end of this book, I once again urge a caveat. It is also a reminder to seize an opportunity. Politics is a tough act. Nevertheless the way to a better future lies through politics: there is in fact no way to continued survival, except through the fire of politics. Politics — the act of seeking power and governing — can enhance your life, can enhance your society, and it can also destroy it. But you cannot do without it, even if you believe you can ignore it with impunity. For politics, at its most fundamental, is the only real alternative we have to war, the only means we have as human beings to stave off and indeed overcome and transcend war. Politics means dealing with, and then also embracing, the other. There inevitably is conflict in this process of encounter with the other: witness what I've written with some candor about our Green struggles! There is also the hope and expectation of finding, and re-finding, common ground. Such dealing, such embracing, and such finding of common ground takes its roots from the way we humans approach nature.

If our approach to nature follows the vision of ecology, if in consequence we truly know ourselves as part of an evolutionary process of life, then we will listen within ourselves to the voice and prompting of nature, we will see ourselves in tune with life, in tune in a manner that suggests interaction, reciprocity, interface, mutual acknowledgment, and yes, love. It is this spirit of give and take, of sharing, of mutual supportive action, that our time cries out for as never before. The ecological crisis is also, therefore, in addition to being a crisis, an incredible opportunity for the expansion and deepening of our human capacities for acknowledging and embracing the other.

The human vis-a-vis nature as the other: an acknowledgment, an embrace, a cooperation of partners, a mutually supportive relationship. The human vis-a-vis other humans as the other: an acknowledgment, an embrace, a negotiation of partners, and a mutually supportive relationship. Politics is an integral part of this process. But if we contemn politics, or ignore it, or leave it to those who are drawn to it for reasons of vanity, greed and hate, then we have missed the message of ecology and we are not going to survive or thrive.

Epilogue
Only the Free Can Choose

There is a silence, a very palpable silence, which you feel before you actually know it's there. It yawns across the great valley of our politics, from left to right and from up to down.

The silence concerns the actual state of our politics and the imperative need there is for someone, or somebodies, to seek its transformation in a serious and responsible way. The silence is a curtain that keeps from view those who, in spite of the silence, and against all odds, are trying to do this.

The silence is puzzling for a country that prides itself on its revolutionary origins, its long and impressive constitutional history, and its well advertised credentials as one of the world's leading democracies. But perhaps therein lies the rub. Are we resting on our laurels? Have we become complacent? We may like to think that we are living up to our revolutionary heritage, our constitutional foundations, but are we?

The political science that is taught to millions of college students yields very little by way of attention to the need for addressing these questions, let alone the need for political transformation. The other parts of the curriculum of higher learning, and the civics courses in our high schools, forswear such concerns altogether. The assumption is that America is a democracy. The assumption has the aura of a known and unalterable truth. Nor does any particular criticism that is voiced, sometimes with great urgency, about such travesties as the unabashed trading of votes for money by elected officials, or the virulence of negative campaigning, or the stunning absence of voters at the polls, or the domination of politics by wealthy special interests, or the persistent and consummate lying of leaders to the people and to each other — none of that dents the over-riding power of the myth that whatever else may be said of America, we are a democracy.

The myth precludes serious attention to the one factor in our perilous planetary situation that if studied and understood and acted upon, would enable us to address the inter-related ecological and economic crises that now threaten to overwhelm us and the world. That one thing is the pressing, though daunting, need to transform, renovate, re-invigorate the political system. The need is identical with the proposition that the one thing we need is to recover, regain, reclaim our freedom. Freedom through politics. Freedom through insisting that we act as citizens in charge of our destiny; freedom as an activity undertaken by citizens in the political sphere to address together the manifest problems that now for lack of political will and the power to choose sink us in a slough of despair and make our problems seem insurmountable.

222

The silence inhabits the Republican Party and the Democratic Party. Both are deeply entrenched in the belief that we are (already) a democracy, we are (already) free. No need to bother with the transformation of our politics or to proceed seriously with measures to regain our political freedom.

The silence also affects the weekly, monthly, and quarterly publications that speak with liberal and progressive voices: *The Nation, The Progressive, The Progressive Populist, In These Times, The Atlantic Monthly, Tikkun, The Utne Reader, E Magazine,* and many others. Much of their content is interesting, insightful, and useful. But there is very little that takes a hard look at the political system, its adequacy, its desperate need for transformation, the fact that it cries out for a fundamental shift in the constellation of power. When it comes to politics, one does find heroic appeals to struggle for the soul of the Democratic Party, as if putting new wine in that old bottle is feasible, or—even assuming that it might yield some positive results—as if such limited reform is worth the energy and is not, instead, a decoy the pursuit of which precludes the transforming action that our current predicament demands. The absence of fundamental political critique coming from liberals and progressives reinforces complacency and deepens the silence.

The silence is deafening when one listens carefully to the voices of non-governmental organizations, which by the thousands kneel on bent knee to the powers-that-be begging/cajoling/demanding favors and the crumbs of policy and perquisites from the table of power for their particular cause, leaving undone and un-noticed the larger question of their own freedom, their own responsibility to challenge the power equations at the table so that justice and truth and mutual support for all might prevail there. Equally problematic is the behavior of protest groups demonstrating and marching for a good cause, expending countless hours and most of their limited financial capital, on actions that become known only to those who already agree with them, impressing few others, and still leaving the field to those at the helm of the ship of state who don't care a fig about "the causes" but do love their own power, and mean to hang on to it. The protesters are mostly silent about seeking the transformation of the political system. Are they afraid, or too fastidious, to get in there directly via the ballot box and a political party built to their own specifications and by these means assert their freedom so that with others they themselves can decide the affairs of state in a manner that becomes a free citizen?

The Silence of Scholars*

A similar silence conditions the scholars and writers of a progressive

*The books and authors cited below are listed in order of mention in the Endnote to this Epilogue.

and liberal way of thinking who write with insight and courage about searing problems afflicting society and economy. Yet they maintain an incorrigible silence about the political realm and what might have to change there if the problems they so eloquently articulate are to receive the attention they cry out for.

Jeremy Rifkin's work, for example, is outstanding in its exposition of the dangers of genetic engineering and he has written feelingly about the meat eating craze of Americans aided and abetted by the agribusiness interests that cause us cruelly to waste infinite resources of land, water, and the lives of countless animals, a waste that only serves to make many Americans sickly and obese. Yet not a word about the transformation of politics in any of his works. It is not that he doesn't look for answers. On occasion he appeals to religion as maybe the answer, but not politics. Why is that?.

Herman Daly, a first-rate economist, is powerful in his analysis of the shortcomings of the corporatized economy and he suggests new economic models and new policies that could well lead us out of the wilderness of distorted priorities and unjust distribution of wealth. But, in a fashion similar to Rifkin, he avoids talking about how those ideas could be implemented or who is to do the implementing, and he considers not at all how the way forward might be, yes must be, can only be, by means of the transformation of the political system. In a fashion similar to Rifkin, he and John Cobb turn to religion as an answer at the end of their book *For The Common Good.*

I think of David Orr's insightful book on ecological literacy. Or I think of Danah Zohar's equally insightful work—*Quantum Society, Human Nature and Consciousness Defined by the New Physics*—applying quantum physics theory to a new reading of how society and its institutions might be organized. Or of Robert D. Bullard's powerful articulation of case study after case study of environmental racism in the United States. Or Theo Colborn, Dianne Dumanoski, and John Peterson Myers who wrote *Our Stolen Future*, a thoroughly compelling and frightening book on the way fossil fuels produce endocrine-disrupting chemicals that destroy the healthy functioning of our bodies.

Or I think of Lester R. Brown et al.'s annual *State of the World* which lavishly compiles statistical information and many convincing analyses of the terrible threat the nations of the planet face from the distortions practiced on the planet's ecology. Or Paul Hawken's *The Ecology of Commerce*, a practical and persuasive analysis of the limitations of our economic system and a book chuck full of do-able things that could be done to pull ourselves out of our predicament. Or of Amory Lovens who has written, lectured, counselled, and demonstrated convincingly at his Rocky

Mountain Institute as to what can be done by way of conservation and the development of renewable energies.

Each one feels the need to probe for and provide answers to the problems and crises they pose ("...we look to the future and think about charting a new course", writes Theo Colborn), yet they all somehow manage to overlook the political system as a critically important avenue through which to chart a new course.

It's no good their expostulating that the political realm is outside their concern, that their subject matter is not about that. Their work cries out for completion, a political completion. Their work inexorably points to such questions as these: are not the problems you address at least partly (indeed, as many might say, mostly) created by the failures of the current political system; and as for the excellent remedies you propose, how are they going to be implemented and who is to do that? Once these questions are raised there is no way to avoid addressing the need to seek in a spirit of freedom and conviction the transformation of the political system. It might not be the only option in their estimation, but surely it is one of the options. And if they would but think about it, they might see that it is a very key option.

The above is just a random selection of authors—they are American thinkers at their best—examining the many different features of the current crisis which they meticulously and honestly address. For each of these authors, one could name a score more, all exhibiting the same pattern of silence. It's a political silence. For one who has spent a bit of time behind the Iron Curtain, as I have, the silence has a familiar ring. Something there is that's not free here!

Earth Odyssey

A few days ago, I received from Ralph Nader a book by Mark Hertsgaard, Earth Odyssey, Around the world in search of our environmental future. I read it immediately and the awareness that had been dawning in my mind for years about the silence was suddenly triggered into full and stark recognition. Hertsgaard's book is outstanding. And yet, here too there is the familiar silence. Fortunately, there is also a small but definite intimation that there really is no other place to look for fundamental answers than through the political system. Even so, he does not enter that realm to look around and see what must be changed there, or who is to do it.

Hertsgaard has spent seven years trekking the continents, searching out the environmental trouble spots of the world, not content with talking only to officials and experts and activists, though he does this very effectively, but going off the beaten path to see the way life is actually lived and suffered (unbearably) by people in the trouble spots: the Horn of Africa (especially southern Sudan), many different areas of China, Thailand, and the farther reaches of the Amazon in Brazil. He intersperses his on-site descriptions, portraits, anecdotes, vignettes, and conversations with ordinary people, with in-depth analyses of environmental degradation, issues of population control, humankind's love affair with the automobile, and the rising conflict between the North and the South on issues of climate change.

At the end he asks with eloquence what can be done, even in the face of disillusion and despair. He provides examples of efforts at amelioration: what some are doing in the market place, what others are doing in and through NGOs (non-governmental organizations), and what still others are doing through individual witness. He offers a counsel of hope. He also recommends and strongly promotes a plan which he describes as the Global Green Deal, suggesting we do something globally on the order of what Franklin Roosevelt undertook in the United States with the New Deal. I return to this idea below.

His book focuses most strongly on the North/South contradiction. As he points out tellingly and vividly, most of the peoples of the Southern nations (and he includes China) want to escape the hardship and crushing material (and consequently spiritual) deprivation of their existence. They've been given to believe that only by imitating the North, its industrial model, can they escape. That it means pernicious environmental degradation, so great that it adds immeasurably to their hardship, is the price they feel they must pay in order eventually to reach a better life.

This way of thinking in the South and this way of trying to come to terms with harsh reality, is a fact of life, Hertsgaard keeps reminding the reader, and it is something that must be acknowledged as real. So real that it directly threatens, in its awesome implications, the health and well-being, not only of Southern populations, but all northern populations as well; and, of course, of the planet as a whole. The immense mountains of coal that China produces and burns are so great that China is now the number two contributor to carbon overload in the planet's atmosphere (the U.S. still is number one). China will continue to burn coal and is headed for even greater use of this dangerous fossil fuel. Brazil continues to raze huge areas of the Amazon. The combination of China burning coal, adding carbon, and of Brazil eviscerating whole forests, the trees of which would otherwise eat carbon, is a pretty lethal one. It is only one example in the book, though a powerful one, of how the world now teeters toward a planetary ecological armageddon.

The trouble is that the South is too poor to do much about it. Nor is their poverty simply a matter of their own doing. The massive debt owed the North, the unfair terms of trade to the detriment of the South, the Southern operations of the multinational corporate complex actuated only by the narrowest concerns of profit in the short term, and the failure of the North, though rich enough do so, to provide the capital for clean industry and post-fossil fuel energy systems either for itself or for the South, even though this would save the North as much as it would save the South— these are additional facts of life that make the outlook for the planet exceedingly gloomy.

Hertsgaard makes these arguments clearly and he makes them stick. But he misses the most salient fact; namely, that there will not be an answer for either the North or the South, nor for the planet as a whole, as long as the constellation of political forces, both North and South, remains the same. There is more to this, obviously, than just getting a "good person" in office, say the presidency of the United States. It's going to take a lot more than that. It's going to take the building of a new political party that can grow, endure, and affect policy directly and decisively so that the constellation of political forces is fundamentally altered. This change, this transformation of the political system, will have to happen in the United States and in Europe; but also in Brazil and China. Political freedom must be on our agendas everywhere.

Hertsgaard says that if you are poor (as in the South or in various parts of the North) one really has no choice. There is merit in that argument. But one can turn this around and say that if you are free then you are on the way to take action that will lead you out of your poverty. Hertsgaard notices this in the case of the millions of women of the South. If they could be free, it they had the power of choice, the problem of population pressure would be much diminished. He does not see the issue of freedom as clearly, however, in regard to China or Brazil. Yet, if the Chinese people could shake off the Communist Party stranglehold, and if Brazil's small farmers could shake off the horrendous landholding monopoly by just a small stratum of landowners, a monopoly created and shored up by the country's oppressive political system, and a monopoly which forces the small farmer to seek land by burning the forests of the Amazon — then each country would by so much have latitude for choice.

They would still come up against the relative scarcity of capital, of course, and so their relative poverty would still be a major factor in preventing them from becoming ecologically sustainable. More is needed and that more turns to what will/can/could happen in the North, what could happen there politically that would release energies and resources for ecological and economic sustainability around the world.

The argument therefore returns full force to the North, especially the

United States. Freedom as the activity of transforming the political system must be put highest on the priority list of concerned people in the North. This could unlock the doors that now are shut against new industrial policies based on solar energy and based on a sophisticated understanding that we live in one world and that the transfer of the best new industrial technology to the South (to say nothing of its immediate application to the North) is an exercise in realism and common sense. Hertsgaard approvingly quotes Philip Shabecoff's *A New Name For Peace* where he says "We know what needs to be done." That is exactly right. The point is we don't now have a political system adequate to the task of applying the knowledge and technology we already possess. We need a new constellation of power.

But Hertsgaard's book is virtually silent on this crucial matter. The most he can muster is supportive words for NGO activity and various initiatives in the market place. But he notes that "the market is rarely free" and can't be relied on to do the job. He might also pay closer attention to NGOs, for they are too fractured and protest-driven to substantially alter the course of public policy. His overall argument therefore moves tantalizingly close to the questions I pose for him and for an entire de-politicized American intellectual class: Where must the job be done if not on the terrain of politics? How can it be done except through a re-affirmation of a citizen inspired freedom that transforms the political system towards truth-telling, integrity, and meticulous attention to the needs of ordinary people? And who are those who will carry the ball if not the builders of a new party dedicated to such transformation?

Hertsgaard strongly advocates a Global Green Deal, as he engagingly calls it, evoking the memory of the man who arguably was the last Tribune of the People that the United States has had in the President's office. He wants it. It would be a great thing. It would be a political thing, and that is the positive part of his proposal. He needs to look farther, to examine the adequacy of the political system and consider what needs to be done there if his proposal is ever to see the light of day. Strangely, he never mentions the Green Party, except once fleetingly when he refers to the Green Party in Germany; but even then it is in a context in which the Green Party is treated as similar in kind to NGOs. Nor does he mention any other third party. Indeed he mentions political parties not at all. There seems to be a kind a self-censorship at work here, masked perhaps by a deep distrust of politics as a whole.

What steps can be taken to reduce, if not dissolve, the silence? An important, and decisive, step is to pose the question : Is there a silence as is claimed in this Epilogue? No need to say there is one; just pose it as a plausible question, a genuine possibility. And then look to see how to probe the question and get it asked in public, to the public. Put the question on

"Face the Nation," have it play for several weeks! Encourage *The Nation* to feature a series of articles on the question. *The Atlantic Monthly* and *The New Yorker* could delve into the question in full length inquiries. It could become the grist of many radio and TV talk shows. The question could be raised persistently throughout cyberspace. High school and college classes could debate the issue. *The New York Times* and *The Washington Post* and *The Los Angeles Times* could feature the question and all the newspapers in all the states could hone in on it. And so forth.

The likelihood of this step being taken, or happening any time soon, is extremely problematic. Efforts to make it happen will only succeed if another more important step is taken at the same time. This step is to build an independent, durable, credible, and sincere political party. It's very existence, once it is perceived as real and vital, puts the question to the media, the scholars, the public, and the two major political parties as nothing else can. Once the banners of such a party are raised, many who now hang back or are unsure will see the point of the question and will act upon it.

The Green Party and the Global Green Deal

The pervasive political silence which I have charted here puts into even sharper perspective, therefore, the efforts of the Greens throughout the world to move seriously into the political terrain to fight for the transformation of the political system and to achieve a new constellation of power. It also puts into sharp perspective the move that Ralph Nader has made and will continue to make, in concert with the Greens, to focus the attention of citizens on what he calls the tools of democracy. He is talking about reshaping the political terrain and making it once again a home for truth-tellers, plain speakers, freedom seekers, and leaders in solidarity with the needs of ordinary people everywhere.

During the same week that I received a copy of Hertsgaard's book, I, along with Greens throughout the country, got an e-mail message from Ralph Monoe in Brussels. Monoe is the chief staff person of the European Federation of Green Parties (EFGP). His message was that the European Federation, comprising Green Parties in 28 countries, had decided "that the Federation recognizes the Association of State Green Parties (ASGP) as our partner in the United States." This was a timely and welcome assist to our efforts in the United States to build a viable, credible, and serious political party at the national level through the ASGP, a process described at some length in Parts III and IV of this book.

But this action by the EFGP also confirms the forward motion of the Green movement and Green political parties and their emergence as a significant and realistic political force in the affairs of the nations and in world affairs. Already, Greens are Ministers of the Environment in several European countries and in one of them, Germany, a Green is Foreign Minister. Federations of Green Parties are forming in the Americas and in Africa and a global gathering of Greens is scheduled for Australia in 2001. A cooperative effort among the Green Parties of the earth for a workable global economic/ecological policy—workable for the individual nations, for the North and the South, and for the planet as a whole—is in the making. It can act to apply brakes to the worst and to provoke, be a catalyst for, the emergence in the 21st century of a Global Green Deal.

The Greens above all stand for a fundamental breakthrough in economic policy so that economic policy henceforth will take ecology fully into account and will measure overall economic performance in accordance with ecological yardsticks. As Greens press on the pulse of power, they will increasingly be a force for the rapid sharing of new industrial technologies and capital with the South and for its rapid application in the North.

It is a race against time. It is also a race for political freedom. The Greens know that their struggle for the power to help accomplish this and other needed changes in policy (health, education, agriculture, military spending) can and must only come by re-affirming the freedom to choose and to build a political system in which freedom truly flourishes. In the North. And in the South. The passion for political freedom dissolves the silence. Only the free can choose.

Appendix

Publishers note: The world enters a new century, a new millennium, in just a few months. Greens around the world, in their many separate nations, are communicating more and more in cyberspace and in regional and continental congresses. They are forming federations, the most mature and best organized of which is the European Federation of Green Parties (EFGP). Given these developments, and fast-moving events, it seems fitting to include in this book, not only various references in the text to the EFGP, but an appendix featuring the following description of The European Greens composed in January 1999 by Ralph Monoe, the Secretary-General, European Federation of Green Parties.

THE EUROPEAN GREENS
by Ralph Monoe, Secretary-General, EFGP

30 member parties in 28 countries

In 1984 the Green parties of Belgium, the Netherlands, Luxembourg, the United Kingdom, France, Germany, Sweden and Switzerland formed the European Coordination of Green Parties. Following end of the cold war, the Greens felt they needed a new common body, mandated to speak on behalf of all the Greens in Europe. Therefore, in June 1993 the Coordination was transformed into the present European Federation of Green Parties - called the EUROPEAN GREENS.

The Federation today includes 30 Green parties in 28 European countries extending from Ireland to Georgia and from Malta to Norway. It facilitates communication between member parties, Green parliamentarians and ministers. It coordinates Green European policy and supports small Green parties in order to strengthen the Green political movement in Europe as a whole.

Committed to a sustainable and socially just Europe

The EUROPEAN GREENS and its member parties are committed to the development of an ecologically sound and socially just Europe. This means developing environmentally sustainable economies, introducing eco-taxes, creating new green job opportunities, elaborating a concept for conflict prevention and nonviolence in Europe as well as supporting the transition of the new democracies in east and central Europe.

Much more than the EU

The development of the European Union and the consequences of this for the rest of Europe is a major political focus. The EUROPEAN GREENS are actively involved in developing a new vision for the European Union. However, the perspective of the EUROPEAN GREENS clearly transcends the boundaries of the European Union and western Europe.

The Green East-West Dialogue is designed to foster cooperation between eastern and western member parties. The EUROPEAN GREENS is committed to developing Green ideas for fruitful relationships around the Mediterranean and the Black Sea. In northern Europe, growing Green cooperation aims at improving the environment in and around the Baltic Sea.

Within the regional context, the EUROPEAN GREENS support small Green parties, something that is essential to strengthening the Green movement in Europe as a whole

Greens in 17 Parliaments and 5 Governments

In 1979 the Swiss Green Party was the first to have a Green elected to a national parliament in Europe. Today, 206 Greens have entered 17 parliaments: Austria, Belgium, Bulgaria, Finland, France, Georgia, Germany, Sweden, Ireland, Italy, Luxembourg, the Netherlands, Portugal, Switzerland, Slovakia, Ukraine as well as the EU Parliament.

There are 28 Green Members of the European Parliament. They form the Green Group in the EP, which is part of the EUROPEAN GREENS. The co-operation with the Green Group is very close, particularly on matters of major EU political significance. The Group is the exclusive partner of the EUROPEAN GREENS in the European Parliament.

The Lithuanian Greens were the first Green party to participate in government in 1990, holding the post of deputy prime minister. The Slovene Greens entered government sometime later, after the first free elections in their country. Today, the Greens participate in national government in Finland, Georgia, France and Italy, where they hold the environment portfolios. In Italy recently, a minister for Equal Opportunities was also elected. Following the elections in September1998, the German Greens have entered into government with the Social Democrats, and 3 Greens have been elevated to ministerial posts; Foreign Affairs Minister (and vice chancellor), Health Minister and Minister for the Environment. In Slovakia, a Green was recently chosen for the position of deputy Environment minister.

Campaigning together

Only through united efforts and a common goal can the Greens of our continent provide new leadership for Europe. The EUROPEAN GREENS therefore work to forge close links between its 30 members, to stimulate bilateral and regional Green initiatives and to organise activities at the European level.

Jointly with the member parties, the EUROPEAN GREENS formulate policies on major political issues. A Common Election Manifesto is being developed for the European elections in 1999. Green leaders and ministers meet to discuss topics of common interest. Non-governmental organisations are brought in for facts and consultations.

Taking Global responsibilities

The EUROPEAN GREENS are part of a global Green movement and have assumed a particular responsibility to contribute to developing closer contacts with Greens worldwide. Links are rapidly being forged with the Green parties of America, Australia, Asia and Africa and maintained through electronic communication and visits.

Our office is in Brussels. The monthly UPDATE newsletter and the EUROPEAN GREENS website (http://www.europeangreens.org) are the main channels for information to the member parties and other interested groups and individuals.

Endnotes

Chapter One

For the discussion in this chapter of new understandings of nature that are important for an emerging political ecology, there is a considerable literature to consult. Especially important to the author are the following works on the science and philosophy of nature, several of which draw out the implications of these new understandings for human institutions, relationships, and ways of knowing.

1. Albert A. Anderson. "The Essence of Universalism." *Dialogue and Universalism*, Vol. I, No. 5-6, pp. 173-83, 1996.
2. Ludwig von Bertalanfy. "The Theory of Open Systems in Physics and Biology." *Science*, Vol. III, pp. 23-29, 1950.
3. David Bohm. *Wholeness and the Implicate Order.* London: Ark Paperbacks, 1980.
4. Murray Bookchin. *The Ecology of Freedom: The Emergence and Dissolution of Hierarchy.* Palo Alto: Cheshire Books. 1982.
5. Charles S. Brown. "Humanism and the Voice of Nature: Challenges for a Universal Metaphilosophy." *Dialogue and Universalism*, Vol. VIII, No. 1-2, pp. 91-98, 1998.
6. John Casti. *Complexification, Explaining a Paradoxical World Through the Science of Surprise.* New York: Harper Perennial. 1995.
7. Pierre Teilhard de Chardin. *The Phenomenon of Man.* New York: Harper and Row, 1995.
8. Edward Goldsmith. *The Way: An Ecological World View.* Boston: Shambala, 1993.
9. Werner Heisenberg. *Physics and Beyond.* New York: Harper and Row, 1971.
10. Erich Jantz. *The Self-Organizing Universe.* New York: Pergamon, 1980.
11. Janusz Kuszynski. "The Ethos of Universalism: Reconciliation with the Co-Created World — the Universe of Man." *Dialogue and Universalism*, Vol. VI, No. 11-12, pp. 210-225, 1996.
12. Jerry Mander. *In the Absence of the Sacred.* San Francisco: Sierra Club Books, 1991.
13. John Mingers. *Self-Producing Systems.* New York: Plenum, 1995.
14. Ilya Prigogine. *From Being to Becoming.* San Francisco: Freeman, 1980; and, with Isabelle Stengers. *Order Out of Chaos.* New York: Bantam, 1984.
15. Daniel Quinn. *Ishmael.* New York: Bantam, 1995.
16. John Rensenbrink. "In the Wake of Post-Modernism: Can a New Universal Emerge?" *Dialogue and Universalism*, Vol. V, No. 11-12, 1995.
17. Rupert Sheldrake. *A New Science of Life.* Los Angeles: Tarcher, 1981.
18. Henryk Skolimowski. *Eco-Philosphy.* London: Marion Boyare, 1981.
19. Charlene Spretnak. *Resurgence of the Real: Body, Nature, and Place in a Hypermodern World.* Reading, MA: Addison-Wesley, 1997.
20. Danah Zohar. *The Quantum Self: Human Nature and Consciousness Defined by the New Physics.* New York: William Morrow. 1990; and, with Ian Marshall. *The Quantum Society: Mind, Physics, and a New Social Vision.* New York: Quill, William Morrow, 1994.

Chapter Three
1. Audry Lorde, *Sister Outsider* (Tumansberg, N.Y. : The Crossing Press, 1984); Maurice Merleau-Ponty *The Visible and the Invisible* (Evanston, Il.: Northwestern University Press, 19568).
2. Carolyn Heilbrun, *Writing a Woman's Life* (New York: Norton, 1988).
3. Robert Michels, *Political Parties, A Sociological Study of Oligarchical Tendencies of Mordern Democracy,* tr. Eden and Ceder Paul (New York: Free Press, 1968).

Chapter Six
1. Walter Lippman, *Essays in the Public Philosophy.* (New York: Transaction Publications, 1989); and Carole Pateman, *Participation and Democratic Theory* (Cambridge, England: Cambridge Univ. Press, 1970.

2.   Georg Lukacs, *History and Class Consciousness:Studies in Marxist Dialectics*, Rodney
     Livingstone, tr. (Cambridge, Mass.: The M.I.T. Press, 1971); and Ivan Ilich, *Tools for Con-
     viviality* (New York: Harper and Row, 1973).

Chapter Seven
1.   Russell Jacoby, *Social Amnesia: A Critique of Conformist Psychology from Adler to Laing*
     (Boston: Beacon Press, 1976).
2.   James Bumham, *The Managerial Revolution: What Is Happening in the World* (Chicago:
     Greenwood, 1972); William G. Domhoff, *Who Rules America?* (Englewood Cliffs,
     N.J.:Prentice Hall, 1967); Edward S. Greenberg, *Serving the Few: Corporate Capitalism
     and the Bias of Government Policy* (New York: John Wiley & Sons, Inc., 1974); C.
     Wxight Mills, *The Power Elite* (New York: Oxford Univ. Press, 1972); David Noble,
     America by Design (New York: Oxford Univ. Press, 1977); Kevin Phillips, *The Politics of
     Rich and Poor: Wealth and the American Electorate in the Reagan Aftermath* (New York:
     Random House, 1990);
3.   Ralph Miliband, *The State in Capitalist Society* (New York: Basic Books, 1969).
4.   Richard Nixon wanted to devolve powers to states and localities in the name of a new feder-
     alism. Jimmy Carter made much out of running against Washington. One of Ronald Reagan's
     major goals on coming to office was to return power to states and localities. In an Op Ed
     piece for *The New York Times*, February 3, 1990, entitled "Two Paralyzed Parties," George
     Will observed that "Federal civilian employment grew 211,000 during the
     Reagan "revolution."
5.   Newsweek, March 19, 1990, p. 23.
6.   Nancy Folbre, et al., *A Field Guide to the U.S. Economy* (New York: Pantheon Books,
     1987) Section 1.5.
7.   David Halberstam, *The Best and the Brightest* (New York: Random House, 1972).
8.   *The Boston Globe*, January 12, 1990.
9.   Mark Hertsgard, *On Bended Knee-the Press and the Reagan Presidency* (New York:
     Schocken Books, Inc., 1989); and Ben Bagdikian, The Media Monopoly (Boston: Beacon
     Press, 1983).
10. Martin Lee and Nonnan Solomon, *Unreliable Sources* (New York: Carol Publishing Group,
     1990).
11. Folbre, et al., op. cit. Section 1.6.
12. Ibid., Section 1.4.
13. Ibid.
14. Ibid., Section 1.8.
15. Ibid., Section 1. 1 1.
16. Ibid., Section 1. 12.
17. Thomas Dye, *Who's Running America? The Carter Years* (Englewood Cliffs, N.J.: Prentice
     Hall, 1979).
18. *The Boston Globe*, May 14, 1990. The Forbes article referred to appeared in the May 28,
     1990, issue of *Forbes Magazine*.
19. Aristotle, *Politics*, translated with an introduction and appendixes by Ernest Barker (New
     York:Oxford Univ. Press, 1962) Book 1.
20. Karl Marx, *Capital* in Robert Tucker, *The Marx/Engels Reader* (New York: Norton, 1972).
21. Georg Lukacs, "Reification and the Consciousness of the Proletariat," in *History and Class
     Consciousness*, Rodney Livingstone, tr. (Cam   bridge: M.I.T. Press, 1971).
22. Toni Morrison, *Tar Baby* (New York: Knopf, 1981).
23. Mary Fricker and Steve Pizzo, "S. &L. Scandal: The Gang's All Here," Op Ed, *The New
     York Times*, July 27, 1990.
24. "U.S. to Reimburse Meese for His Legal Bills," *The New York Times*, July 13, 1990.
25. "I.R.S. Sought $90,000 from Mitch Snyder," ibid.

Chapter Eight
1.   John Kenneth Galbraith, *The Affluent Society* (New York: New American Library, 1963);
     and Daniel Bell, *End of Ideology* (Cambridge: Harvard University Press, 1988).
2.   Debord, Guy, *Society of the Spectacle* (Detroit: Black and Red, 1978); and Elisabeth
     Sussman, *On the Passage of a Few People Through a Rather Brief Moment in Time: The
     Situationist International* Cambridge, Mass.: M.I.T. Press, 1990).
3.   Lester W. Milbrath, *Envisioning a Sustainable Society: Learning Our Way Out* (Albany:
     State University of New York Press, 1,989).

Chapter Nine
1.   Matthew Rothschild, "Third Party Time?" *The Progressive*, October 20, 1989.
2.   Bruce Johanson, *Forgotten Founders: Benjamin Franklin, Iroquois, and the Rationale
     for American Rationale for American Revolution* (Cambridge, Mass.: Harvard Common
     Press, 1982); and Bruce Johanson, *How the American Indians Helped Shape Democracy*
     (Cambridge, Mass.: Harvard Common Press, 1987).

Chapter Ten
1.   Tim Feller, "Green Party of Alaska Report," ICBulletin, December 1990 (Kansas City,
     Missouri: Green Clearing House, POB 30208).
2.   Green Party Organizing Committee: "Founding Document," available from the GPOC Clear
     ing House, Huntington, New York, 31 Clearview Street 11743.
3.   M. Scott Peck, *The Different Drum: Community Making and Peace,* (New York: Simon
     and Schuster, 1987).

Chapter Eleven

1.   John Vasconcellos, interview with author, March 6, 1990.
2.   Audrey Lorde, *Sister Outsider* (Trumansburg, New York: The Crossing Press, 1984), 116
3.   Jeff Fishel, "Leadership for Social Change: Assemblyman John Vasconcellos (D-CA) and
     the Promise of Humanistic Psychology in Public Life," paper presented at the American
     Political Science Association annual convention panel on Transformational Psychology,
     August 30-September 2, 1990, San Francisco.
4.   Robert D. Bullard, *Dumping in Dixie: Race, Class, and Environmental Quality* (Denver:
     Westview Press, 1990); Commission for Racial Justice: United Church of Christ, *Toxic
     Wastes and Race in the United States: A National Repoit on the Racial and Socio-Eco
     nomic Characte 'Yistics of Communities with Hazardous Waste Sites* (New York: Public
     Data Access, 1987); Richard Kazis and Richard Grossman, *Fear at Work: Job Blackmail,
     Labor, and the Environment* (New York: The Pilgrim Press, 1982). Lucinda Wyckle,
     Ward Morehouse, and David Dembo, *Jobs versus the Environment: the Superfund for
     Workers* (1991, Council on International and Public Affairs, New York City); and "Group
     to Recruit Minorities for Ecology Jobs," *The Boston Globe*, April 9, 1990.
5.   "Gay Republican Says Bias Cost Him His Post," *The Boston Globe*, April 14, 1990, p. 21.
6.   Louis Harris, "The Gender Gulf," *The New York Times*, Op Ed, December 7, 1990.

Chapter Twelve
1.   Barry Commoner, *New Yorker Magazine*, June 1987.
2.   EPA Journal, Special Earthday Issue, January/February 1990.
3.   Herman E. Daly and John B. Cobb, Jr., with contributions by Clifford W. Cobb, *For the
     Common Good: Redirecting the Economy Toward Community, the Environment, and a
     Sustainable Future* (Boston: Beacon, 1989).
4.   Lynn White, Jr., "The Historic Roots of Our Ecologic Crisis," *Science*, v. 155 n. 3767,

March, 1967, 1203-1207.

5. Hannah Arendt, *The Human Condition* (Chicago: Univ. of Chicago Press, 1958); Joseph Conrad, *The Heart of Darkness* and *The Secret Sharer* (New York: New American Library, 1960); Mary E. Clark, *Ariadne's Thread: In Search of a Greener Future* (New York: St. Martin's Press, 1989); C. S. Lewis, *That Hideous Strength* (New York: Macmillan, 1968); Wilham Leiss, *Domination of Nature* (New York: Brazilier, 1972); Karl Polanyi, *1 The Great Transformation: The Political and Economic Origins of Our Time* (Boston: Beacon Press, 1957); Carolyn Merchant, *The Death of Nature: Women, Ecology, and the Scientific Revolution* (San Francisco: Harper and Row, 1980); Simone Weil, *The Need for Roots: Prelude to a Declaration of Duties Towards Mankind*, tr. Arthur Wills (Boston: Beacon Press, 1960).

6. The Caracas Report on Alternative Development Indicators, Redefining Wealth and Progress: New Ways to Measure Economic, Social and Environmental Change (New York: The Boot strap Press, 1989); Lester R. Brown, "The Illusion of Progress," in Lester R. Brown, et al., *State of the World 1990* (New York: Norton, 1990); Daly and Cobb, op. cit., have come up with a new measure, the per capita Index of Sustainable Economic Welfare (ISEW).

7. Daly and Cobb, ibid., on the liniitations of comparative advantage.

8. Harry Braverrnan, *Labor and Monopoly Capital: The Degradation of Work in the 20th Century* (New York: Monthly Review Press, 1975); Paul Hawken, *The Next Economy* (New York: Holt, Rinehart and Winston, 1983); John Naisbett and Patricia Aburdene, *Reinventing the Corporation: Transforming Your Company for the New Infonnation Society* (New York: Warner Books, 1985).

9. Alan B. Durning, "Mobilizing at the Grassroots," in Lester R. Brown, et al., *State of the World*, 1989 (New York: Norton, 1989).

10. Douglas Amy, *The Politics of Environmnetal Mediation* (New York: Columbia Univ. Press, 1987).

Endnotes for the Epilogue

The books referred to in this chapter are as follows, in the order mentioned:

1. Jeremy Rifkin, *Biosphere Politics, A New Consciousness for a New Century*, New York: Crown Publishers, Inc. 1991.

2. Jeremy Rifkin, *Declaration of a Heretic*, Boston: Routledge, 1985

3. Herman E. Daly and John B. Cobb, *For the Common Good: Redirecting the Economy toward Community, the Enviornment, and a Sustainable Future*, Boston: Beacon Press, 1989.

4. David Orr, *Ecological Literacy*, Albany: State Univesity of New York Press, 1992

5. Robert D. Bullard, *Unequal Protection: Environmental Justice and Communities of Color*

6. Dana Zohar, *The Quantum Society, Human Nature and Consciousness Defined by the New Physics*, New York: William Morrow, 1994.

7. Theo Colborn, Dianne Dumanoski, and John Peterson Myers, *Our Stolen Future, Are We Threatening Our Fertility, Intelligence, and Survival? —A Scientific Detective Story*.

8. Lester R. Brown, et al., *State of the World*, annual publication 1984-98, New York: W.W. Norton, 1984-98.

9. Paul Hawken, *The Ecology of Commerce, A Declaration of Sustainability*, NewYork: Harper Collins, 1993.

10. Mark Hertsgaard, *Earth Odyssey: Around the world in search of our environmental future*, New York: Broadway Books, 1998.

Bibliography

Adair, Margo, and Sharon Howell. *Breaking Old Patterns, Weaving New Ties*. San Francisco: Tools for Change, POB 14141, San Francisco, CA, 1990.

Adorno, Theodor W., and Max Horkheimer. *The Dialectic of Enlightenment*, trans. John Cumming. New York: Continuum Publishing Co., 1975.

Albert Michael. *What Is to Be Undone: A Modern Revolutionary Discussion of Classical Left Ideologies*. Boston: An Extending Horizons Book (Porter Sargent Publisher), 1974.

Alperovitz, Gar, and Jeff Faux. *Rebuilding America*. New York: Pantheon Books, 1984.

Althusser, Louis. "Marx's Immense Theoretical Revolution," *The Structuralists from Marx to Levi-Strauss*, ed. Richard and Fernande De George. Garden City, N.Y.: Doubleday Anchor Books, 1977.

Amy, Douglas J. *Proportional Representation: The Case for a Better Election System*. Northampton, MA: Crescent Street Press, 1997.

Amy, Douglas J. *The Politics of Environmental Mediation*. New York: Columbia Univ. Press, 1987.

Anderson, Walter Truett. *To Govern Evolution: Further Adventures of the Political Animal*. Boston: Harcourt, Brace, Jovanovich, 1987.

Arendt, Hannah. *On Revolution*. New York: The Viking Press, 1965.

———. *The Human Condition*. Chicago: Univ. of Chicago Press, 1958.

Argyris, Chris, and Donald Schon. *Organizational Learning: A Theory of Action Perspective*. Reading, Mass.: Addison-Wesley, 1978.

Aristotle. *Politics*, trans. Ernest Barker. Oxford: Clarendon Press, 1962.

Aronowitz, Stanley, and Henry A. Giroux. *Postmodern Education, Politics, Culture, and Social Criticism*. Minneapolis: University of Minnesota Press, 1991.

Bagdikian, Ben. *The Media Monopoly*. Boston: Beacon Press, 1983.

Bahro, Rudolf. *Building the Green Movement*. Philadelphia: New Society Publishers, 1985.

Bakhtin, Mikhail M. *Toward a Philosophy of the Act*. Translation and notes by Vadım Liapunov, edited by Vadim Liapunov and Michael Holquist. Austin: University of Texas Press, 1993.

Bakhtin, Mikhail. *The Dialogic Imagination*, trans. Caryl Emerson and Michael Holquist. Austin: University of Texas, 1981.

Barnett, Lincoln. *The Universe and Dr. Einstein*. New York: Bantam Books, 1975.

Bateson, Gregory. *Steps to an Ecology of Mind*. New York: Ballantine, 1972.

Benda, Julien. *The Treason of the Intellectuals (La Trahison des Clercs)*, trans. Richard Aldington. New York: W.W. Norton & Co., 1928.

Berry, Dee. *A Green Story*. Kansas City, Mo.: Kansas City Greens, POB 30353, 1990.

Berry, Thomas. *The Dream of the Earth*. San Francisco: Sierra Club Books, 1988.

Berry, Wendell. *The Unsettling of America: Culture and Agriculture*. New York: Avon Books, 1977. 2d ed.; San Francisco: Sierra Club Books, 1986.

Bertalanffy, Ludwig von. "The Theory of Open Systems in Physics and Biology," *Science*, vol. 111, pp. 23-29, 1950.

Black Elk Speaks, "Being the Life Story of a Holy Man of the Oglala Sioux", as told through John S. Neihardt. Lincoln, Neb.: University of Nebraska Press, 1972.

Boggs, Carl. *Social Movements and Political Power: Emerging Forms of Radicalism in the West*. Philadelphia: Temple University Press, 1986.

Boggs, James, and Grace Lee Boggs. *Conversations in Maine: Explaining Our Nation's Future*. Boston: South End Press, 1978.

Bookchin, Murray. *The Ecology of Freedom: The Emergence and Dissolution of Hierarchy*. Palo Alto: Cheshire Books, 1982.

———. *The Modern Crisis*. Philadelphia: New Society Publishers, 1986.

Boyte, Harry C. *The Backyard Revolution: Understanding the New Citizen Movement*. Philadelphia: Temple University Press, 1980.

Bohm, David. *Wholeness and the Implicate Order*. London: Ark Paperbacks, 1980.

Brown, Dee. *Bury My Heart at Wounded Knee: An Indian History of the American West*. New York: Holt, Reinhart & Winston, 1974.

Brown, Lester R. et al. *State of the World 1984-1998* (14 volumes), New York: W.W. Norton & Co,, 1984 through 1998, annually.

Brown, Lester, Michael Renner, and Christopher Flavin. *Vital Signs 1997, the Environmental Trends That Are Shaping Our Future*. New York: W.W. Norton, 1997.

Bruyn, Severyn T,, and James Meehan. *Beyond the Market and the State: New Direction*. Philadelphia: Temple University Press, 1987.

Bryan, Frank, and John McClaughry. *The Vermont Papers: Recreating Democracy on a Human Scale*. Chelsea, Vt.: Chelsea Green Publishing Co., 1989.

Bryant, Dorothy. *The Kin of Ata Are Waiting For You*. New York and Berkeley: Moon Books via Random House, 1971. Buber, Martin. *Between Man and Man*, 2nd ed., trans. Ronald G. Smith. New York: Macmillan Publishing Co., 1985.

Bullard, Robert D. *Dumping in Dixie: Race, Class, and Environmental Quality*. Denver:

Westview Press, 1990.

Bullard, Robert D. *Unequal Protection: Environmental Justice and Communities of Color.* San Francisco, Sierra Club Books, 1996.

Cabral, Amilcar. *Return to the Source,* edited by Africa Information Services. New York: Review Press, 1973.

Caldecott, Helen. *Missile Envy: The Arms Race and Nuclear War.* New York: Morrow, 1984.

Caldecott, Leonie, and Stephanie Leland. *Reclaim the Earth: Women Speak Out for Life on Earth.* Salem, N.H.: Salem House Publishers, 1984.

Callenbach, Ernest, *Ecotopia: The Notebooks and Reports of William Weston.* New York: Bantam Books, Inc., 1990.

Callicote, J. Baird. *In Defense of the Land Ethic: Essays in Environmental Philosophy.* Albany: State University of New York Press, 1990.

Cameron, Anne. *Daughters of Copper Woman.* Vancouver, B.C.: Press Gang, 1981.

Camus, Albert. *The Rebel.* New York: Vintage Books, 1956.

Capra, Bernt. *Mindwalk* (film). Hollywood, CA: Atlas Production Company in association with Mindwalk productions, 1990.

Capra, Fritjof. *The Web of Life.* New York: Doubleday, Anchor Books, 1996.

Capra, Fritjof. *The Tao of Physics.* New York: Bantam Books, 1975.

———. *The Turning Point: Science, Society, and the Rising Culture.* New York: Simon & Schuster, 1982.

Carson, Rachel. *Silent Spring.* Cambridge, Mass.: Riverside Press, 1962.

Carter, Forrest. *The Education of Little Tree.* Albuquerque: University of New Mexico Press, 1976.

Casti, John. *Complexification, Explaining a Paradoxical World Through the Science of Surprise.* New York: Harper Perennial, 1995.

Cheng, Chung-ying. "On the Environmental Ethics of the Tao and the Chi," *Environmental Ethics,* v. 8, n. 4 (June 1987), 17-24.

Childs, John Brown. *Leadership, Conflict, and Cooperation in AfroAmerican Social Thought.* Philadelphia: Temple University Press, 1989.

Clark, Mary E. *Ariadne's Thread: In Search of a Greener Future.* New York: St. Martin's Press, 1989.

Colborn, Theo and Dianne Dumanoski and John Peterson Myers. *Our Stolen Future, Are We Threatening our Fertility, Intelligence, and Survival?—A Scientific Detective Story.* New York: Dutton, 1996

Collingwood, R.G. *An Autobiography.* Oxford: Oxford University Press, 1951.

Commission for Racial Justice: United Church of Christ. *Toxic Wastes and Race in the United States: A National Report on the Racial and Socio-Economic Characteristics of Communities with Hazardous Waste Sites.* New York: Public Data Access, 1987.

Commoner, Barry. *The Politics of Energy.* New York: Alfred A. Knopf, 1979.

———. *The Poverty of Power: Energy and Economic Crisis.* New York: Bantam Books, 1976.

Covering the Candidates: Role & Responsibilities of the Press, Proceedings of the Fourth Annual J. Montgomery Curtis Memorial Seminar. Reston, Va.: American Press Institute, Sept. 9-11, 1987.

Crick, Bernard. *In Defense of Politics.* New York: Penguin Books, 1982.

Crotty, William and Gary C. Jacobson. *American Parties in Decline.*

Daly, Herman E. and John B. Cobb, Jr. *For the Common Good: Redirecting the Economy Toward Community, the Environment, and a Sustainable Future* Boston: Beacon Press, 1989.

Damman, Erik. *Revolution in the Affluent Society.* London: Heretic, 1984.

Davis, Donald Edward. *Ecophilosophy: A Field Guide to the Literature,* San Pedro, Calif.: R. & E. Miles, 1989.

De Beauvoir, Simone. *The Second Sex,* trans. H.M. Parshley, New York: Alfred A. Knopf, Inc., 1953.

DeChardin, Pierre Teilhard. *The Phenomenon of Man.* New York: Harper and Row Publishers, 1955.

Deloria, Vine, Jr. *Custer Died for Your Sins.* New York: Collier Macmillan, 1969.

Descartes, Rene. *Discourse on Method and Other Writings.* New York: Penguin, 1968.

DeToequeville, Alexis. *Democracy in America,* ed. H.S. Commager. New York: 1947.

Devall, Bill, and George Sessions. *Deep Ecology.* Salt Lake City: Gibbs and Smith, 1985.

Diamond, Irene, and Gloria Feman Orenstein, eds. *Reweaving the World: The Emergence of Ecofeminism,* edited and with essays. San Francisco, Calif.: Sierra Club Books, 1990.

Die Grünen, Programme of the Green Party. Available in English from Die Grünen, Colmantstrame 36, 5200 Bonn 1, West Germany (Also pamphlets entitled "Ecology and the Economy" and "The Peace Manifesto".)

Dinnerstein, Dorothy, *The Mermaid and the Minotaur.* New York: Harper and Row Publishers, 1963.

Djilas, Milovan. *The New Class: An Analysis of the Communist System.* New York: Frederick

A. Praeger, Publisher, 1957.

Domhoff, G, William. *The Power Elite and the State, How Policy Is Made in America.* Hawthorne, N.Y.: Aldine de Gruyter, 1990.

_____. *Who Rules America?* Englewood Cliffs, N.J.: Prentice Hall, 1967.

Dowd, Douglas. *The Waste of Nations: Dysfunction in the World Economy.* Boulder, Colo.: Westview Press, 1989.

Drengson, Alan R. *Beyond Environmental Crisis: From Technocrat to Planetary Person.* New York: P. Lang, 1989.

Dye, Thomas. *Who's Running America? The Carter Years.* Englewood Cliffs, N.J.: Prentice Hall, 1979.

Dowie, Mark. *Losing Ground, American Environmentalism at the Close of the Twentieth Century.* Cambridge, Massachusetts: The MIT Press, 1995. Boston: Little, Brown and Co., 1980.

Eckersley, Robyn. *The Political Theory of Environmentalism: Toward an Eco-Centric Approach.* Albany: State University of New York Press.

Ehrlich, Paul. *The Population Bomb.* New York: Ballantine Books, 1968.

Eisler, Riane. *The Chalice and the Blade: Our History, Our Future.* San Francisco: Harper & Row, 1987.

Ekins, Paul. *The Living Economy.* New York: Routledge and Kegan Paul, Ltd., 1986.

Elgin, Duane. *Awakening Earth, Exploring the Evolution of Human Culture and Consciousness.* New York: William Morrow, 1993.

Epstein, Edwin M. *The Corporation in American Politics.* Englewood Cliffs, N.J.: Prentice-Hall, Inc., 1969.

Evernden, Neil. *The Natural Alien: Humankind and Environment.* University of Toronto Press, 1985.

Feinstein, Mike. *Sixteen Weeks with European Greens.* San Pedro, CA: Distributed by R & E Miles, 1992.

Fingarette, Herbert. *Confucius-The Secular as Sacred.* New York: Harper and Row Publishers, 1963.

Firestone, Shulamith. *The Dialectics of Sex: The Case for Feminist Revolution.* New York: William Morrow & Co., 1974.

Fischer, Roger, and William Ury. *Getting to Yes: Negotiating Agreement Without Giving In.* New York: Penguin, 1983.

Folbre, Nancy. *A Field Guide to the U.S. Economy.* New York: Pantheon Books, 1987.

Fox, Matthew. *The Coming of the Cosmic Christ: Healing of Mother Earth and the Birth of a Global Renaissance.* San Francisco: Harper & Row, 1988.

Fox, Warwick. *Toward a Transpersonal Ecology: Developing New Foundations for Environmentalism,* ed. Jeremy Hayward. Boston: Shambhala Publications, Inc., 1990.

Freire, Paulo. *Pedagogy of the Oppressed,* trans. Myra Bergynan Ramos. New York: Herder and Herder, 1970.

French, Marilyn. *Beyond Power: On Women, Men and Morals.* New York: Summit Books, 1985.

Freud, Sigmund. *Civilization and Its Discontents,* ed. James Strachey. New York: W.W. Norton & Co., 1962.

Fromm, Erich. *The Sane Society.* New York: Fawcett, 1955.

Frondizi, Risieri. *The Nature of the Self: A Functional Interpretation.* Carbondale, Ill.: Southern Illinois University Press, 1953.

Gelbspan, Ross. *The Heat is On: The High Stakes Battle Over the Earth's Threatened Climate.* Reading, Massachusetts: Addison-Wesley, 1997.

Galbraith, John Kenneth. *The New Industrial State.* Boston: Houghton Mifflin Co., 1967.

Garland, Anne W. *Women Activists.* New York: Feminist Press at the City University of New York, 1990.

Gerson, Joseph. *The Deadly Connection: Nuclear War and U.S. Intervention.* Cambridge, Mass.: American Friends Service Committee, 1982.

Gerritt, Greg. *A Campaign for the Forest: The Campaign to Ban Clearcutting in Maine in 1996.* Raymond, Maine: Leopold Press, 1997.

Gilligan, Carol, *In a Different Voice.* Cambridge: Harvard University Press, 1982.

Gilman, Charlotte Perkins. *Herland,* New York: Pantheon Books, 1979.

Gitlin, Todd. *The Sixties: Years of Hope, Days of Rage.* New York: Bantam Books, Inc., 1987.

Glendinning, Chellis. *When Technology Wounds: The Human Consequences of Progress.* New York: Morrow, 1990.

Goldsmith, Edward. *The Way: An Ecological World-View.* Boston: Shambala, 1993.

Goldsmith, Edward. *The Great U-Turn: De-Industrializing Society.* Hartland, U.K.: Green Books, 1988.

Gorz, Andre. *Ecology as Politics,* trans. Patsy Vigderman and Jonathan Cloud. Boston: South End Press, 1980.

Gramsci, Antonio. *Selections from the Prison Notebooks,* trans. Lynne Lawner. New York:

Harper and Row, 1975.

Greenberg, Edward S. *The American Political System: A Radical Approach*, 2d ed. Cambridge, Mass.: 1980.

Griffin, Susan. *Women and Nature: The Roaring Insider Her*, 1st ed, New York: Harper & Row, 1978.

Grofman, Bernard, and Arend Lijpshart, eds. *Electoral Laws and Their Political Consequences.* New York: Agathon Press, Inc., 1986.

Grossman, Richard, and Frank Adams. *Taking Care of Business: Citizenship and the Charter of Incorporation.* Cambridge, MA: Charter, Inc., 1993.

Grumet, Madeleine R. *Bitter Milk: Women and Technology.* Amherst, Mass.: University of Massachusetts Press, 1988.

Guérin, Daniel, *Anarchism*, trans. Mary Klopper. New York: Monthly Review Press, 1970.

Habermas, Jürgen. *Legitimation Crisis*, trans. Thomas McCarthy. Boston: Beacon Press, 1973.

Hagopian, Mark N. *The Phenomenon of Revolution.* New York: Dodd, Mead & Company, 1975.

Hall, Bob, ed. *Environmental Politics: Lessons from the Grassroots.* Durham, N.C.: Institute for Southern Studies, 1988.

Hamaker, John D. *The Survival of Civilization.* Burlingame, Calif.: Hamaker-Weaver Publishers, 1982.

Hamilton, Alexander, James Madison, and John Jay. *The Federalist or The New Constitution.* New York: The Heritage Press, 1945.

Hamilton, Edward K., ed. *America's Global Interests: A Global Agenda.* New York: W.W. Norton & Co., 1989.

Hardin, Garrett. "The Tragedy of the Commons," *Science*, 162 (December 13, 1968), 1243-1248.

Harris, Adrienne and Ying, Ynestra, eds. *Rocking the Ship of State: Toward a Feminist Peace Politics.* Boulder, Colo.: Westview Press, 1989.

Hawken, Paul. *The Next Economy.* New York: Holt, Rinehart and Winston, 1983.

Hawken, Paul. *The Ecology of Commerce: A Declaration of Sustainability.* New York: HarperCollins, 1993.

Hawkins, Howard. *The Potential of the Green Movement.* Burlington, Vt.: Green Program Project, POB 111, Burlington, VT, 05402,1988.

Hazen, Dan. *Money and Politics: Electoral Reform as If Democracy Matters.* Media and Democracy Project, 100 East 85th St., New York, NY 10028.

Hegi, Ursula. *Stones from the River.* New York: Simon & Shuster, Scribner Paperback, 1994

Heisenberg, Werner. *Physics and Beyond.* New York: Harper and Row, 1971.

Henderson, Hazel. *Paradigms in Progress.* San Francisco: Berrett-Koehler, 1995.

Hermson, Paul S. and John C. Green. *Multiparty Politics in America.* New York: Rowman and Littlefield, 1997.

Hertsgaard, Mark. *Earth Odyssey: Around the world in search of our environmental future.* New York: Broadway Books, 1998.

Jacoby, Russell. *Social Amnesia: A Critique of Conformist Psychology from Adler to Laing.* Boston: Beacon Pres, 1976.

Jackson, Wes. *Altars of Unhewn Stone: Science and the Earth.* San Francisco: North Point Press, 1987.

Jaggar, Allison. *Feminist Politics and Human Nature.* Totowa, N.J.: Rowan and Littlefield, Publishers, Inc., 1983.

Jantsch, Erich. *The Self-Organizing Universe.* New York: Pergamon, 1980.

Jefferson, Thomas. *The Political Writings of Thomas Jefferson: Representative Selections*, ed. Edward Dumbauld. New York: The Liberal Arts Press, 1955.

Jencks, Christopher, et al. *Inequality: A Reassessment of the Effect of Family and Schooling in America.* New York: Basic Books Inc., 1972.

Johnson, Chalmers. *Revolutionary Change.* Boston: Little, Brown and Co., 1966.

Jones, Ken. *Beyond Optimism: A Buddhist Political Ecology.* Oxford: John Carpenter Publishers, 1993.

Jung, C.G. *Memories, Dreams, Reflections*, ed. Jaffé Anelia; trans. Richard and Clara Winston. New York: Random House, 1965.

Jung, Hwa Yol. *Existential Phenomenology and Political Theory: A Reader.* Chicago: Gateway Edition (Henry Regenery Company), 1972.

Kant, Immanuel. *Perpetual Peace*, ed. Lewis White Beek. Indianapolis: The Library of Liberal Arts (Bobbs-Merrill Educational Publishing), 1957.

Kassiola, Joel-Jay. *The Death of Industrial Civilization, the Limits to Economic Growth and the Repoliticization of Advanced Industrial Society.* Albany: State University of New York Press, 1990.

Katsiaficas, George. *The Imagination of the New Left.* Boston: South End Press, 1987.

Kelly, Petra. *Fighting for Hope.* Boston: South End Press, 1985.

Keyes, Ken Jr., *The Hundredth Monkey.* St. Mary, Ky.: Vision Books, 1982.

King, Martin Luther Jr. *A Testament of Hope: The Essential Writings of Martin Luther King Jr.*, ed. James Melvin Washington. San Francisco: Harper & Row, 1986.
Kohr, Leopold. *The Breakdown of Nations.* New York: E. P. Dutton, 1978.
Kuhn, Thomas S. *The Structure of Scientific Revolutions,* 2d ed. Chicago: The University of Chicago Press, 1970.
Laing, R.D. *The Dispossessed.* New York: Avon Books, 1974,
Lee, Martin, and Norman Soloman. *Unreliable Sources: A Guide to Detecting Bias in News Media.* New York: Carol Publishing Group, 1990.
Legge, James. *The Texts of Taoism.* New York: Dover Press, 1959.
Leiss, William. *Domination of Nature.* New York: G. Brazilier, 1972.
Lenin, Vladimir Ilich. *The Lenin Anthology,* 2nd ed., Robert Tucker, ed. New York: W.W. Norton & Co., 1975.
Leopold, Aldo. *A Sand County Almanac.* New York: Oxford University Press 1962.
Lerner, Michael. *Surplus Powerlessness.* New York, Humanities Press, 1991.
Lewis, C. S. *That Hideous Strength.* New York: The Macmillan Co., 1946.
Lippmann, Walter. *Essays in the Public Philosophy.* New York, 1956.
Locke, John. *Two Treatises of Government.* With a supplement, Patriarchas, by Robert Filmer, ed. Thomas I. Cook. New York: Hafner Publishing Co., 1947.
Lovelock, J.E. *Gaia: A New Look at Life on Earth.* London: Oxford University Press, 1979.
Lovins, Amory. *Soft Energy Paths.* New York: Harper & Row, 1977.
Lukacs, Georg. *History and Class Consciousness: Studies in Marxist Dialectics,* trans. Rodney Livingstone. Cambridge, Mass.: The M.I.T. Press, 1971.
Machiavelli, Niccolò. *The Prince and The Discourses.* New York: The Modern Library, 1950.
Macpherson, C. B. *The Real World of Democracy: The Massey Lectures.* Oxford: Clarendon Press, 1966.
Mander, Jerry. *In the Absence of the Sacred.* San Francisco: Sierra Club Books, 1991.
Mander, Jerry and Edward Goldsmith. *The Case Against the Global Economy and for a turn toward the local.* San Francisco: Sierra Club Books, 1996.
Mansbridge, Jane. *Beyond Adversary Democracy.* Chicago: University of Chicago Press, 1980.
Mao Tse-Tung. *Four Essays on Philosophy.* Pelcing: Foreign Languages Press, 1968.
Marcus, Greil. *Lipstick Traces: A Secret History of the Twentieth Century.* Cambridge, Mass.: Harvard University Press, 1989.
Marcuse, Herbert. *One-Dimensional Man; Studies in the Ideology of Advanced Industrial Socioty.* Boston: Beacon Pres, 1964.
Martinez-Alier, Juan. *Ecological Economies: Energy, Environment and Society.* New York: Basil Blackwell Inc., 1987.
Marx, Karl, and Friedrich Engels. *The Marx-Engels Reader,* 2nd ed., Robert Tucker, ed. New York: W.W. Norton & Co., 1978.
McLaughlin, Corinne, and Gordon Davidson. *Builders of the Dawn: Community Lifestyles in a Changing World.* Shutesbury, Mass.: Sirius Publishing, 1986.
Meadows, Donella, Denis Meadows and Jorgen Randers. *Beyond the Limits: Confronting Global Collapse, Envisioning a Sustainable Future.* Post Mills, Vt.: Chelsea Green Publishing Co., 1992.
Meadows, Donella H., Denis L. Meadows, Jorgen Randers, and William W. Behrens III. *The Limits to Growth: A Report for the Club of Rome's Project on the Predicament of Mankind.* New York: Signet, 1972.
Meeker-Lowry, Susan. *Economics as If the Earth Really Mattered: A Catalyst Guide to Socially Conscious Investing.* Philadelphia: New Society Publishers, 1988.
Merchant, Carolyn. *The Death of Nature: Women, Ecology, and the Scientific Revolution.* New York: Harper Religious Books, 1983.
Merleau-Ponty, Maurice. *Consciousness and the Acquisition of Language.* Evanston: Northwestern University Press, 1973.
_____. *Phenomenology of Perception,* trans. Colin Wilson. New York: Humanities Press, 1962.
Michael, Donald N. "Neither Hierarchy nor Anarchy: Notes on Norms for Govemance in a Systemic World," in Walter Truitt Anderson, ed., *Rethinking Liberalism.* New York: Avon Books, 1983.
Milbrath, Lester W. *Envisioning a Sustainable Society.* Albany, N.Y.: State University of New York Press, 1990.
Miliband, Ralph. *Marxism and Politics.* Oxford: Oxford University Press, 1977.
Mill, John Stuart. *A Selection of His Works,* ed. John M. Robson. New York: St. Martin's Press, 1966.
_____. *Considerations on Representative Government.* New York: The Liberal Arts Press, 1958.
_____. *The Subjection of Women,* ed. Susan Moller Oldn. Indianapolis: Hackett Publishers, 1988.
Milosz, Czeslaw. *The Captive Mind.* New York: Vintage Books, 1981.

Mingers, John. *Self-Producing Systems*. New York: Plenum, 1995.

Mohawk, John, Jose Barreiro, and Akwesasne Notes. *Basic Call to Conscience*. Akwesasne Notes Mohawk Nation, Via Roosevelt Town, NY, NY 13683, 3d revised edition, 1986.

Mokhiber, Russell. *Corporate Crime and Violence: Big Business Power and the Abuse of the Public Trust*. San Francisco: Sierra Club Books, 1988.

More, Thomas. *Utopia*, trans. Paul Turner. New York: Penguin Books, 1965.

Morehouse, Ward, and M. Arum Subramaniam. *The Bhopol Tragedy, What Really Happened and What It Means for American Workers and Communities at Risk*. New York: Penguin Books, 1986.

Morris, William. *News from Nowhere and Selected Writings and Designs*, ed. Asa Briggs. New York: Penguin Books, 1962.

Morrison, Roy. *Ecological Democracy*. Boston: South End Press, 1995.

Muller-Rommel, Ferdinand, ed.,*New Politics in Western Europe: The Rise and Success of Green Parties and Alternative Lists*. Boulder, Colo.: Westview Press, 1989.

Naess, Arne. "The Shallow and the Deep, Long Range Ecology Movements: A Summary," *Inquiry*, 16(1973), 95-100.

_____. "Intrinsic Value: Will the Defenders of Nature Please Rise?" Keynote Address, Second International Conference on Conservation Biology. University of Michigan, May 1985.

Naisbitt, John, and Patricia Aburdene. *Re-inventing the Corporation*. New York: Warner Books, Inc., 1986.

Nash, George H. *The Conservative Intellectual Movement in America since 1945*. New York: Harper & Row, 1976.

New World Alliance. *A Transformational Platform: The Dialogue Begins*. Washington, D.C.: New World Alliance, 1981.

Nichols, Robert. *Arrival: Book I of Daily Lives in Nghsi-Altai*. New York: New Directions Publishing Cor., 1977.

_____. *Garh City: Book II of Daily Lives in Nghsi-Altai*. New York: New Directions Publishing Corp., 1978.

Nietzsche, Friedrich. *On the Genealogy of Morals*. New York: 1969.

_____. *The Use and Abuse of History*, trans. Adrian Collins. Indianapolis: The Library of Liberal Arts (Bobbs-Meriill Educational Publishing), 1957.

Nisbet, Robert. *The Quest for Community*. New York: Oxford University Press, 1962.

Nozick, Robert. *Anarchy, State, and Utopia*, NewYork: Basic Books, Inc., 1974.

O'Brien, Mary. *The Politics of Reproduction*. Boston: Routledge & Kegan Paul, 1981.

Odendahl, Teresa. *Charity Begins at Home: Generosity and Self-Interest among the Philanthropic Elite*. New York: Basic Books, 1990.

Oldenberg, Ray. *The Great Good Place: Cafes, Coffee Shops, Community Centers, Beauty Parlors, General Stores, Bars, Hang-outs, and How They Get You Through the Day*. New York: Paragon, 1989.

Ophuls, Williama. *Ecology and the Politics of Scarcity: Prologue to a Political Theory of the Steady State*. San Francisco: W.H. Freeman and Co., 1977.

Orr, David. *Ecological Literacy*. Albany: State University of New York Press, 1992.

Ortega y Gasset, José. *The Revolt of the Masses*. New York: W.W. Norton & Co., 1932.

Orwell, George. *Animal Farm*. New York: Signet, 1946.

Paehlke, Robert. *Environmentalism and the Future of Progressive Politics*. New Haven: Yale University Press, 1989.

Parenti, Michael. *Power and the Powerless*. New York: St. Martin's Press, 1978.

Parkin, Sara. *Green Parties: An International Guide*. London: Heretic Books, 1989.

Pateman, Carole. *Pailicipation and Democratic Theory*. Cambridge, England: 1970.

Peck, M. Scott, M.D. *The Different Drum*. New York: Simon and Schuster, 1987.

Phillips, Kevin. *The Politics of Rich and Poor: Wealth and the American Electorate in the Reagan Aftermath*. New York: Random House, 1990.

Piercy, Marge. *Woman on the Edge of Time*. New York: Ballantine Books, 1976.

Pirsig, Robert M. *Zen and the Art of Motorcycle Maintenance*. New York: Morrow, William & Co., Inc., 1974.

Piven, Francis Fox, and Richard A. Cloward. *Why Americans Don't Vote*. New York: Pantheon Books, 1988.

Piven, Francis Fox and Richard Cloward. *The Breaking of the American Social Contract*. New York: The New Press, 1997.

Plato. *The Republic*, trans. Francis MacDonald Cornford. New York: Oxford University Press, 1945.

Plumwood, Val. "The Eco-Politics Debate and the Politics of Nature," in Karen J. Warren, ed., *Ecological Feminism*, New York and London: Routledge, 1994.

Politics for Life: The 1983 Election Manifesto of Britain's Ecology Party. Available from the Ecology Party (Now Green Party) 36/38 Clapham Road, London SW9 OJQ England.

Polyani, Karl. *The Great Transformation*. New York: Farrar, Rinehart, Inc., 1944.

Porritt, Jonathan. *Seeing Green: The Politics of Ecology Explained*. Oxford: Basil Blackwell,

Ltd., 1985.

Prigogine, Ilya. *From Being to Becoming*. San Francisco: Freeman, 1980.

Prigogine, Ilya and Isabelle Stengers. *Order out of Chaos*. New York: Bantam, 1984.

Quinn, Daniel. *Ishmael*. New York: Bantam Books Paperback, 1995.

Rand, Ayn. *For the New Intellectual*. New York: Random House, 1961.

Redefining Wealth and Progress: New Ways to Measure Economic, Social, and Environmental Change. The Caracas Report on Alternative Development Indicators. Indianapolis: Knowledge Systems; New York: Bootstrap Press, 1990.

Reed, David, ed. *Structural Adjustment, the Environment, and Sustainable Development*. London: Earthscan, 1992

Reich, Robert B. *Tales of a New America: The Anxious Liberal's Guide to the Future*. New York: Vintage Books, 1987.

Reich, Wilhelm. *The Function of the Orgasm: Sex-economic problems of biological energy*, trans. Vincent R. Carfagno. New York: Farrar, Strauss, & Giroux, 1973.

Reinsch, J. Leonard. *Getting Elected: From Radio and Roosevelt to Television and Reagan*. New York: Hippocrene Books, 1988.

Rensenbrink, John C. *Poland Challenges a Divided World*. Baton Rouge, La.: Louisiana State University Press, 1988.

_____. *The Greens and the Politics of Transformation*. San Pedro, CA: R. & E. Miles, 1992.

Report from, Iron Mountain on the Possibility and Desirability of Peace. New York: The Dial Press, Inc., 1967.

Reynolds, David. *Democracy Unbound*. Boston: South End Press, 1997.

Richardson, George P. *Feedback Thought in Social Science and Systems Theory*. Philadelphia: University of Pennsylvania Press, 1992.

Rickover, Hyman. *No Holds Barred: The Final Congressional Testimony of Admiral Hyman Rickover*. Washington, D.C.: Center for Study of Responsive Law, 1982.

Rifkin, Jeremy. *Biosphere Politics, A New Consciousness for a New Century*. New York: Crown Publishers, Inc., 1991.

_____. *Time Wars: The Primary Conflict in Human History*. New York: Holt, 1987.

Sale, Kirkpatrick. *Dwellers in the Land: the Bioregional Vision*. San Francisco: Sierra Club Books, 1985.

Satin, Mark. *New Age Politics: Healing Self and Society: The Emerging New Alternative to Marxism and Liberalism*. Vancouver, B.C.: Fairweather Press, 1978.

Schmookler, Andrew B. *The Parable of the Tribes: The Problem of Power in Social Evolution*. Berkeley, Calif.: University of California Press, 1984.

Schon, Donald A. *Beyond the Stable State*. New York: W.W. Norton & Co., Inc., 1971.

Schumacher, E.F. *Small Is Beautiful: Economics as if People Mattered*. New York: Harper & Row, 1973.

Seed, John, et al. *Thinking Like a Mountain: Towards a Council of All Beings*. Philadelphia: New Society Publishers, 1988.

Shabecoff, Philip. *A Fierce Green Fire: The American Environmenta Movement*. New York: Hill and Wang1993.

Shabecoff, Philip. *A New Name for Peace: International Environmentalism, Sustainable Development and Democracy*. University of New England Press, 1996.

Sharp, Gene. *The Politics of Non-Violent Action* (3 parts) ed. Marina Finkelstein. Boston: Porter Sargent Publishers, Inc., 1974.

Sheldrake, Rupert. *A New Science of Life*. Los Angeles: Tarcher, 1981.

Simon, Julian L., and Hennan Kahn, eds. *The Resourceful Earth: A Response to Global 2000*. New York: Basil Blackwell Inc., 1984.

Simon, Yves R. *Philosophy of Democratic Government*. Chicago: The University of Chicago Press, 1951.

Skinner, B.F. *Walden Two*. New York: The Macmillan Co., 1948.

Sklar, Holly, ed. *Trilateralism: The TTilateral Commission and Elite Planning*. Boston: South End Press, 1980.

Skolimowski, Henryk. *Eco-Philosophy*. London: Marion Boyare, 1981.

Slater, Philip E. *The Pursuit of Loneliness*. Boston: Beacon Press, 1971.

Smith, Sam. *Sam Smith's Great American Political Repair Manual: How to rebuild our country so the politics aren't broken and politicians aren't fixed*. New York: W.W. Norton, 1997.

Spence, Larry. *The Politics of Social Knowledge*. University Park, Pa.: Pennsylvania State University Press, 1978.

Spretnak, Charlene. *The Spiritual Dimension of Green Politics*. Santa Fe, N.M.: Bear & Co., 1986.

Spretnak, Charlene, and Fritjof, Capra. *Green Politics*. Santa Fe: Bear and Co., 1986.

Spretnak, Charlene. *Resurgence of the Real, Body, Nature and Place in a Hypermodern World*. Reading, MA: Addison-Wesley,1997.

Spretnak, Charlene. *States of Grace: The Recovery of Meaning in the Postmodern Age.* San Francisco: Harper, 1991.

Starbawk. *Dreaming the Dark: Magic, Sex, and Politics.* Boston: Beacon Press, 1982.

Stein, Arthur. *Seeds of the Seventies.* Hanover, N.H.: University Press of New England, 1985.

Steingraber, Sandra. *Living Downstream, An Ecologist Looks at Cancer and the Environment.* Reading, Massachusetts: Addison-Wesley, 1997.

Strauss, Leo. *Natural Right and History.* Chicago: The University of Chicago Press, 1953.

Sumner, William Graham. *What Social Classes Owe to Each Other.* Caldwell, Idaho: The Caxton Printers, Ltd., 1954.

Sun-tzu. *The Art of War,* trans. Samuel B. Griffith. New York: Oxford University Press, 1963.

The Global Tomorrow Coalition. *The Global Ecology Handbook, What You Can Do About the Environmental Crisis.* Boston: Beacon Press, 1990.

Theobald, Robert. *The Rapids of Change: Leadership in a World of Discontinuities.* Wickenburg, Ariz.: Participation Publishers, 1986.

Thompson, E.P. *William Morris: Romantic to Revolutionary.* New York: Pantheon Books, 1976.

Thurow, Lester C. *The Zero-Sum Society: Distribution and the Possibilities for Economic Change.* New York: Penguin Books, 1980.

Tokar, Brian. *Earth for Sale: Reclaiming Ecology in the Age of Corporate Greenwash.* Boston: South End Press, 1997

Tokar, Brian. *The Green Alternative: Creating an Ecological Future.* San Pedro, Calif.: R. & E. Miles, 1987.

Toynbee, Arnold J. *A Study of History.* New York: Oxford University Press, 1947.

Trungpa, Chogyam. *Shambhala: The Sacred Path of the Warrior,* ed. Carolyn Rose Gimian. Boston: Shambhala Publications, 1984.

Vogel, Steven. *Against Nature: The Concept of Nature in Critical Theory.* Albany: State University of New York Press, 1997.

Waring, Marilyn. *If Women Counted, A New Feminist Economics.* San Francisco: Harper, 1988.

Warren, Karen. "Feminism and Ecology: Making Connections," *Environmental Ethics,* (Spring 1987).

Weil, Simone. *The Need for Roots.* Boston: The Boston Press, 1952.

White, Lynn, Jr. "The Historic Roots of our Ecologic Crisis," *Science,* v. 155 n. 3767 (March 1967), 1203-1207.

Wheatley, Margaret J. *Leadership and the New Science, Learning About Organization from an Orderly Universe.* San Francisco: Barrett-Koehler, 1992.

Whitehead, Alfred North. *The Function of Reason.* Boston: Beacon Press, 1929.

Wiener, Norbeft. *The Human Use of Human Beings: Cybernetics and Society.* Garden City, N.Y.: Doubleday Anchor Books, 1954.

Winner, Langdon. *The Whale and the Reactor: A Search for Limits in an Age of High Technology.* Chicago: Chicago University Press, 1986.

World Commission on Environment and Development. *Our Common Future.* New York: Oxford University Press, 1987.

X, Malcolm. *The Autobiography of Malcolm X.* With the assistance of Alex Haley. New York: Grove Press, 1965.

Zamiatin, Engene. *We,* trans. Gregory Zilboorg. New York: E.P. Dutton & Co., Inc., 1959.

Zinn, Howard. *A People's History of the United States.* New York:Harper, 1980.

Zisk, Betty H. *Money, Media, and the Grass Roots: State Ballot Issues and the Electoral Process.* Newbury Park, Calif.: Sage Publications, 1987.

Zisk, Betty H. *The Politics of Transformation: Local Activism in the Peace and Environmental Movments.* Westport, CT: Praeger, 1992.

Zohar, Danah. *The Quantum Self: Human Nature and Consciousness Defined by the New Physics.* New York: William Morrow, 1990.

Zohar, Danah and Ian Marshall. *The Quantum Society: Mind, Physics, and a New Social Vision.* New York: Quill, William Morrow, 1994.